GOOD ORDER

Right *Answers to* Contemporary Questions

EDITED BY BRAD MINER

A TOUCHSTONE BOOK
Published by Simon & Schuster

New York   London   Toronto   Sydney   Tokyo   Singapore

TOUCHSTONE
Rockefeller Center
1230 Avenue of the Americas
New York, New York 10020

TOUCHSTONE and colophon are registered trademarks
of Simon & Schuster Inc.

Designed by Irving Perkins Associates

Manufactured in the United States of America

10   9   8   7   6   5   4   3   2   1

Library of Congress Cataloging-in-Publication Data
Good Order : right answers to contemporary questions / edited by Brad Miner.
p.   cm.
"A Touchstone book."
1. Conservatism—United States. 2. Conservatism—Religious aspects. I. Miner, Brad.
JC573.2.U6G66   1995
320.5'2'0973—dc20   94-3712
                                                                                   CIP

ISBN: 0-671-88235-X

The compilation of *Good Order* was supported in part
by a grant from the Lynde and Harry Bradley Foundation.

The following selections in this anthology are reproduced by permission of the authors, their publishers, or their agents:

"The Vulnerability of the Naked Square" from *The Naked Public Square: Religion and Democracy in America* by Richard John Neuhaus. Copyright © 1984 by Richard John Neuhaus. Used by permission of Wm. B. Eerdmans Publishing Co.

"Are There Any Moral Absolutes? Finding Black and White in a World of Grays" from *Making Choices* by Peter Kreeft. Copyright © 1990 by Peter Kreeft. Used by permission of Servant Publications.

"Character and Community: The Problem of Broken Windows" from *On Character: Essays* by James Q. Wilson. Copyright © 1991 by the American Enterprise Institute. Used by permission of the American Enterprise Institute.

"The Hole in the Theory" from *The Dream and the Nightmare: The Sixties' Legacy to the Underclass* by Myron Magnet. Copyright © 1993 by Myron Magnet. Used by permission of William Morrow and Company, Inc.

"The Feminist Perversion" by Carol Iannone. (A shorter version of this article appeared in *Second Thoughts: Former Radicals Look Back at the Sixties,* edited by Peter Collier and David Horowitz, published by Madison Books and ©1989 by the National Forum Foundation.) Revision copyright © 1994 by Carol Iannone. Used by permission of the author.

"The Last Metaphysical Right" from *Ideas Have Consequences* by Richard M. Weaver. Copyright © 1948 by Richard M. Weaver. Used by permission of the University of Chicago Press.

"The Kinetic Economy" from *Wealth and Poverty* by George Gilder. Copyright © 1981 by George Gilder. Used by permission of Georges Borchardt, Inc., for the author.

"Little Platoons" from *In Pursuit: Of Happiness and Good Government.* Copyright © 1988 by Cox and Murray, Inc. Used by permission of International Creative Management.

"The Original Intent Controversy" from *The Conservative Constitution* by Russell Kirk. Copyright © 1989 Russell Kirk. Used by permission of Regnery Gateway, Inc., Washington, D.C.

"The Revival of Classical Republicanism" from *Restoration: Congress, Term Limits and the Recovery of Deliberative Democracy* by George F. Will. Copyright © 1992 by George F. Will. Used by permission of The Free Press, a division of Macmillan, Inc.

"Assorted Dogmas" from *Inside American Education* by Thomas Sowell. Copyright © 1993 by Thomas Sowell. Used by permission of The Free Press, a division of Macmillan, Inc.

"Sex and Separateness" from *The Closing of the American Mind* by Allan Bloom. Copyright © 1987 by Allan Bloom. Used by permission of Simon & Schuster Inc.

Note: For purposes of consistency in typographical style, footnotes that appear in some of the original essays have been deleted in *Good Order*. Readers are, of course, urged to consult the books in which these essays first appeared for the fullest appreciation of each author's argument.

*To the memory of
Russell Kirk*

Thus says the Lord, Stand in the ways and see, and ask for the old paths and see where is the good way, and walk in it and find rest for your souls.

—JEREMIAH 6:16

Contents

Individual religious belief can be dismissed scornfully as superstition, for it finally poses little threat to the power of the state. No, the chief attack is upon the *institutions* that bear and promulgate belief in a transcendent reality by which the state can be called to judgment. Such institutions threaten the totalitarian proposition that everything is to be within the state, nothing is to be outside the state.

All of us know from our own experience that hard, unyielding moral absolutes are often very inconvenient. We would very much like to bend the laws a bit; therefore we bend our *beliefs* about the law. It takes only a little knowledge of modern psychology to reveal how much we all rationalize rather than reason, how often our arguments are supports for our desires rather than honest searches after truth.

The citizen who fears the ill-smelling drunk, the rowdy teenager, or the importuning beggar is not merely expressing his distaste for unseemly behavior; he is also giving voice to a bit of folk wisdom that happens to be a correct generalization: namely, that serious street crime flourishes in areas in which disorderly behavior goes unchecked.

Nothing tells these young women that getting pregnant without being married and having illegitimate babies they can't support and aren't equipped to nurture well is wrong. The culture they live in, both the larger culture and the culture of the underclass, tells them that a life on welfare is perfectly acceptable and, arguably, just as good as any other kind of life. Under those circumstances, who can wonder that no inner voice condemns them for choosing such a fate?

First of all, feminism is a series of self-indulgent contradictions and anyone
following it for a while is going to find her thought coarsened. Women are
the same as men, women are different from men, according to the ideological need. Women are strong and capable. And yet have been the slaves and
victims of men throughout history. Women are angry, rebellious, even murderous in patriarchy, but also superior to men because loving and tender.

PART III   THE ECONOMIC ORDER

When we survey the scene to find something which the rancorous leveling
wind of utilitarianism has not brought down, we discover one institution,
shaken somewhat, but still strong and perfectly clear in its implications.
This is the right of private property, which is, in fact, the last metaphysical
right remaining to us. The ordinances of religion, the prerogatives of sex
and vocation, all have been swept away by materialism, but the relationship of a man to his own has until the present largely escaped attack.

The more comprehensive the regulatory systems, the more surely they will
be dominated by mediocrities, and the more surely mediocre will be the
growth of the U.S. economy. Excessive regulation to save us from all risks
will create the greatest danger of all: a stagnant society in a changing
world. The choice is not between comfortable equilibrium and reckless
progress. It is between random deterioration by time and change and creative destruction by human genius.

PART IV   THE POLITICAL ORDER

Strongly bound communities, fulfilling complex public functions, are not
creations of the state. They form because they must. Human beings have

needs as individuals (never mind the "moral sense" or lack of it) that cannot be met except by cooperation with other human beings. To this degree, the often-lamented conflict between "individualism" and "community" is misleading. The pursuit of individual happiness cannot be an atomistic process; it will naturally and always occur in the context of communities.

Men and women in a tolerable society ought to be able to feel confident that the body of rules which we call law will be much the same tomorrow as it was yesterday. It becomes difficult to obey the law if the law is changed greatly from time to time, and changed almost unpredictably. People like to live by rules; to have the assurance that if they behave conformably to certain rules called the law, mischief will not be done to them. Permanence and continuity in the law are virtually essential to a society's material success.

[I]f term limitation is inscribed as a constitutional value it will perform, as law frequently does, an expressive and affirming function. It will express an idea central to the civic culture of republicanism (of the American, if not necessarily the Burkean, variety). The idea is that representation is not a function beyond the capacities of any reasonably educated and attentive citizen. Term limitation will affirm the democratic faith in the broad diffusion in the public of the talents necessary for the conduct of the public's business.

PART V   THE CULTURAL ORDER

The ideological component of multiculturalism can be summarized as a cultural relativism which finds the prominence of Western civilization in the world or in the schools intolerable. Behind this attitude is often a seething hostility to the West, barely concealed even in public statements designed to attract wider political support for the multicultural agenda. That such attitudes or opinions exist, and are expressed by some people, is to be expected in a free society. It is not these beliefs, as such, which are the real problem. The real *educational* problem is the attempt to impose such views as a new orthodoxy . . .

The immediate promise of sexual liberation was, simply, happiness understood as the release of energies that had been stored up over millennia during the dark night of repression, in a great continuous Bacchanalia. However, the lion roaring behind the door turned out, when the door was opened, to be a little, domesticated cat.

Herewith as fine and concise a definition of the conservative view as one is likely to find:

> Let me, then, warn the reader that I was a Conservative when I went to Mexico and that everything I saw there strengthened my opinions. I believe that man is, by nature, an exile and will never be self-sufficient or complete on this earth; that his chances of happiness and virtue, here, remain more or less constant through the centuries and, generally speaking, are not much affected by the political and economic conditions in which he lives; that the balance of good and ill tends to revert to a norm; that sudden changes of physical condition are usually ill, and are advocated by the wrong people for the wrong reasons; that the intellectual communists of today have personal, irrelevant grounds for their antagonism to society, which they are trying to exploit. I believe in government; that men cannot live together without rules but that these should be kept at the bare minimum of safety; that there is no form of government ordained from God as being better than any other; that the anarchic elements in society are so strong that it is a whole-time task to keep the peace. I believe that inequalities of wealth and position are inevitable and that it is therefore meaningless to discuss the advantages of their elimination; that men naturally arrange themselves in a system of classes; that such a system is necessary for any form of co-operative work, more particularly the work of keeping a nation together. I believe in nationality; not in terms of race or of divine commissions for world conquest, but simply thus: mankind inevitably organizes itself in communities according to its geographical distribution; these communities by sharing a common history develop common characteristics and inspire a local loyalty; the individual family develops most happily and fully when it accepts these natural limits. . . . I believe that war and conquest are inevitable; that is how history has been made and that is how it will develop. I believe that Art is a natural function of man. . . .

—EVELYN WAUGH, *Mexico: An Object Lesson* (1939)

Foolish Virgins

"Among democratic nations, each new generation is a new people."
—ALEXIS DE TOCQUEVILLE. *Democracy in America*

HAS MODERN AMERICA BECOME a "conservative" nation? It's an interesting question, although unanswerable since no dependable standard exists for measuring conservatism (or any other persuasion) on such a grand scale, and since—as conservatives themselves know only too well—there's substantial disagreement in the so-called conservative movement about what constitutes the True Faith. Still, I've often wondered if a team of social scientists might not usefully develop a Worldview Quotient: a battery of tests measuring spiritual, social, economic, political, and cultural attitudes, from which a score would result—high negative scores indicating the deepest fathoms of liberal fantasy, high positive scores demonstrating the furthest reaches of right-wing wackiness. Unlike its cousin IQ, in which higher is universally acknowledged as better, stratospheric WQ scores would probably be inversely proportional to the public esteem. The -200s and the +200s would find that it's lonely on the margins—not that they'd care, of course.

Some conservatives might speculate that a WQ distribution curve would look like a wave swelling from left to right and breaking after passing the center. But, if so, how far after? Well, only our scientists could tell us, but the truth is probably not as far right as many liberals fear, more centered than most conservatives hope.

But turn the question around: Is contemporary America a "liberal" nation? I don't think so (at least not as the word is popularly used), although let's admit that majority opinion swings rather widely issue to issue. As many commentators have pointed out, most Americans are usually inattentive to politics. Watch out though when they do pay heed. Their opinions shift with breathtaking speed.

Opinion research on this matter is inconclusive. (What a surprise.) Inferences derived from various polls conflict, although one does hear that the young especially are more conservative than at any time since the fifties, which, given the spirit of the intervening decades, isn't saying much. And anyway what these kids seem to be is more *libertarian*: They want limited government and unlimited fun.

But although the American majority may sometimes think and act on the negative (liberal) half of the WQ scale, more often than not we all *live* on the positive side. This is most obviously true in fundamental matters. A few examples follow, which, although I state them in parochial terms, probably apply generically (as equally in France and Russia as in the United States):

• We Americans speak English, and language itself derives its power and utility precisely from its conservative nature: Words and their meanings must largely be fixed; if they were ever-changing, we'd have a hard time indeed understanding our neighbors. You could even argue we'd have no neighbors. Language does often find radical employment, but only superficially and briefly.

• We Americans (better than 90 percent according to Mr. Gallup) believe in God, the One and Only, who is certainly not some second-string demigod like old Proteus, able to utter prophecies well enough, but always changing his shape. Every theological innovation must assert that Man's *understanding* evolves; any suggestion that God evolves is beneath even heresy.

• We Americans, most of us anyway, still admire the Constitution; we carry its precepts with us, as Willmoore Kendall used to say, "in our hips," which is to say *almost* instinctively. The Constitution is a very conservative document. As Margaret Thatcher has noted, America is the only nation founded on an idea: individual liberty.

• And we Americans know that summer follows spring, night follows day, and that the world is eternally obedient to law. Nature is conservative.

In each case we are talking about order. Reality itself is a series of orders: of orders within orders. Our most "progressive" liberals typically deny it. Order is Man's invention, they say (and, therefore, one made-up scheme is as good as any other). This is one of the intelligentsia's more baronial half-truths. Civilization and culture are indeed processes through which Man's creativity is most dramatically (occasionally clumsily) manifest, but the true and enduring order is *uncovered* more than it is invented. In this we are like Michelangelo, who said that as a sculptor he was simply chipping away stone to discover the form beneath. And those few avant-garde theorists who disclaim the importance of order are really just fooling themselves. As Robert Conquest has pointed out (this is his First Law), "Everybody is a reactionary on the subject he is expert about," which means even the most radical of radicals—say, a red-hot literary theorist—clings to a kind of order. Madmen may not; everybody else does.

So no matter how you choose to look at order's genesis—as divinely instituted or as culturally contrived—Edmund Burke's observation about its *primacy* holds true: "Good order is the foundation of all good things." Without it, we can see no future for ourselves.

But all that proves nothing about the "American character," which—if the very idea of a meaningful *national* ethos isn't bogus to begin with—is probably an indecipherable stew of contradictions. Besides, from the conservative point of view victory in the court of public opinion isn't even a goal. "Right is right, even if nobody does it," G. K. Chesterton observes. "Wrong is wrong, even if everybody is wrong about it."

Pluses and minuses aside, one may fairly ask who is closer to the truth about how best to live: the pursuit of truth being the concern of the best people, left, right, and center. Less so in matters spiritual, but more so in matters social, economic, political, and cultural, the *understanding* of truth emerges from debate, from the marketplace of competing ideas. I'm not suggesting here that truth itself is *determined* (in the sense of being created) by competition. If one believes in objective truth one must believe that it exists independently of our perceptions of it. I am suggesting that the ideas *embodying* truth must be refined and strengthened to withstand the endless assaults of illusion. And, given the complexity of everyday life and the limits of human intellect, *nobody* ever gets it all exactly right.

Like the ten maidens in the twenty-fifth chapter of Matthew's Gospel, we are virgins, one and all, with just one life to live. But if, as the parable has it, some of us can live with prudence and humility, perhaps our fundamental ignorance won't betray us in the midnight of our long loss of innocence.

Credo: Close to Home

What's at issue here is what people believe about the things that matter. This collection of conservative essays, some actually written by conservatives, is divided into five sections, which together represent one view of the broader categories of American experience: spiritual, social, economic, political, and cultural. Each of those words is a definitional morass, although none is quite so deep a pool of quicksand as *conservative* itself. Think of it: Back about 1989, one read daily that both "American conservatives" and "Soviet conservatives" opposed vigorous support of Gorbachev's reforms, and one whose ear was not delicately tuned to the shades of meaning might actually have believed that those two groups had something in common, whereas *our* opposition was intended to speed the expiration of communism, and *theirs* was meant to resuscitate it.

Conservative? It's a peculiar term. I'm not the first to say it: It is a *dreadful* word. And, heaven knows, for a century at least (the word gained currency here about 1850) American conservatives have wished to discover a better word, one that more adequately describes the spirit of the Right, one that does not so fixedly imply veneration of the status quo. After all, the political status quo—the Reagan years notwithstanding—increasingly resembles a conservative's nightmare.

Even sympathetic observers may dwell on this association with, as they said in the 1950s, "standpattism." In his *New Political Dictionary*, William Safire defines conservative as "a defender of the status quo who, when change becomes necessary in tested institutions or practices, prefers that it come slowly, and in moderation."

That's fine in part, although, again, "status quo" is just a bit too sweeping. (Conservatives are not confortable with Alexander Pope's assertion that whatever is, is good. Better is Viscount Falkland's famous dictum: "When it is not necessary to change, it is necessary not to change.") We need a word that captures not only conservatism's scruples but also its ethics.

In pursuit of most tenets of the conservative's good order, *libertarian* may be preferable to *conservative*. Trouble is, most traditionalists (paradoxically, both those described as *neo*conservative and as *paleo*conservative) can't accept that particular part of their ethos as properly descriptive of the whole. Nearly all conservatives are libertarian in their view of the state's *presence* in the lives of its citizens, but they disagree about its ends (and, therefore, about the degree of the presence). Traditionalists are more concerned with virtue; libertarians, as the name implies, with liberty. Traditionalists tend to see the community as the center of order; libertarians tend to place the individual at the core. As a result, traditionalists may see a greater role for institutions than do libertarians. "Do good," the traditionalist says to our leaders, whereas the libertarian says, "Go away."

Still, nearly all would agree with Lord Acton: "Liberty is not a means to a higher political end. It is itself the highest political end." And I don't believe I have ever met a conservative of any description who, practically as a first principle, did not favor limited government. Yes, some libertarians strike one as half-a-step removed from anarchism, and, true, some traditionalists seem too inclined to use expanded government power in the pursuit of goodness, but most American conservatives remain committed to the principle of limited, enumerated powers. ("Big-government conservative," an oxymoron if ever there was one, is an epithet sometimes hurled at neocons, who reply that it's not that government should be huge, but that it should be strong and effective when needed. Few conservatives, even the most libertarian, really believe government ought to be weak, although at times one is tempted.)

A word that is currently popular among many conservatives is *subsidiarity*. It's a term borrowed from Catholic social theory, and expressed most succinctly by Pope Pius XI: "[I]t is . . . unjust to turn over to a greater society of higher rank functions and services which can be performed by lesser bodies on a lower plane." The principle does not simply mean that federal power should be turned over to local authorities. As Richard John Neuhaus wrote in *Doing Well and Doing Good,* "The notion of devolving or decentralizing state functions assumes that the functions belong to the state in the first place. Subsidiarity is based on exactly the opposite assumption." Or as Abe Lincoln put it: "In all that the people can individually do as well for themselves, government ought not to interfere."

Whether in pursuit of virtue, liberty, or any other goal (most notably justice), government's enumerated powers need to be limited because its real powers are limited. Before the collapse of state socialism it was less possible to assert this with confidence, but it is now clear that even the apparatus of terror, mastered in this century by Nazis and communists, is unable to reshape the complex aspirations of a people.

F. A. Hayek emphasized that "not all order that results from the interplay of human actions is the result of design." We tend to think that order must be designed, because we are such designing creatures. But all intentional efforts to create a social order, Hayek wrote (in "The Confusion of Language in Political Thought"), "take place within a more comprehensive spontaneous order which is not the result of such a design."

The key phrase is "spontaneous order," another word for which is *tradition.* Conservatives are extremely suspicious of attempts to plan and control outcomes in society. The traditional orderly, evolved community—however flawed—is preferable to one melted and molded by contemporary enthusiasms—however noble. We may not know why things are as they are, but we do well to recall Proverbs (22:28): "Remove not the ancient landmark the fathers have set." As Burke observed of the social experimenters of his day, "With them it is a sufficient motive to destroy an old scheme because it is old. As to the new one, they are in no sort of fear with regard to the duration of a new building run up in haste; because duration is no object to those who think little or nothing has been done before their time."

The modern American liberal has trouble accepting tradition unless he understands how it has evolved, but in many, if not most cases such reasons are unknowable. In place of tradition the liberal would put reason itself, which seems perfectly reasonable at first. It's just a matter of goals and strategies, isn't it? In closed systems perhaps, but not in real life. The trouble with reason is its dependence upon facts, and the trouble with the facts of any traditional structure in a society is that they are too many and too hidden. As Pascal had it: "The last function of reason is to recognize that there are an infinity of things which surpass it." Reason, after all, is—and these words are being used in their philosophical senses—instrumental, not essential. If reason is not anchored by such fundamental matters as faith, law, and tradition, it can become dangerously brutal, even revolutionary. The early—which is to say, political—success of any revolutionary proposal is in large measure due to its novelty and simplicity. Its later failures arise when winning but facile policies collide with complex reality. This is why such proposals must always be implemented with coercion. And when the American government gets coercive, as it does whenever it ratchets up its taxing power (but also does when it propagates foolish regulations that proliferate inefficient bureaucracies), then the American people begin to behave in a positively conservative manner. It's the next thing to an instinct: Don't Tread On Me.

THE OLD PARADIGM

Limited governments of balanced powers, such as the one embodied by America's Constitution, are meant to leave most decisions, large and small, to the people in their communities and in their voluntary institutions—institutions that are as important as government, if not more important than government. Our unity, our nationhood, is predicated upon the strength and *power* of our most basic political units: families, neighborhoods, communities. Some power is ceded to the county (or big city), to the state, and finally to the national government, but each assignment of power is supposed to be legally enumerated. Today we live in a system in which great chunks of power have been assumed de facto by one of the three federal branches. Certain state capitals have become nearly as imperial as Washington, D.C. And in this political debate, wherein liberals and conservatives aim their respective constitutional weapons (the Fourteenth Amendment, theirs, versus the Tenth, ours), we often lose sight of why empowered communities—*subsidiarities*—are so important. "*There must be a stopping point,*" Charles Murray writes (in the chapter from his *In Pursuit: Of Happiness and Good Government* that appears in this book on page 175, "*some rule by which governments limit what they do for people*—not just because of budget constraints, not just because of infringements on freedom (though either of these might be a sufficient reason in itself), but because happiness is impossible unless people are left alone to take trouble over important things."

But this whole discussion raises a messy, chicken-egg question: Which comes first, the tradition or the principle? At first look, most of us would say the principle (in the foregoing discussion, limited government) would surely precede any institution (such as an independent judiciary). Yet Hayek for one argued somewhat differently: *Cosmos,* the evolved society, contains within it the *taxis* of organized institutions. Hayek spoke of *cosmos* as forming spontaneously—without purpose. This, I think, is simply another, and more elegant, way of describing the unplumbable complexities of everyday life, and it's a view that echoes Tocqueville's observation in *Democracy in America* that, "Every central government worships uniformity: uniformity relieves it from inquiry into an infinity of details, which must be attended to if rules have to be adapted to different men, instead of indiscriminately subjecting all men to the same rule."

Our best "taxic" principles will be those that were first "cosmic." Tradition certainly looms large, and conservatism's respect of it, of *cosmos,* demands formulated principles that look far beyond mere partisan intent and attempt to describe good order.

Which leads me to Richard Weaver's famous definition of conservatism: *a paradigm of essences towards which the phenomenology of the world is in continuing approximation.* Made thus (with great good humor), the claim is bold: this *philosophy of life* corresponds to—it mirrors—the *meaning of life.*

But those essences in Professor Weaver's paradigm, those principles, do stand apart from tradition. More and more, American conservatives champion American tradition. They do not champion tradition, per se: do not champion, for instance, *Romanian* tradition, and—this is the point—would primarily offer American principles, not American *traditions,* to those in Bucharest who today struggle to liberate their nation from its communist past.

And so . . . one wonders if the word *conservative* even plausibly signifies the views of conservatives. Increasingly, those whom we call *conservative* stand for certain principles that may have their roots in tradition, but which have little to do with the regnant mood in Hollywood, New York, or Washington.

Of course, tradition has always been a dicey word. Too often it is conceived of as a single, knowable entity, unchanging and rigid. In fact, no one can define tradition, except as its etymology suggests, as *a handing down.* For someone to offer the general statement, "I believe in tradition," is to invite queries concerning the specifics. One can probably as easily argue that there is a *tradition* of wife beating as that there is a tradition of marriage. Are conservatives in favor of both? No, of course not. And, in fact, the tradition we do favor is that process most adequately described as . . . *democracy*. Again we turn to Chesterton: "I have never been able to understand where people got the idea that democracy is in some way opposed to tradition. It is obvious that tradition is only democracy extended through time. It is trusting to a consensus of common human voices rather than to some isolated or arbitrary record."

Among those voices Chesterton included our ancestors', and in what has become perhaps his most famous aphorism defined tradition thusly: "It is the democracy of the dead." Not ignoring those who oppose it, G.K.C. went on to declare that tradition "refuses to submit to the small and arrogant oligarchy of those who happen merely to be walking about."

RADICAL FAITH

But, besides belief in limited government, what other views are definitively conservative? Only a few, none of them universally accepted on the Right: faith in God, skepticism about human nature, advocacy of free markets and private ownership, acceptance of inequality, belief in truth. Of these, the most important is faith.

Not that all conservatives are religious, of course. But the more religious a person is the more likely he is to be a conservative, whether or not he so describes himself. Although not widely so acknowledged, America's most *influential* conservative spokesman is *probably* not William F. Buckley, Jr., although he is conservatism's most eloquent champion, nor is it George Will, although he is conservatism's keenest analyst; nor is it Norman Podhoretz, although he is conservatism's most daring commentator; nor is it Irving Kristol, although he is conservatism's finest intellect. It is probably not even Rush Limbaugh, although his is conservatism's most *popular* voice. American conservatism's most influential voice is probably . . . Pat Robertson's. Why? Because his Evangelical conservatism is the most radical—*radical* in the etymological sense: it goes down deep; to the roots. According to recent Gallup surveys, Evangelicals are "the most conservative group in the country on social issues," although (no surprise here) this "conservative orientation does not always translate into conservative positions. . . . " Still, belief in God—of the kind, anyway, that acknowledges *divine rule*—gives rise to an almost organic conservatism. The "return to orthodoxy" by Protestants, Catholics, and Jews is showily proclaimed by our glossiest magazines. The character of that orthodoxy is explicated in G. K. Chesterton's "The Eternal Revolution," beginning on page 37.

PLAYING THE ANGELS

A conservative, whether religious or agnostic, does not necessarily believe that Man is evil or fallen, but such a view is closer to what most conservatives do believe than is the idea, common among liberals, that Man is perfectible. As with so many of the broad differences between conservatives and liberals, another chicken-egg dispute is at issue here. Many of America's more doctrinaire liberals believe the Sartrean formula: existence precedes essence. Man is malleable; change the environment, and you can change the man. To which the conservative replies: *Absurdité!*

The conservative emphasis on individual responsibility can at times seem to embrace the notion that a man is wholly what *he* makes of himself, which might literally mean his "essence" is self-created, but in fact Man's essence and his *existential* dilemma are transcendent. Changes in circumstances can and do matter, especially as they awaken individuals to the joys and sorrows of accountability, but evil cannot be repealed (or deprogrammed) because the selfishness from which it arises is an inevitability.

Man is full of passions. The soul of civilization, and particularly of religious civilization, is the ordering of those passions. Lately it seems we want to abolish the hierarchy and proclaim the equality of all desires. The claim is even made that the old hierarchy itself is the source of evil. But far from creating Utopia, the impulse to homogenize the "tempers"—to equate, for example, love and lust—is actually the incitement of Hell.

Conservative skepticism about human nature has a telling effect upon conservative views not only of Man but of society and government as well. The famous observation of James Madison in the *Federalist* is worth repeating: "If men were angels, no government would be necessary. If angels were to govern men, neither internal nor external controls on government would be necessary. In framing a govern-

ment which is to be administered by men over men, the great difficulty lies in this: you must first enable the government to control the
governed; and in the next place oblige it to control itself." Or, as
Michael Novak put it in *The Catholic Ethic and the Spirit of Capitalism:* "The reason behind these checks and balances is a classical
Christian and Jewish observation: *Every human sometimes sins.*
From this fact is drawn a political principle: *Trust no one with excessive power.* Trust no institution, either."

THE MESSY MARKET

The notion that a man ought to have the right to buy from and sell to
whomever he wishes is both a fundamental expression of his economic liberty and the essential ingredient of his commercial success.
Now at that the statement is one most people—right, center, and even
left—have little difficulty accepting, except for those who hold what
William F. Buckley, Jr., has called the "protectionist heresy."

The paradoxes abound. Because conservatives admire free markets—and, therefore, must accept capitalism's "creative destructiveness" (about which see George Gilder's "The Kinetic Economy" on
page 158)—they will often and increasingly find themselves at odds
with their own moral sense, as for instance, in the case of certain
innovations that express our boundless creativity but challenge our
received wisdom. In *Unbinding Prometheus,* physicist Donald
Cowan describes the conflict as "like the compulsion to open the
yellow envelope of a telegram—you must open it and at the same
time you dread opening it: it has your name on it and, you suppose,
your destiny in it. Most of us will open the envelope, must open it,
for if we do not, then we become the mediocre, the lukewarm, who,
as we have it on good authority, will be spewed out at the day of
judgment. We shall not have existed at all. The end of man is to
know." Who would not wish to return knowledge of nuclear
weapons to the Pandora's box of human creativity and then lock the
lid? Who would not want to protect workers from the loss of their
jobs in the wake of innovations, foreign or domestic? A free market
is risky, but it remains the best way for determining value and producing quality. And this is a principle as much at work in politics as
in economics. What we call democracy, a concept that has often

caused queasiness among conservatives, is preferable to all other forms of governance precisely because it maximizes individual choices and tends (in the long run anyway) to upset the schemes of elites. It is *antignostic,* by which I mean it facilitates the emergence of grass-roots truths—which tend to be grounded in tradition—and inhibits the imposition of avant-garde illusions. It is our best protection against tyranny.

And, as Richard M. Weaver notes (in "The Last Metaphysical Right," included in part III of this book), state ownership of the economy may provide "temporary amelioration and the illusion of future security," but Americans have so far successfully resisted its allure. Our agrarian roots, our expansionist history (think of the Homestead Act), and our never-wavering passion for real estate have created and maintained the "American exceptionalism" that Marx and Engels bemoaned, and that makes us instinctively hostile to collectivism.

INEQUALITY AND JUSTICE FOR ALL

One of the most fascinating subjects for students of American thought is the perennial debate about one of our most ubiquitous notions, equality.

As the great Tocqueville wrote: "Whatever may be the general endeavor of a community to render its members equal and alike, the personal pride of individuals will always seek to rise above the line, and to form somewhere an inequality to their own advantage." It is, therefore, an utter and dangerous fantasy to imagine that equality ought rightly to be a goal of public policy. Human life in all its complexity is set by nature against leveling. And yet the cry continues to be heard that the problem of American society is principally the problem of inequality. That may be so. But if there's no solution, there's no problem. To make a problem of that which cannot be solved is to invite forms of oppression that would be comical if they weren't so often brutal.

On the risible side, I think of Joseph Sobran's tongue-in-cheek proposition that if we are to grant rights to animals, we have a corresponding duty to demand that the animals in their turn act responsibly. The lion *must* lie down with the lamb. If they are to be equal with us—to share human rights—then animals must also be equal with one another, and, frankly, until *those* carnivores start eating tofu instead of flesh, don't bother asking this one to.

The goal of most preferential policies, such as affirmative action, is to see all groups in a society represented within all institutions and professions more or less as in their proportion to the population at large. If we make a temporary set-aside of jobs for one group, pretty soon that group will catch up, or so the rationale proposes. But as Shelby Steele points out (in *The Content of Our Character*), such attempts to enforce *diversity*, the current buzz word embodying egalitarian aspirations, apply "democratic principles to races and cultures rather than to citizens, despite the fact that there is nothing to indicate that real diversity is the same thing as proportionate representation."

As Irving Kristol has written:

> Purely egalitarian communities are certainly feasible—but only if they are selective in their recruitment and are relatively indifferent to economic growth and change, which encourages differentiation. Aristocratic societies are feasible too—most of human history consists of them—but only under conditions of relative economic lethargy, so that the distribution of power and wealth is insulated from change. But once you are committed to the vision of a predominantly commercial society, in which flux and change are "normal"—in which men and resources are expected to move to take advantage of new economic opportunities—then you find yourself tending toward the limited inequalities of a bourgeois kind.

("About Equality" in *Two Cheers for Capitalism*)

EPISTEMOLOGY MADE SIMPLE

The American academy is currently roiling with the suspicion that we cannot know anything for certain. Various forms of what both outsiders and insiders—with more or less equal glibness—call *deconstruction* have led some to conclude that *objective truth* is an idea with about as much currency as witchcraft, except that witchcraft is taken a bit more seriously. One observer has called the cachet of deconstruction "the squiggle of fancy French mustard on the hot dog of banal observation," and that it is, but what it isn't is particularly new. According to Paul Johnson, this all began with a half-educated understanding of Einstein's Special Theory of Relativity. "At the beginning of the 1920s the belief began to circulate," Johnson writes in *Modern Times*, "that there were no longer any absolutes: of time and space, of good and evil, of knowledge, above all of value. Mistakenly but perhaps inevitably, relativity became confused with relativism."

This is a Great Divide. If it weren't for the fact that conservatives are right about Truth, which I capitalize here to indicate that point towards which all lines of argument must converge, those on either side of the divide would be helpless even to discuss it. But because Truth does exist, those who deny it are able to do so only by using the forms that are derived from it.

This is not the place to detail proofs for the existence of objective truth. In the essay that begins on page 78, Peter Kreeft reminds us that none other than Jean-Paul Sartre opposed the Nuremberg trials because their judicial reference was natural law:

> The trial assumed that such a universal moral law really existed. Sartre had always taught that it didn't. So he was consistent. The democracies had no right to judge the Nazis if all values were relative to different cultures or different individuals.
>
> That was consistent. It was also moral bankruptcy—intolerable, unendurable, unlivable. Thank God for consistent moral relativists like Sartre: they show us what relativism really comes to.

• • •

My hope is that this anthology presents the beginnings of an outline of the conservative view of the Good Order. It is a complex view that by its nature eludes precise definition. Most people I know sure don't get it.

I disclaim any interest in being understood and appreciated by liberals, although I speak here as a conservative, not as a man. To say that many of my best friends are liberals is to state what, for one who has lived nearly twenty years among the Manhattanites, must be a given for all but the very lonely. Still, I might hope for at least a smidgen more forbearance from some of them.

Once at a Fifth Avenue cocktail party I found myself the ham sandwiched between two liberal women from the Heartland. I was literary editor of *National Review* at the time, and they expressed some amazement at meeting an *Eastern* conservative, so inured were they to the notion of liberal New York. I admitted that I'm a native Buck-eye, which helped explain me, and then one of the women asked:

"But you are prochoice, aren't you?"

"Am I proabortion? No," I admitted.

"Why do you say 'proabortion'?" the other woman asked.

"It's more precise. I'm antiabortion, not *prolife*. We're grown-ups, right? We can call things by their true names."

"What about your wife?"

"She's over there. Ask her," I said.

"I don't have to," the first woman said. "She's prochoice."

Knowing that they hadn't discussed the subject with my wife, I wondered aloud how they could possibly be so sure.

"She's obviously an intelligent woman," one of them said, "and I've never met an intelligent woman who's prolife."

Now this is a problem. I suppose it comes down to divergent views of the genesis of truth. Conservatives believe truth comes from God. Liberals believe that truth evolves from history, which for many of them begins only when they themselves, unaborted, are born.

But I do hope some fair-minded folks will read the essays that follow and gain from them, as I have, vivid knowledge of the numinous world. Each of these essays describes what your editor considers a conservative position, even though not every author may consider himself conservative.

There are questions, problems. We believe there must be answers, solutions. And if the whole of conservative thought comes close to the truth—that is, well describes the order, the *proper* order, of the world—we will first sense it and then cleave to it as we note the efficacy of specific conservative ideas. That efficacy ought to ring the bell of common sense. Those ideas ought to make folks nod, and say, "Well, that just about settles it." This does not mean that all good, conservative ideas ought to be reducible to mere slogans. Still, the conservative ethos ought always to reject the frenzied obscurantism of the Left, and be comfortable with its aphoristic tendency. "When guns are outlawed," the old bumper sticker reads, "only outlaws will have guns." No proponent of gun control has ever refuted the truth of the assertion; none ever will. *Veritas simplex oratio est,* I always say. The language of truth is simplicity.

PART I

The Spiritual Order

A great historian's view of why the state has to accept the supremacy of spiritual needs:

This is why our modern machine-made civilisation, in spite of the material benefits that it has conferred, is marked by a feeling of moral unrest and social discontent which was absent from the old religious cultures, although the lot of the ordinary man in them was infinitely harder from the material point of view.

You can give men food and leisure and good conditons of work, and still they will remain unsatisfied. You can deny them all these things, and they will not complain so long as they feel that they have something to die for.

—CHRISTOPHER DAWSON, *The Modern Dilemma: The Problem of European Unity (1933)*

The Eternal Revolution

G. K. Chesterton's Orthodoxy: The Romance of Faith *(1908) is an incomparable classic of Western spirituality. There may be another twentieth-century book that is more quotable, but I don't know it. Gilbert Keith Chesterton was an astonishingly erudite man whose opinions—about everything under the sun—were always presented with an authority that in a lesser man would have been fantastic arrogance. Who else could call Nietzsche a "very timid thinker"?*

Edmund Burke asserted that "change is the instrument of preservation," which from conservatism's beginnings ought to have given the lie to all the claptrap about standpattism. For Chesterton, the preferred word was reform. *It is, he wrote, "a metaphor for reasonable and determined men: it means that we can see a certain thing out of shape and we mean to put it into shape. And we know what shape." His insight that we must progress toward a fixed ideal gets to the heart of the conservative's vision of the world.*

THE FOLLOWING PROPOSITIONS HAVE BEEN URGED: First, that some faith in our life is required even to improve it; second, that some dissatisfaction with things as they are is necessary even in order to be satisfied; third, that to have this necessary content and necessary discontent it is not sufficient to have the obvious equilibrium of the Stoic. For mere resignation has neither the gigantic levity of pleasure nor the superb intolerance of pain. There is a vital objection to the advice merely to grin and bear it. The objection is that if you merely bear it, you do not grin. Greek heroes do not grin: but gargoyles do—because they are Christian. And when a Christian is pleased, he is (in the most exact sense) frightfully pleased; his pleasure is frightful. Christ prophesied the whole of Gothic architecture in that hour when nervous and respectable people (such people as now object to barrel organs) objected to the shouting of the gutter-snipes of Jerusalem. He said, "If these were silent, the very stones would cry out." Under the impulse of His spirit arose like a clamorous chorus the façades of the mediæval cathedrals, thronged with shouting faces and open mouths. The prophecy has fulfilled itself: the very stones cry out.

If these things be conceded, though only for argument, we may take up where we left it the thread of the thought of the natural man, called by the Scotch (with regrettable familiarity), "The Old Man." We can ask the next question so obviously in front of us. Some satisfaction is needed even to make things better. But what do we mean by making things better? Most modern talk on this matter is a mere argument in a circle—that circle which we have already made the symbol of madness and of mere rationalism. Evolution is only good if it produces good; good is only good if it helps evolution. The elephant stands on the tortoise, and the tortoise on the elephant.

Obviously, it will not do to take our ideal from the principle in nature; for the simple reason that (except for some human or divine theory), there is no principle in nature. For instance, the cheap anti-democrat of to-day will tell you solemnly that there is no equality in nature. He is right, but he does not see the logical addendum. There is no equality in nature; also there is no inequality in nature. Inequality, as much as equality, implies a standard of value. To read aristocracy into the anarchy of animals is just as sentimental as to read democracy into it. Both aristocracy and democracy are human ideals: the one saying that all men are valuable, the other that some men are more valuable. But nature does not say that cats are more valuable than mice; nature makes no remark on the subject. She does not even say that the cat is enviable or the mouse pitiable. We think the cat superior because we have (or most of us have) a particular philosophy to the effect that life is better than death. But if the mouse were a German pessimist mouse, he might not think that the cat had beaten him at all. He might think he had beaten the cat by getting to the grave first. Or he might feel that he had actually inflicted frightful punishment on the cat by keeping him alive. Just as a microbe might feel proud of spreading a pestilence, so the pessimistic mouse might exult to think that he was renewing in the cat the torture of conscious existence. It all depends on the philosophy of the mouse. You cannot even say that there is victory or superiority in nature unless you have some doctrine about what things are superior. You cannot even say that the cat scores unless there is a system of scoring. You cannot even say that the cat gets the best of it unless there is some best to be got.

We cannot, then, get the ideal itself from nature, and as we follow here the first and natural speculation, we will leave out (for the present) the idea of getting it from God. We must have our own vision. But the attempts of most moderns to express it are highly vague.

Some fall back simply on the clock: they talk as if mere passage through time brought some superiority; so that even a man of the first mental calibre carelessly uses the phrase that human morality is never up to date. How can anything be up to date?—a date has no character. How can one say that Christmas celebrations are not suitable to the twenty-fifth of a month? What the writer meant, of course, was that the majority is behind his favourite minority—or in front of it. Other vague modern people take refuge in material metaphors; in fact, this is the chief mark of vague modern people. Not daring to define their doctrine of what is good, they use physical figures of speech without stint or shame, and, what is worst of all, seem to think these cheap analogies are exquisitely spiritual and superior to the old morality. Thus they think it intellectual to talk about things being "high." It is at least the reverse of intellectual; it is a mere phrase from a steeple or a weathercock. "Tommy was a good boy" is a pure philosophical statement, worthy of Plato or Aquinas. "Tommy lived the higher life" is a gross metaphor from a ten-foot rule.

This, incidentally, is almost the whole weakness of Nietzsche, whom some are representing as a bold and strong thinker. No one will deny that he was a poetical and suggestive thinker; but he was quite the reverse of strong. He was not at all bold. He never put his own meaning before himself in bald abstract words: as did Aristotle and Calvin, and even Karl Marx, the hard, fearless men of thought. Nietzsche always escaped a question by a physical metaphor, like a cheery minor poet. He said, "beyond good and evil," because he had not the courage to say, "more good than good and evil," or, "more evil than good and evil." Had he faced his thought without metaphors, he would have seen that it was nonsense. So, when he describes his hero, he does not dare to say, "the purer man," or "the happier man," or "the sadder man," for all these are ideas; and ideas are alarming. He says "the upper man," or "over man," a physical metaphor from acrobats or alpine climbers. Nietzsche is truly a very timid thinker. He does not really know in the least what sort of man he wants evolution to produce. And if he does not know, certainly the ordinary evolutionists, who talk about things being "higher," do not know either.

Then again, some people fall back on sheer submission and sitting still. Nature is going to do something some day; nobody knows what, and nobody knows when. We have no reason for acting, and no reason for not acting. If anything happens it is right: if anything is prevented it was wrong. Again, some people try to anticipate nature by doing something, by doing anything. Because we may possibly grow wings they cut off their legs. Yet nature may be trying to make them centipedes for all they know.

Lastly, there is a fourth class of people who take whatever it is that they happen to want, and say that that is the ultimate aim of evolution. And these are the only sensible people. This is the only really healthy way with the word evolution, to work for what you want, and to call *that* evolution. The only intelligible sense that progress or advance can have among men, is that we have a definite vision, and that we wish to make the whole world like that vision. If you like to put it so, the essence of the doctrine is that what we have around us is the mere method and preparation for something that we have to create. This is not a world, but rather the material for a world. God has given us not so much the colours of a picture as the colours of a palette. But he has also given us a subject, a model, a fixed vision. We must be clear about what we want to paint. This adds a further principle to our previous list of principles. We have said we must be fond of this world, even in order to change it. We now add that we must be fond of another world (real or imaginary) in order to have something to change it to.

We need not debate about the mere words evolution or progress: personally I prefer to call it reform. For reform implies form. It implies that we are trying to shape the world in a particular image; to make it something that we see already in our minds. Evolution is a metaphor from mere automatic unrolling. Progress is a metaphor from merely walking along a road—very likely the wrong road. But reform is a metaphor for reasonable and determined men: it means that we see a certain thing out of shape and we mean to put it into shape. And we know what shape.

Now here comes in the whole collapse and huge blunder of our age. We have mixed up two different things, two opposite things. Progress should mean that we are always changing the world to suit the vision. Progress does mean (just now) that we are always changing the vision. It should mean that we are slow but sure in bringing justice and mercy among men: it does mean that we are very swift in doubting the desirability of justice and mercy: a wild page from any Prussian sophist makes men doubt it. Progress should mean that we are always walking towards the New Jerusalem. It does not mean that the New Jerusalem is always walking away from us. We are not altering the real to suit the ideal. We are altering the ideal: it is easier.

Silly examples are always simpler; let us suppose a man wanted a particular kind of world; say, a blue world. He would have no cause to complain of the slightness or swiftness of his task; he might toil for a long time at the transformation; he could work away (in every sense) until all was blue. He could have heroic adventures; the putting of the last touches to a blue tiger. He could have fairy dreams; the dawn of a blue moon. But if he worked harm, that high-minded reformer would certainly (from his own point of view) leave the world better and bluer than he found it. If he altered a blade of grass to his favourite colour every day, he would get on slowly. But if he altered his favourite colour every day, he would not get on at all. If, after reading a fresh philosopher, he started to paint everything red or yellow, his work would be thrown away: there would be nothing to show except a few blue tigers walking about, specimens of his early bad manner. This is exactly the position of the average modern thinker. It will be said that this is avowedly a preposterous example. But it is literally the fact of recent history. The great and grave changes in our political civilization all belonged to the early nineteenth century, not to the later. They belonged to the black and white epoch when men believed fixedly in Toryism, in Protestantism, in Calvinism, in Reform, and not unfrequently in Revolution. And whatever each man believed in he hammered at steadily, without scepticism: and there was a time when the Established Church might have fallen, and the House of Lords nearly fell. It was because Radicals were wise enough to be constant and consistent; it was because Radicals were wise enough to be Conservative. But in the existing atmosphere there is not enough time and tradition in Radicalism to pull anything down. There is a great deal of truth in Lord Hugh Cecil's suggestion (made in a fine speech) that the era of change is over, and that ours is an era of conservation and repose. But probably it would pain Lord Hugh Cecil if he realized (what is certainly the case) that ours is only an age of conservation because it is an age of complete unbelief. Let beliefs fade fast and frequently, if you wish institutions to remain the same. The more the life of the mind is unhinged, the more the machinery of matter will be left to itself. The net result of all our political suggestions, Collectivism, Tolstoyanism, Neo-Feudalism, Communism, Anarchy, Scientific Bureaucracy—the plain fruit of all of them is that the Monarchy and the House of Lords will remain. The net result of all the new religions will be that the Church of England will not (for heaven knows how long) be disestablished. It was Karl Marx, Nietzsche, Tolstoy, Cunninghame Grahame, Bernard Shaw and Auberon Herbert, who between them, with bowed gigantic backs, bore up the throne of the Archbishop of Canterbury.

We may say broadly that free thought is the best of all the safeguards against freedom. Managed in a modern style the emancipation of the slave's mind is the best way of preventing the emancipation of the slave. Teach him to worry about whether he wants to be free, and he will not free himself. Again, it may be said that this instance is remote or extreme. But, again, it is exactly true of the men in the streets around us. It is true that the negro slave, being a debased barbarian, will probably have either a human affection of loyalty, or a human affection for liberty. But the man we see every day—the worker in Mr. Gradgrind's factory, the little clerk in Mr. Gradgind's office— he is too mentally worried to believe in freedom. He is kept quiet with revolutionary literature. He is calmed and kept in his place by a constant succession of wild philosophies. He is a Marxian one day, a Nietzscheite the next day, a Superman (probably) the next day; and a slave every day. The only thing that remains after all the philosophies is the factory. The only man who gains by all the philosophies is Gradgrind. It would be worth his while to keep his commercial helotry supplied with sceptical literature. And now I come to think of it, of course, Gradgrind is famous for giving libraries. He shows his sense. All modern books are on his side. As long as the vision of heaven is always changing, the vision of earth will be exactly the same. No ideal will remain long enough to be realized, or even partly realized. The modern young man will never change his environment; for he will always change his mind.

This, therefore, is our first requirement about the ideal towards which progress is directed; it must be fixed. Whistler used to make many rapid studies of a sitter; it did not matter if he tore up twenty portraits. But it would matter if he looked up twenty times, and each time saw a new person sitting placidly for his portrait. So it does not matter (comparatively speaking) how often humanity fails to imitate its ideal; for then all its old failures are fruitful. But it does frightfully matter how often humanity changes its ideal; for then all its old failures are fruitless. The question therefore becomes this: How can we keep the artist discontented with his pictures while preventing him from being vitally discontented with his art? How can we make a man always dissatisfied with his work, yet always satisfied with working? How can we make sure that the portrait painter will throw the portrait out of window instead of taking the natural and more human course of throwing the sitter out of window?

A strict rule is not only necessary for ruling; it is also necessary for rebelling. This fixed and familiar ideal is necessary to any sort of revolution. Man will sometimes act slowly upon new ideas; but he will only act swiftly upon old ideas. If I am merely to float or fade or evolve, it may be towards something anarchic; but if I am to riot, it must be for something respectable. This is the whole weakness of certain schools of progress and moral evolution. They suggest that there has been a slow movement towards morality, with an imperceptible ethical change in every year or at every instant. There is only one great disadvantage in this theory. It talks of a slow movement towards justice; but it does not permit a swift movement. A man is not allowed to leap up and declare a certain state of things to be intrinsically intolerable. To make the matter clear, it is better to take a specific example. Certain of the idealistic vegetarians, such as Mr. Salt, say that the time has now come for eating no meat; by implication they assume that at one time it was right to eat meat, and they suggest (in words that could be quoted) that some day it may be wrong to eat milk and eggs. I do not discuss here the question of what is justice to animals. I only say that whatever is justice ought, under given conditions, to be prompt justice. If an animal is wronged, we ought to be able to rush to his rescue. But how can we rush if we are, perhaps, in advance of our time? How can we rush to catch a train which may not arrive for a few centuries? How can I denounce a man for skinning cats, if he is only now what I may possibly become in drinking a glass of milk? A splendid and insane Russian sect ran about taking all the cattle out of all the carts. How can I pluck up courage to take the horse out of my hansom-cab, when I do not know whether my evolutionary watch is only a little fast or the cabman's a little slow? Suppose I say to a sweater, "Slavery suited one stage of evolution." And suppose he answers, "And sweating suits this stage of evolution." How can I answer if there is no eternal test? If sweaters can be behind the current morality, why should not philanthropists be in front of it? What on earth is the current morality, except in its literal sense—the morality that is always running away?

Thus we may say that a permanent ideal is as necessary to the innovator as to the conservative; it is necessary whether we wish the king's orders to be promptly executed or whether we only wish the king to be promptly executed. The guillotine has many sins, but to do it justice there is nothing evolutionary about it. The favorite evolutionary argument finds its best answer in the axe. The Evolutionist says, "Where do you draw the line?" the Revolutionist answers, "I draw it *here:* exactly between your head and body." There must at any given moment be an abstract right and wrong if any blow is to be struck; there must be something eternal if there is to be anything sudden. Therefore for all intelligible human purposes, for altering things or for keeping things as they are, for founding a system for ever, as in China, or for altering it every month as in the early French Revolution, it is equally necessary that the vision should be a fixed vision. This is our first requirement.

When I had written this down, I felt once again the presence of something else in the discussion: as a man hears a church bell above the sound of the street. Something seemed to be saying, "My ideal at least is fixed; for it was fixed before the foundations of the world. My vision of perfection assuredly cannot be altered; for it is called Eden. You may alter the place to which you are going; but you cannot alter the place from which you have come. To the orthodox there must always be a case for revolution; for in the hearts of men God has been put under the feet of Satan. In the upper world hell once rebelled against heaven. But in this world heaven is rebelling against hell. For the orthodox there can always be a revolution; for a revolution is a restoration. At any instant you may strike a blow for the perfection which no man has seen since Adam. No unchanging custom, no changing evolution can make the original good any thing but good. Man may have had concubines as long as cows have had horns: still they are not a part of him if they are sinful. Men may have been under oppression ever since fish were under water; still they ought not to be, if oppression is sinful. The chain may seem as natural to the slave, or the paint to the harlot, as does the plume to the bird or the burrow to the fox; still they are not, if they are sinful. I lift my prehistoric legend to defy all your history. Your vision is not merely a fixture: it is a fact." I paused to note the new coincidence of Christianity: but I passed on.

I passed on to the next necessity of any ideal of progress. Some people (as we have said) seem to believe in an automatic and impersonal progress in the nature of things. But it is clear that no political activity can be encouraged by saying that progress is natural and inevitable; that is not a reason for being active, but rather a reason for being lazy. If we are bound to improve, we need not trouble to improve. The pure doctrine of progress is the best of all reasons for not being a progressive. But it is to none of these obvious comments that I wish primarily to call attention.

The only arresting point is this: that if we suppose improvement to be natural, it must be fairly simple. The world might conceivably be working toward one consummation, but hardly towards any particular arrangement of many qualities. To take our original simile: Nature by herself may be growing more blue; that is, a process so simple that it might be impersonal. But Nature cannot be making a careful picture made of many picked colours, unless Nature is personal. If the end of the world were mere darkness or mere light it might come as slowly and inevitably as dusk or dawn. But if the end of the world is to be a piece of elaborate and artistic chiaroscuro, then there must be design in it, either human or divine. The world, through mere time, might grow black like an old picture, or white like an old coat; but if it is turned into a particular piece of black and white art—then there is an artist.

If the distinction be not evident, I give an ordinary instance. We constantly hear a particularly cosmic creed from the modern humanitarians; I use the word humanitarian in the ordinary sense, as meaning one who upholds the claims of all creatures against those of humanity. They suggest that through the ages we have been growing more and more humane, that is to say, that one after another, groups or sections of beings, slaves, children, women, cows, or what not, have been gradually admitted to mercy or to justice. They say that we once thought it right to eat men (we didn't); but I am not here concerned with their history, which is highly unhistorical. As a fact, anthropophagy is certainly a decadent thing, not a primitive one. It is much more likely that modern men will eat human flesh out of affectation than that primitive man ever ate it out of ignorance. I am here only following the outlines of their argument, which consists in maintaining that man has been progressively more lenient, first to citizens, then to slaves, then to animals, and then (presumably) to plants. I think it wrong to sit on a man. Soon, I shall think it wrong to sit on a horse. Eventually (I suppose) I shall think it wrong to sit on a chair. That is the drive of the argument. And for this argument it can be said that it is possible to talk of it in terms of evolution or inevitable progress. A perpetual tendency to touch fewer and fewer things might—one feels, be a mere brute unconscious tendency, like that of a species to produce fewer and fewer children. This drift may be really evolutionary, because it is stupid.

Darwinism can be used to back up two mad moralities, but it cannot be used to back up a single sane one. The kinship and competition of all living creatures can be used as a reason for being insanely cruel or insanely sentimental; but not for a healthy love of animals. On the evolutionary basis you may be inhumane, or you may be absurdly humane; but you cannot be human. That you and a tiger are one may be a reason for being tender to a tiger. Or it may be a reason for being as cruel as the tiger. It is one way to train the tiger to imitate you, it is a shorter way to imitate the tiger. But in neither case does evolution tell you how to treat a tiger reasonably, that is, to admire his stripes while avoiding his claws.

If you want to treat a tiger reasonably, you must go back to the garden of Eden. For the obstinate reminder continued to recur: only the supernatural has taken a sane view of Nature. The essence of all pantheism, evolutionism, and modern cosmic religion is really in this proposition: that Nature is our mother. Unfortunately, if you regard Nature as a mother, you discover that she is a step-mother. The main point of Christianity was this: that Nature is not our mother: Nature is our sister. We can be proud of her beauty, since we have the same father; but she has no authority over us; we have to admire, but not to imitate. This gives to the typically Christian pleasure in this earth a strange touch of lightness that is almost frivolity. Nature was a solemn mother to the worshippers of Isis and Cybele. Nature was a solemn mother to Wordsworth or to Emerson. But Nature is not solemn to Francis of Assisi or to George Herbert. To St. Francis, Nature is a sister, and even a younger sister: a little, dancing sister, to be laughed at as well as loved.

This, however, is hardly our main point at present; I have admitted it only in order to show how constantly, and as it were accidentally, the key would fit the smallest doors. Our main point is here, that if there be a mere trend of impersonal improvement in Nature, it must presumably be a simple trend towards some simple triumph. One can imagine that some automatic tendency in biology might work for giving us longer and longer noses. But the question is, do we want to have longer and longer noses? I fancy not; I believe that we most of us want to say to our noses, "thus far, and no farther; and here shall thy proud point be stayed": we require a nose of such length as may ensure an interesting face. But we cannot imagine a mere biological trend towards producing interesting faces; because an interesting face is one particular arrangement of eyes, nose, and mouth, in a most complex relation to each other. Proportion cannot be a drift: it is either an accident or a design. So with the ideal of human morality and its relation to the humanitarians and the anti-humanitarians. It is conceivable that we are going more and more to keep our hands off things: not to drive horses; not to pick flowers. We may eventually be bound not to disturb a man's mind even by argument; not to disturb the sleep of birds even by coughing. The ultimate apotheosis would appear to be that of a man sitting quite still, nor daring to stir for fear of disturbing a fly, nor to eat for fear of incommoding a microbe. To so crude a consummation as that we might perhaps unconsciously drift. But do we want so crude a consummation? Similarly, we might unconsciously evolve along the opposite or Nietzschian line of development—superman crushing superman in one tower of tyrants until the universe is smashed up for fun. But do we want the universe smashed up for fun? It is not quite clear that what we really hope for is one particular management and proposition of these two things; a certain amount of restraint and respect, a certain amount of energy and mastery? If our life is ever really as beautiful as a fairy-tale, we shall have to remember that all the beauty of a fairy-tale lies in this: that the prince has a wonder which just stops short of being fear. If he is afraid of the giant, there is an end of him; but also if he is not astonished at the giant, there is an end of the fairy-tale. The whole point depends upon his being at once humble enough to wonder, and haughty enough to defy. So our attitude to the giant of the world must not merely be increasing delicacy or increasing contempt: it must be one particular proportion of the two—which is exactly right. We must have in us enough reverence for all things outside us to make us tread fearfully on the grass. We must also have enough disdain for all things outside us, to make us, on due occasion, spit at the stars. Yet these two things (if we are to be good or happy) must be combined, not in any combination, but in one particular combination. The perfect happiness of men on the earth (if it ever comes) will not be a flat and solid thing, like the satisfaction of animals. It will be an exact and perilous balance; like that of a desperate romance. Man must have just enough faith in himself to have adventures, and just enough doubt of himself to enjoy them.

This, then, is our second requirement for the ideal of progress. First, it must be fixed; second, it must be composite. It must not (if it is to satisfy our souls) be the mere victory of some one thing swallowing up everything else, love or pride or peace or adventure; it must be a definite picture composed of these elements in their best proportion and relation. I am not concerned at this moment to deny that some such good culmination may be, by the constitution of things, reserved for the human race. I only point out that if this composite happiness is fixed for us it must be fixed by some mind; for only a mind can place the exact proportions of a composite happiness. If the beautification of the world is a mere work of nature, then it must be as simple as the freezing of the world, or the burning up of the world. But if the beautification of the world is not a work of nature but a work of art, then it involves an artist. And here again my contemplation was cloven by the ancient voice which said, "I could have told you all this a long time ago. If there is any certain progress it can only be my kind of progress, the progress towards a complete city of virtues and dominations where righteousness and peace contrive to kiss each other. An impersonal force might be leading you to a wilderness of perfect flatness or a peak of perfect height. But only a personal God can possibly be leading you (if, indeed, you are being led) to a city with just streets and architectural proportions, a city in which each of you can contribute exactly the right amount of your own colour to the many coloured coat of Joseph."

Twice again, therefore, Christianity had come in with the exact answer that I required. I had said, "The ideal must be fixed," and the Church had answered, "Mine is literally fixed, for it existed before anything else." I said secondly, "It must be artistically combined, like a picture"; and the Church answered, "Mine is quite literally a picture, for I know who painted it." Then I went on to the third thing, which, as it seemed to me, was needed for an Utopia or goal of progress. And of all the three it is infinitely the hardest to express. Perhaps it might be put thus: that we need watchfulness even in Utopia, lest we fall from Utopia as we fell from Eden.

We have remarked that one reason offered for being a progressive is that things naturally tend to grow better. But the only real reason for being a progressive is that things naturally tend to grow worse. The corruption in things is not only the best argument for being progressive; it is also the only argument against being conservative. The conservative theory would really be quite sweeping and unanswerable if it were not for this one fact. But all conservatism is based upon the idea that if you leave things alone you leave them as they are. But you do not. If you leave a thing alone you leave it to a torrent of change. If you leave a white post alone it will soon be a black post. If you particularly want it to be white you must be always painting it again; that is, you must be always having a revolution. Briefly, if you want the old white post you must have a new white post. But this which is true even of inanimate things is in a quite special and terrible sense true of all human things. An almost unnatural vigilance is really required of the citizen because of the horrible rapidity with which human institutions grow old. It is the custom in passing romance and journalism to talk of men suffering under old tyrannies. But, as a fact, men have almost always suffered under new tyrannies; under tyrannies that had been public liberties hardly twenty years before. Thus England went mad with joy over the patriotic monarchy of Elizabeth; and then (almost immediately afterwards) went mad with rage in the trap of the tyranny of Charles the First. So, again, in France the monarchy became intolerable, not just after it had been tolerated, but just after it had been adored. The son of Louis the well-beloved was Louis the guillotined. So in the same way in England in the nineteenth century the Radical manufacturer was entirely trusted as a mere tribune of the people, until suddenly we heard the cry of the Socialist that he was a tyrant eating the people like bread. So again, we have almost up to the last instant trusted the newspapers as organs of public opinion. Just recently some of us have seen (not slowly, but with a start) that they are obviously nothing of the kind. They are, by the nature of the case, the hobbies of a few rich men. We have not any need to rebel against antiquity; we have to rebel against novelty. It is the new rulers, the capitalist or the editor, who really hold up the modern world. There is no fear that a modern king will attempt to override the constitution; it is more likely that he will ignore the constitution and work behind its back; he will take no advantage of his kingly power; it is more likely that he will take advantage of his kingly powerlessness, of the fact that he is free from criticism and publicity. For the king is the most private person of our time. It will not be necessary for any one to fight again against the proposal of a censorship of the press. We do not need a censorship of the press. We have a censorship by the press.

This startling swiftness with which popular systems turn oppressive is the third fact for which we shall ask our perfect theory of progress to allow. It must always be on the look out for every privilege being abused, for every working right becoming a wrong. In this matter I am entirely on the side of the revolutionists. They are really right to be always suspecting human institutions; they are right not to put their trust in princes nor in any child of man. The chieftain chosen to be the friend of the people becomes the enemy of the people; the newspaper started to tell the truth now exists to prevent the truth being told. Here, I say, I felt that I was really at last on the side of the revolutionary. And then I caught my breath again: for I remembered that I was once again on the side of the orthodox.

Christianity spoke again and said: "I have always maintained that men were naturally backsliders; that human virtue tended of its own nature to rust or to rot; I have always said that human beings as such go wrong, especially happy human beings, especially proud and prosperous human beings. This eternal revolution, this suspicion sustained through centuries, you (being a vague modern) call the doctrine of progress. If you were a philosopher you would call it, as I do, the doctrine of original sin. You may call it the cosmic advance as much as you like; I call it what it is—the Fall."

I have spoken of orthodoxy coming in like a sword; here I confess it came in like a battleaxe. For really (when I came to think of it) Christianity is the only thing left that has any real right to question the power of the well-nurtured or the well-bred. I have listened often enough to Socialists, or even to democrats, saying that the physical conditions of the poor must of necessity make them mentally and morally degraded. I have listened to scientific men (and there are still scientific men not opposed to democracy) saying that if we give the poor healthier conditions vice and wrong will disappear. I have listened to them with a horrible attention, with a hideous fascination. For it was like watching a man energetically sawing from the tree the branch he is sitting on. If these happy democrats could prove their case, they would strike democracy dead. If the poor are thus utterly demoralized, it may or may not be practical to raise them. But it is certainly quite practical to disfranchise them. If the man with a bad bedroom cannot give a good vote, then the first and swiftest deduction is that he shall give no vote. The governing class may not unreasonably say: "It may take us some time to reform his bedroom. But if he is the brute you say, it will take him very little time to ruin our country. Therefore we will take your hint and not give him the chance." It fills me with horrible amusement to observe the way in which the earnest Socialist industriously lays the foundation of all aristocracy, expatiating blandly upon the evident unfitness of the poor to rule. It is like listening to somebody at an evening party apologising for entering without evening dress, and explaining that he had recently been intoxicated, had a personal habit of taking off his clothes in the street, and had, moreover, only just changed from prison uniform. At any moment, one feels, the host might say that really, if it was as bad as that, he need not come in at all. So it is when the ordinary Socialist, with a beaming face, proves that the poor, after their smashing experiences, cannot be really trustworthy. At any moment the rich may say, "Very well, then, we won't trust them," and bang the door in his face. On the basis of Mr. Blatchford's view of heredity and environment, the case for the aristocracy is quite overwhelming. If clean homes and clean air make clean souls, why not give the power (for the present at any rate) to those who undoubtedly have the clean air? If better conditions will make the poor more fit to govern themselves, why should not better conditions already make the rich more fit to govern them? On the ordinary environment argument the matter is fairly manifest. The comfortable class must be merely our vanguard in Utopia.

Is there any answer to the proposition that those who have had the best opportunities will probably be our best guides? Is there any answer to the argument that those who have breathed clean air had better decide for those who have breathed foul? As far as I know, there is only one answer, and that answer is Christianity. Only the Christian Church can offer any rational objection to a complete confidence in the rich. For she has maintained from the beginning that the danger was not in man's environment, but in man. Further, she has maintained that if we come to talk of a dangerous environment, the most dangerous environment of all is the commodious environment. I know that the most modern manufacture has been really occupied in trying to produce an abnormally large needle. I know that the most recent biologists have been chiefly anxious to discover a very small camel. But if we diminish the camel to his smallest, or open the eye of the needle to its largest—if, in short, we assume the words of Christ to have meant the very least that they could mean, His words must at the very least mean this—that rich men are not very likely to be morally trustworthy. Christianity even when watered down is hot enough to boil all modern society to rags. The mere minimum of the Church would be a deadly ultimatum to the world. For the whole modern world is absolutely based on the assumption, not that the rich are necessary (which is tenable), but that the rich are trustworthy, which (for a Christian) is not tenable. You will hear everlastingly, in all discussions about newspapers, companies, aristocracies, or party politics, this argument that the rich man cannot be bribed. The fact is, of course, that the rich man is bribed; he has been bribed already. That is why he is a rich man. The whole case for Christianity is that a man who is dependent upon the luxuries of this life is a corrupt man, spiritually corrupt, politically corrupt, financially corrupt. There is one thing that Christ and all the Christian saints have said with a sort of savage monotony. They have said simply that to be rich is to be in peculiar danger of moral wreck. It is not demonstrably un-Christian to kill the rich as violators of definable justice. It is not demonstrably un-Christian to crown the rich as convenient rulers of society. It is not certainly un-Christian to rebel against the rich or to submit to the rich. But it is quite certainly un-Christian to trust the rich, to regard the rich as more morally safe than the poor. A Christian may consistently say, "I respect that man's rank, although he takes bribes." But a Christian cannot say, as all modern men are saying at lunch and breakfast, "a man of that rank would not take bribes." For it is a part of Christian dogma that any man in any rank may take bribes. It is a part of Christian dogma; it also happens by a curious coincidence that it is a part of obvious human history. When people say that a man "in that position" would be incorruptible, there is no need to bring Christianity into the discussion. Was Lord Bacon a bootblack? Was the Duke of Marlborough a crossing sweeper? In the best Utopia, I must be prepared for the moral fall of any man in any position at any moment; especially for my fall from my position at this moment.

Much vague and sentimental journalism has been poured out to the effect that Christianity is akin to democracy, and most of it is scarcely strong or clear enough to refute the fact that the two things have often quarrelled. The real ground upon which Christianity and democracy are one is very much deeper. The one specially and peculiarly un-Christian idea is the idea of Carlyle—the idea that the man should rule who feels that he can rule. Whatever else is Christian, this is heathen. If our faith comments on government at all, its comment must be this—that the man should rule who does *not* think that he can rule. Carlyle's hero may say "I will be king"; but the Christian saint must say "Nolo episcopari." If the great paradox of Christianity means anything, it means this—that we must take the crown in our hands, and go hunting in dry places and dark corners of the earth until we find the one man who feels himself unfit to wear it. Carlyle was quite wrong; we have not got to crown the exceptional man who knows he can rule. Rather we must crown the much more exceptional man who knows he can't.

Now, this is one of the two or three vital defences of working democracy. The mere machinery of voting is not democracy, though at present it is not easy to effect any simpler democratic method. But even the machinery of voting is profoundly Christian in this practical sense—that it is an attempt to get at the opinion of those who would be too modest to offer it. It is a mystical adventure; it is specially trusting those who do not trust themselves. That enigma is strictly peculiar to Christendom. There is nothing really humble about the abnegation of the Buddhist; the mild Hindoo is mild, but he is not meek. But there is something psychologically Christian about the idea of seeking for the opinion of the obscure rather than taking the obvious course of accepting the opinion of the prominent. To say that voting is particularly Christian may seem somewhat curious. To say that canvassing is Christian may seem quite crazy. But canvassing is very Christian in its primary idea. It is encouraging the humble; it is saying to the modest man, "Friend, go up higher." Or if there is some slight defect in canvassing, that is in its perfect and rounded piety, it is only because it may possibly neglect to encourage the modesty of the canvasser.

Aristocracy is not an institution: aristocracy is a sin; generally a very venial one. It is merely the drift or slide of men into a sort of natural pomposity and praise of the powerful, which is the most easy and obvious affair in the world.

It is one of the hundred answers to the fugitive perversion of modern "force" that the promptest and boldest agencies are also the most fragile or full of sensibility. The swiftest things are the softest things. A bird is active, because a bird is soft. A stone is helpless, because a stone is hard. The stone must by its own nature go downwards, because hardness is weakness. The bird can of its nature go upwards, because fragility is force. In perfect force there is a kind of frivolity, an airiness that can maintain itself in the air. Modern investigators of miraculous history have solemnly admitted that a characteristic of the great saints is their power of "levitation." They might go further; a characteristic of the great saints is their power of levity. Angels can fly because they can take themselves lightly. This has been always the instinct of Christendom, and especially the instinct of Christian art. Remember how Fra Angelico represented all his angels, not only as birds, but almost as butterflies. Remember how the most earnest mediæval art was full of light and fluttering draperies, of quick and capering feet. It was the one thing that the modern Pre-raphaelites could not imitate in the real Pre-raphaelites. Burne-Jones could never recover the deep levity of the Middle Ages. In the old Christian pictures the sky over every figure is like a blue or gold parachute. Every figure seems ready to fly up and float about in the heavens. The tattered cloak of the beggar will bear him up like the rayed plumes of the angels. But the kings in their heavy gold and the proud in their robes of purple will all of their nature sink downwards, for pride cannot rise to levity or levitation. Pride is the downward drag of all things into an easy solemnity. One "settles down" into a sort of selfish seriousness; but one has to rise to a gay self-forgetfulness. A man "falls" into a brown study; he reaches up at a blue sky. Seriousness is not a virtue. It would be a heresy, but a much more sensible heresy, to say that seriousness is a vice. It is really a natural trend or lapse into taking one's self gravely, because it is the easiest thing to do. It is much easier to write a good *Times* leading article than a good joke in *Punch*. For solemnity flows out of men naturally; but laughter is a leap. It is easy to be heavy: hard to be light. Satan fell by the force of gravity.

Now, it is the peculiar honour of Europe since it has been Christian that while it has had aristocracy it has always at the back of its heart treated aristocracy as a weakness—generally as a weakness that must be allowed for. If any one wishes to appreciate this point, let him go outside Christianity into some other philosophical atmosphere. Let him, for instance, compare the classes of Europe with the castes of India. There aristocracy is far more awful, because it is far more intellectual. It is seriously felt that the scale of classes is a scale of spiritual values; that the baker is better than the butcher in an invisible and sacred sense. But no Christianity, not even the most ignorant or perverse, ever suggested that a baronet was better than a butcher in that sacred sense. No Christianity, however ignorant or extravagant, ever suggested that a duke would not be damned. In pagan society there may have been (I do not know) some such serious division between the free man and the slave. But in Christian society we have always thought the gentleman a sort of joke, though I admit that in some great crusades and councils he earned the right to be called a practical joke. But we in Europe never really and at the root of our souls took aristocracy seriously. It is only an occasional non-European alien (such as Dr. Oscar Levy, the only intelligent Nietzscheite) who can even manage for a moment to take aristocracy seriously. It may be a mere patriotic bias, though I do not think so, but it seems to me that the English aristocracy is not only the type, but is the crown and flower of all actual aristocracies; it has all the oligarchical virtues as well as all the defects. It is casual, it is kind, it is courageous in obvious matters; but it has one great merit that overlaps even these. The great and very obvious merit of the English aristocracy is that nobody could possibly take it seriously.

In short, I had spelled out slowly, as usual, the need for an equal law in Utopia; and, as usual, I found that Christianity had been there before me. The whole history of my Utopia has the same amusing sadness. I was always rushing out of my architectural study with plans for a new turret only to find it sitting up there in the sunlight, shining, and a thousand years old. For me, in the ancient and partly in the modern sense, God answered the prayer, "Prevent us, O Lord, in all our doings." Without vanity, I really think there was a moment when

I could have invented the marriage vow (as an institution) out of my own head; but I discovered, with a sigh, that it had been invented already. But, since it would be too long a business to show how, fact by fact and inch by inch, my own conception of Utopia was only answered in the New Jerusalem, I will take this one case of the matter of marriage as indicating the converging drift, I may say the converging crash of all the rest.

When the ordinary opponents of Socialism talk about impossibilities and alterations in human nature they always miss an important distinction. In modern ideal conceptions of society there are some desires that are possibly not attainable: but there are some desires that are not desirable. That all men should live in equally beautiful houses is a dream that may or may not be attained. But that all men should live in the same beautiful house is not a dream at all; it is a nightmare. That a man should love all old women is an ideal that may not be attainable. But that a man should regard all old women exactly as he regards his mother is not only an unattainable ideal, but an ideal which ought not to be attained. I do not know if the reader agrees with me in these examples; but I will add the example which has always affected me most. I could never conceive or tolerate any Utopia which did not leave to me the liberty for which I chiefly care, the liberty to bind myself. Complete anarchy would not merely make it impossible to have any discipline or fidelity; it would also make it impossible to have any fun. To take an obvious instance, it would not be worth while to bet if a bet were not binding. The dissolution of all contracts would not only ruin morality but spoil sport. Now betting and such sports are only the stunted and twisted shapes of the original instinct of man for adventure and romance, of which much has been said. And the perils, rewards, punishments, and fulfilments of an adventure must be real, or the adventure is only a shifting and heartless nightmare. If I bet I must be made to pay, or there is no poetry in betting. If I challenge I must be made to fight, or there is no poetry in challenging. If I vow to be faithful I must be cursed when I am unfaithful, or there is no fun in vowing. You could not even make a fairy tale from the experiences of a man who, when he was swallowed by a whale, might find himself at the top of the Eiffel Tower, or when he was turned into a frog might begin to behave like a flamingo. For the purpose even of the wildest romance results must be real; results must be irrevocable. Christian marriage is the great example of a real and irrevocable result; and that is why it is the chief subject and centre of all our romantic writing. And this is my last instance of the things that I should ask, and ask imperatively, of any social paradise; I should ask to be kept to my bargain, to have my oaths and engagements taken seriously; I should ask Utopia to avenge my honour on myself.

All my modern Utopian friends look at each other rather doubtfully, for their ultimate hope is the dissolution of all special ties. But again I seem to hear, like a kind of echo, an answer from beyond the world. "You will have real obligations, and therefore real adventures when you get to my Utopia. But the hardest obligation and the steepest adventure is to get there."

The Vulnerability of the Naked Square

If any phrase coined in the last several decades deserves to permanently enter the language of everyday understanding, it is "the naked public square." Then Pastor, now Father Neuhaus was not mounting an argument in favor of crèches in the town square at Christmastime. No, his sights are set on the much larger target of the "secular city" and its implications: a place destined to become like Narnia under the reign of the White Queen, a place where it is always winter but never Christmas.

Take religion out of public life, and you have a naked public square. But not for long. The state will quickly fill the void, which is a frightening prospect indeed. Imagine the feds in charge of moral truth; imagine us believing in them. Impossible? Ask the survivors of fascism and communism.

We need, as Father Neuhaus concludes, "the critical tutelage of traditions that refuse to leave 'man on his own.'" Or, as Edmund Burke put it, "People will not look forward to posterity, who never look backward to their ancestors."

MARTIN LUTHER KING, JR. AND JERRY FALWELL. Friends of both would likely be offended by the suggestion that they are in any way similar. And yet they are, I believe. Of course they are also strikingly different figures, with quite different analyses of what is wrong

with America and what ought to be done about it. They were on opposite sides of the civil rights struggle in the fifties and sixties. (Without going so far as to say that King was right, the Falwells regularly
acknowledge that they were wrong on race.) There is the sharpest
contrast between King's enprincipled nonviolence and Falwell's advocacy of bellicose toughness in dealing with the Communists. Numerous other differences, political and theological, could be itemized.
But in this they are similar: both Martin Luther King and Jerry Falwell disrupt the business of secular America by an appeal to religiously based public values.

Although in quite different ways, both are profoundly patriotic
figures. Dr. King's dream was of America as an exemplar of racial and
social justice, an anticipation of that "beloved community" promised
by God. The patriotic fervor with which Dr. King invoked an American promise is often forgotten. But the March on Washington, for instance, can never be forgotten by those who were there, nor, one
hopes, by the millions who have watched its replay on television doc-
umentaries. On that oppressively hot Wednesday afternoon of August
28, 1963, before the Lincoln Memorial, a baritone trumpet sought to
recall America to its better self. "Five score years ago, a great American, in whose symbolic shadow we stand, signed the Emancipation
Proclamation," Dr. King began. He then described the ways in which
the promise had not been kept and rhetorically etched the shape of its
fulfillment. "This will be the day when all God's children will be able
to sing with new meaning 'My country 'tis of thee, sweet land of liberty, of thee I sing. Land where my fathers died, land of the pilgrim's
pride, from every mountain side, let freedom ring.'" Lest we succumb
to the prejudice that patriotic rhetoric is by definition ignoble, the
peroration deserves to be committed to memory:

> When we let freedom ring, when we let it ring from every village and
> every hamlet, from every state and every city, we will be able to speed up
> that day when all God's children, black men and white men, Jews and
> Gentiles, Protestants and Catholics, will be able to join hands and sing
> in the words of that old Negro spiritual, "Free at last! Free at last!
> Thank God almighty, we are free at last!"

A biographer of King, who had learned in the school of economic
determinism that moral appeals are but the instrumental disguise of

class conflict, says of the March on Washington speech: "This was rhetoric almost without content, but this was, after all, a day of heroic fantasy." Such a comment suggests that the impingement of religious vision upon the public square can be permitted from time to time—if it is employed in the right causes, and if it is not taken too seriously. Thus also today's discharge of religious language in public space is assumed to hide narrow partisan interests. Although immeasurably less eloquent or persuasive than Dr. King's, contemporary religious rhetoric of populist patriotism deserves to be treated as seriously. To treat it seriously does not, of course, mean that one agrees. But when today's political preachers lift up a vision of a morally rejuvenated America serving as the base for global evangelism and as the defense against atheistic totalitarianism, there is no good reason to doubt that they are—to use that much overworked word—sincere. That is, it is not necessarily suspect language, language employed to advance some purpose other than the purpose indicated by the language itself.

To be sure, activists in whatever cause employ—and even, in the negative sense of the term, exploit—language in order to conceal loyalties and heighten emotional commitment. Activism is inescapably concerned not for disinterested truth but for *effective* truth, truth that is effective in advancing the purpose at hand. From this reality derives the pervasive mendacity that distorts all political engagement, to a greater or lesser degree. That being said, it remains important to note which rhetoric is chosen to advance the cause. Few leaders are so false to the core as to choose a rhetoric for its manipulative effect alone. As skeptical as we may rightly be about appeals to moral ideals, it is reasonable to believe that the ideals by which leaders would call others to judgment are the ideals by which, at least in their more reflective moments, they believe they are themselves judged. This observation is not invalidated by La Rochefoucauld's famous maxim, "Hypocrisy is the homage that vice pays to virtue." The truth of the maxim does not allow even the greatest cynic to be dismissive about moral ideals in public discourse. On the contrary, the hypocrisies by which we know ourselves to fail are of decisive importance. Be they hypocrisies or be they truths nobly adhered to, they are the moral points of reference by which communities are called to accountability. My point is not to suggest that either Dr. King or current political preachers are hypocritical. It is to emphasize that they are alike in proposing a vision of public virtue and that that vision is religiously based.

The assertion that binds together otherwise different causes is the claim that only a transcendent, a religious, vision can turn this society from certain disaster and toward the fulfillment of its destiny. In this connection "destiny" is but another word for purpose. From whatever point on the political spectrum such an assertion is made, it challenges the conventional wisdom that America is a secular society. In recent decades we have become accustomed to believe that *of course* America is a secular society. That, in the minds of many, is what is meant by the separation of church and state. But this way of thinking is of relatively recent vintage. As late as 1931 the Supreme Court could assert without fear of contradiction, "We are a Christian people, according to one another the equal right of religious freedom, and acknowledging with reverence the duty of obedience to the will of God." The 1931 case had to do with whether a conscientious objector to war could become a citizen. After the above statement about obedience to God, the court concluded, "But, also, we are a nation with the duty to survive." Citizenship was denied *(US v. Macintosh)*.

In 1952, in a dispute over students getting off from public schools in released time for religious instruction, Justice Douglas, hardly a religiously observant man, wrote, "We are a religious people whose institutions presuppose a Supreme Being" *(Zorach v. Clauson)*. As time went on, however, the court's references to religion had less and less to do with what is usually meant by religion. That is, religion no longer referred to those communal traditions of ultimate beliefs and practices ordinarily called religion. Religion, in the court's meaning, became radically individualized and privatized. Religion became a synonym for conscience. For instance, in cases again related to conscientious objection, exemption from the military draft was to be allowed on the "registrant's moral, ethical, or religious beliefs about what is right and wrong [provided] those beliefs be held with the strength of traditional religious convictions" *(Welsh v. U.S., 1970)*. Thus religion is no longer a matter of content but of sincerity. It is no longer a matter of communal values but of individual conviction. In short, it is no longer a public reality and therefore cannot interfere with public business.

Such a religious evacuation of the public square cannot be sustained, either in concept or in practice. When religion in any traditional or recognizable form is excluded from the public square, it does not mean that the public square is in fact naked. This is the other side of the "naked public square" metaphor. When recognizable religion is excluded, the vacuum will be filled by *ersatz* religion, by religion bootlegged into public space under other names. Again, to paraphrase Spinoza: transcendence abhors a vacuum. The reason why the naked public square cannot, in fact, remain naked is in the very nature of law and laws. If law and laws are not seen to be coherently related to basic presuppositions about right and wrong, good and evil, they will be condemned as illegitimate. After having excluded traditional religion, then, the legal and political trick is to address questions of right and wrong in a way that is not "contaminated" by the label "religious." This relatively new sleight-of-hand results in what many have called "civil religion." It places a burden upon the law to act religiously without being suspected of committing religion. While social theorists might talk about "civil religion," the courts dare not do so, for that too would be an unconstitutional "establishment" of religion.

Admittedly, it is all very confusing. The late Alexander Bickel of Yale recognized more clearly than most that law inevitably engages ultimate beliefs about right and wrong. If law is to be viewed as legitimate, it must be backed by moral judgment. But, it is argued, in a society where moral judgments differ in source and conclusion, the final grounding of moral judgment must be disguised so as not to give democratic offense. It must be grounded so *generally* so as to obscure the particularities of religious disagreement in a pluralistic society. Bickel proposes a way in which this might be done:

> The function of the Justices . . . is to immerse themselves in the tradition of our society and of kindred societies that have gone before, in history and in the sediment of history which is law, and in the thought and the vision of the philosophers and the poets. The Justices will then be fit to extract "fundamental presuppositions" from their deepest selves, but in fact from the evolving morality of our tradition. . . . The search for the deepest controlling sources, for the precise "how" and the final "whence" of the judgment may, after all, end in the attempt to express the inexpressible. This is not to say that the duty to judge the judgment might as well be abandoned. The inexpressible can be recognized, even though one is unable to parse it.

This is an elegantly convoluted way of thinking about right and wrong in a democratic society that in fact understands its morality to be derived from the Judeo-Christian tradition. Bickel's proposal is for a semi-sanitized public square, for a legal process that is religious in function but dare not speak the name of religion. ("Philosophers and poets" are admitted, be it noted, but not prophets or religious ethicists and teachers.) The tortured reasoning required by the exclusion of identifiable religion is surely a puzzle to many, perhaps most, Americans. It may be that they are puzzled because they do not understand the requirements of a pluralistic society. Or they may be puzzled because they are more impressed by the claim that this is a democratic society. In a democratic society, presumably, the public business is carried on in conversation with the actual values of people who *are* the society. In a survey of North Carolinians in the 1970s, seventy-four percent agree with the statement: "Human rights come from God and not merely from laws." Seventy-eight percent claim the U.S. flag is "sacred." And, despite Vietnam and all that, a third assent to the proposition, "America is God's chosen nation today." North Carolinians may be more "traditional" than other Americans on these scores although there is no reason to assume that. One suspects, rather, that there is among Americans a deep and widespread uneasiness about the denial of the obvious. The obvious is that, in some significant sense, this is, as the Supreme Court said in 1931, a Christian people. The popular intuition is that this fact ought, somehow, to make a difference. It is not an embarrassment to be denied or disguised. It is an inescapable part of what Bickel calls the "tradition of our society and of kindred societies that have gone before." Not only is it tradition in the sense of historic past; it is demonstrably the present source of moral vitalities by which we measure our virtues and hypocrisies.

The notion that this is a secular society is relatively new. It might be proposed that, while the society is incorrigibly religious, the state is secular. But such a disjunction between society and state is a formula for governmental delegitimation. In a democratic society, state and society must draw from the same moral well. In addition, because transcendence abhors a vacuum, the state that styles itself as secular will almost certainly succumb to secular*ism*. Because government cannot help but make moral judgments of an ultimate nature, it must, if it has in principle excluded identifiable religion, make those judgments by "secular" reasoning that is given the force of religion. Because this process is already advanced in the spheres of law and public education, there is a measure of justice in the complaints about "secular humanism." Secular humanism, in this case, is simply the term unhappily chosen for *ersatz* religion.

More than that, the notion of the secular state can become the prelude to totalitarianism. That is, once religion is reduced to nothing more than privatized conscience, the public square has only two actors in it—the state and the individual. Religion as a mediating structure—a community that generates and transmits moral values—is no longer available as a countervailing force to the ambitions of the state. Whether in Hitler's Third Reich or in today's sundry states professing Marxist-Leninism, the chief attack is not upon individual religious belief. Individual religious belief can be dismissed scornfully as superstition, for it finally poses little threat to the power of the state. No, the chief attack is upon the *institutions* that bear and promulgate belief in a transcendent reality by which the state can be called to judgment. Such institutions threaten the totalitarian proposition that everything is to be within the state, nothing is to be outside the state.

It is to be expected that the move in this discussion from the naked public square to the dangers of totalitarianism will be resisted by some readers. It may seem too abrupt and even extreme. We will be coming back to the subject in order to fill in some of the intermediate steps. At the moment, suffice it to register a degree of sympathy with those who resist talk about the dangers of totalitarianism. They object, quite rightly, that many discussions of the threat of totalitarianism are only thinly veiled attacks upon Communism. A one-sided attack upon Communism, they protest, tends to overlook the many forms of authoritarian government that also violate our understandings of democratic freedom. Authoritarian, sometimes brutally authoritarian, regimes with which the United States is allied end up being tolerated or even lauded in order to maintain a common front against the Communist adversary. There is considerable merit to this critique, unfortunately. Anti-Communism is a necessary but hardly a sufficient basis for understanding the perils of our day. In this light, then, one can sympathize with those who resist much contemporary talk about the threat of totalitarianism.

A less admirable component in that resistance, however, is the naive notion that "it can't happen here." Those who subscribe to this notion are too often oblivious of the novelty and fragility of liberal democracy as a political system. They are inadequately sensitive to the distinctly minority status of such an order in our world. It is thought that liberal democracy and the freedoms associated with it are somehow "normal," part of the "establishment." The new and exciting thing, in this view, is the proposal of alternatives to liberal democracy. In the longer reaches of history, however, liberal democracy appears as a curious exception to the various tyrannies under which human beings have suffered. Of the 160 member nations of the United Nations, probably less than thirty qualify as democracies in the sense that we tend to take for granted. This historical and contemporary perspective is essential. Without such a perspective, it is impossible to understand what Americans from Jefferson to Lincoln to John F. Kennedy intended when they spoke of America as an "experiment" launched and sustained in defiance of the "normal" course of history.

Those who think all talk about a totalitarian threat to be exaggerated also evidence an insouciance, sometimes a willful ignorance, with respect to the fact that liberal democracy does have declared adversaries. There are adversaries such as the authoritarian regimes of South America, South Africa, and the Philippines. In a significant way, however, these authoritarian regimes are not adversaries. That is, they do not *claim* to be adversaries, they do not oppose liberal democracy in principle; rather, they often claim to aspire to liberal democracy, asserting that their denial of democratic freedoms is only a temporary expedient on the way to that goal. And in fact we are not without recent examples of authoritarian societies that have been moved toward democracy; Spain, Portugal, and Nigeria are cases in point. In both the long and short term, the more ominous adversaries of liberal democracy are those forces that are totalitarian *in principle*. The only global, systematic movement of this kind today is Marxist-Leninism. In the 1930s, Mussolini's Fascism and Hitler's National Socialism represented another such movement. After World War II and despite loose talk that equates any repressive regime with "fascism," only Marxist-Leninism is left as a theoretically comprehensive and, to many, morally compelling global adversary of liberal democracy.

In such a world it is not extreme but elementary common sense to be concerned about the threat of totalitarianism. "It can't happen here" is but a form of whistling in the dark. It is strange that among the foremost whistlers are some civil libertarians who are otherwise always reminding us of how precarious are the constitutional freedoms that we are too inclined to take for granted. The threat of totalitarianism is not posed chiefly by the prospect of defeat as a result of nuclear war. Nor is the main anxiety that the Soviet Union will launch a victorious march across Alaska and down through Canada. The chief threat comes from a collapse of the idea of freedom and of the social arrangements necessary to sustaining liberal democracy. Crucial to such a democratic order is a public square in which there are many actors. The state is one actor among others. Indispensable to this arrangement are the institutional actors, such as the institutions of religion, that make claims of ultimate or transcendent meaning. The several actors in the public square—government, corporations, education, communications, religion—are there to challenge, check, and compete with one another. They also cooperate with one another, or sometimes one will cooperate with an other in competition with the others. In a democracy the role of cooperation is not to be deemed morally superior to the roles of checking and competing. Giving unqualified priority to the virtue of cooperation, as some Christians do, is the formula for the death of democracy.

There is an inherent and necessary relationship between democracy and pluralism. Pluralism, in this connection, does not mean simply that there are many different kinds of people and institutions in societal play. More radically than that, it means that there are contenders striving with one another to define what the play is about—what are the rules and what the goal. The democratic soul is steeled to resist the allure of a "cooperation" that would bring that contention to a premature closure. Indeed, within the bond of civility, the democratic soul exults in that contention. He exults not because contention is a good in itself, although there is a legitimate joy in contending, but because it is a necessary provisional good short of the coming of the kingdom of God. He strives to sustain the contention within the bond of civility, also, because he recognizes the totalitarianism that is the presently available alternative to such democratic contention.

John Courtney Murray, the great Jesuit analyst of American democracy, understood the nature of the contest in which we are engaged. For many years his work was viewed as suspect by church authorities but he was soundly vindicated by Vatican Council II. Christian thinkers such as Murray and Reinhold Niebuhr are frequently discounted today as old hat. Such mindless dismissal results in part from a desire to espouse the latest thing. It is a bias of the superficially educated that books written thirty years ago, not to say three hundred years ago, are passé. In Christian circles this dismissal takes the curious twist of being conducted in the name of the most current version of "true Christianity," based upon biblical books written two thousand and more years ago. Murray, a deeply educated man, understood that epochs are not demarcated by publishers' seasons. The test of our epoch, he understood, is to sustain the democratic "proposition" in the face of the human yearning for monism. Monism is another word for totalitarianism, and Murray described it this way:

> [The] cardinal assertion is a thorough-going monism, political, social, juridical, religious: there is only one Sovereign, one society, one law, one faith. And the cardinal denial is of the Christian dualism of powers, societies, and laws—spiritual and temporal, divine and human. Upon this denial follows the absorption of the Church in the community, the absorption of the community in the state, the absorption of the state in the party, and the assertion that the party-state is the supreme spiritual and moral, as well as political authority and reality. It has its own absolutely autonomous ideological substance and its own absolutely independent purpose: it is the ultimate bearer of human destiny. Outside of this One Sovereign there is nothing. Or rather, what presumes to stand outside is "the enemy."

The prelude to this totalitarian monism is the notion that society can be ordered according to secular technological reason without reference to religious grounded meaning. Murray again:

> And if this country is to be overthrown from within or from without, I would suggest that it will not be overthrown by Communism. It will be overthrown because it will have made an impossible experiment. It will have undertaken to establish a technological order of most marvelous intricacy, which will have been constructed and will operate without relations to true political ends: and this technological order will hang, as it were, suspended over a moral confusion; and this moral confusion will itself be suspended over a spiritual vacuum. This would be the real danger resulting from a type of fallacious, fictitious, fragile unity that could be created among us.

This "vacuum" with respect to political and spiritual truth is the naked public square. If we are "overthrown," the root cause of the defeat would lie in the "impossible" effort to sustain that vacuum. Murray is right: not Communism, but the effort to establish and maintain the naked public square would be the source of the collapse. Totalitarian monism would be the consequence of such a collapse. Because it is the only totalitarian ideology in play today, the consequence would likely be Marxist-Leninist; which is to say it would be, in one form or another, Communism. The probability that it would be a distinctively American form of Communism will not vindicate those who now say "It can't happen here." Americans may, with a little help from their adversaries, find their own distinctive way to terminate the democratic experiment to which they gave birth. The fact that democracy's demise bears the marking "Made in America" will console only national chauvinists. It will be little comfort to those whose devotion to America was derived from their devotion to the democratic idea.

The naked public square is, as Murray suggests, an "impossible" project. That, however, does not deter people from attempting it. In the minds of some secularists the naked public square is a desirable goal. They subscribe to the dogma of the secular Enlightenment that, as people become more enlightened (educated), religion will wither away; or, if it does not wither away, it can be safely sealed off from public consideration, reduced to a private eccentricity. Our argument is that the naked public square is not desirable, even if it were possible. It is not desirable in the view of believers because they are inescapably entangled in the belief that the moral truths of religion have a universal and public validity. The Ten Commandments, to take an obvious example, have a normative status. They are not, as it has been said, Ten Suggestions or Ten Significant Moral Insights to be more or less appreciated according to one's subjective disposition. Even if one is not a believer, the divorce of public business from the moral vitalities of the society is not desirable if one is committed to the democratic idea. In addition to not being desirable, however, we have argued that the naked public square is not possible. It is an illusion, for the public square cannot and does not remain naked. When particularist religious values and the institutions that bear them are excluded, the inescapable need to make public moral judgments will result in an elite construction of a normative morality from sources and principles not democratically recognized by the society.

The truly naked public square is at best a transitional phenomenon. It is a vacuum begging to be filled. When the democratically affirmed institutions that generate and transmit values are excluded, the vacuum will be filled by the agent left in control of the public square, the state. In this manner, a perverse notion of the disestablishment of religion leads to the establishment of the state as church. Not without reason, religion is viewed by some as a repressive imposition upon the public square. They would cast out the devil of particularist religion and thus put the public square in proper secular order. Having cast out the one devil, they unavoidably invite the entrance of seven devils worse than the first.

The totalitarian alternative edges in from the wings, waiting impatiently for the stage to be cleared of competing actors. Most important is that the stage be cleared of those religious actors that presume to assert absolute values and thus pose such a troublesome check upon the pretensions of the state. The state is not waiting with a set of absolute values of its own or with a ready-made religion. Far from waiting with a package of absolutes, in a society where the remnants of procedural democracy survive the state may be absolutely committed only to the relativization of all values. In that instance, however, the relativity of all things becomes the absolute. Without the counterclaims of "meaning-bestowing" institutions of religion, there is not an absence of religion but, rather, the triumph of the religion of relativity. It is a religion that must in principle deny that it is religious. It is the religion that dare not speak its name. In its triumph there is no contender that can, in Peter Berger's phrase, "relativize the relativizers."

The entrance of the seven devils that take over the cleansed public square is not an alarmist scenario. Conceptually there is no alternative to it, unless of course one believes that a society can get along without a normative ethic. Admittedly, there are those who do believe this. They are, as Alisdair MacIntyre contends, the barbarians. "This time," writes MacIntyre, "the barbarians are not waiting beyond the frontiers; they have already been governing us for quite some time." That the barbarians are composed of the most sophisticated and educated elites of our society makes them no less barbarian. The barbarians are those who in principle refuse to recognize a normative ethic or the reality of public virtue.

The barbarians are the party of emancipation from the truths civilized people consider self-evident. The founding fathers of the American experiment declared certain truths to be self-evident and moved on from that premise. It is a measure of our decline into what may be the new dark ages that today we are compelled to produce evidence for the self-evident. Not that it does much good to produce such evidence, however, for such evidences are ruled to be inadmissible since, again in principle, it is asserted that every moral judgment is simply an instance of emotivism, a statement of subjective preference that cannot be "imposed" upon others. MacIntyre's dismal reading of our times is no doubt an accurate description of the *logic* of contemporary philosophical, moral, and legal reasoning. Fortunately, the real world is not terribly logical. The vitalities of democracy protest that dour logic. Populist resentment against the logic of the naked public square is a source of hope. That resentment is premised upon an alternative vision that calls for a new articulation. When it finds its voice, it will likely sound very much like the voice of Christian America. That voice will not be heard and thus will not prevail in the public square, however, unless it is a voice that aims to reassure those who dissent from the vision.

We have said that conceptually there is no alternative to a *de facto* state religion once traditional religion is driven from the public square. Even if some were to argue that an alternative could be hypothetically conceived, we must attend to actual historical experience. We have witnessed again and again the entrance of the seven devils worse than the first. In every instance except that of Italian Fascism and the Third Reich, in this century they have entered under the banner of Communism. We who embrace the liberal tradition have suffered from a debilitating obtuseness on this score. It has too often been left to conservatives and reactionaries to point out that the emperor carries a very nasty club. Afraid to be thought anti-Communist, a species of liberalism has degenerated to fevered anti-anti-Communism.

This is the unpopular truth underscored by Susan Sontag in the dramatic 1982 confrontaton at Town Hall in New York City. The meeting, the reader may recall, was for the purpose of expressing solidarity with Solidarity, the Polish labor movement that had been brutally repressed under martial law. The meeting was sponsored in part by the *Nation*, a magazine of self-consciously liberal orthodoxy. An impressive lineup of literary and entertainment celebrities were expected to say nice things about the revolutionary proletariat in Poland and the dangers of fascist repression in the United States. Ms. Sontag went beyond expectations. She pointed out that the repression in Poland was not an aberration but inherent in the theory and practice of Marxist-Leninism. She noted that the left routinely railed against the threat of fascism.

> We had identified the enemy as fascism. We heard the demonic language of fascism. We believed in, or at least applied a double standard to, the angelic language of communism. . . . The emigres from communist countries we didn't listen to, who found it far easier to get published in the *Reader's Digest* than in *The Nation* or the *New Statesman*, were telling the truth. Now we hear them. Why didn't we hear them before? . . . The result was that many of us, and I include myself, did not understand the nature of the communist tyranny. . . . What the recent Polish events illustrate is a truth that we should have understood a very long time ago: that communism *is* fascism. . . . Not only is fascism the probable destiny of all communist societies, but communism is in itself a variant of fascism. Fascism with a human face.

The conclusion to be drawn is not that the *Reader's Digest* is the oracle of truth. Anti-Communism combined with American boosterism is not a sufficient political philosophy. But, as Ms. Sontag would argue, neither is anti-anti-Communism sufficient. Alexander Solzhenitsyn comes closer to being an oracle on these questions. Commenting on the Polish developments following the emergence of Solidarity in 1981, he notes the ways in which sundry socialists of a Marxist bent attempt to dissociate themselves from what is happening in that tortured land, or even try to claim Solidarity as a representative of "true socialism" in protest against socialism's Communist distortion. "It is the Communist ideology that, with its heavy steps, is crushing Poland," writes Solzhenitsyn, "and let us admit it is not entirely alien to the socialists, though they are protesting vehemently: The ideology of any communism is based on the coercive power of the state. Let's not be mistaken: Solidarity inspired itself not by socialism but by Christianity." Beyond reasonable doubt, it is the presence of the Catholic Church in the Polish public square that prevents the regime from realizing its ambition for total control.

A literal example of the consistently denuded public square is, of course, Red Square in Moscow. Because it is in the nature of public squares not to remain naked, there is the sacred shrine of Lenin's tomb where thousands are transported each day to stand in line, waiting their turn to pay homage. Within this circumscribed space the maxim,

"All within the state, nothing outside the state," is fulfilled. On several occasions in the early eighties a few bold Soviet citizens attempted to unfold banners appealing for peace and disarmament. They were promptly arrested and hustled off to psychiatric clinics. As Murray tried to help us understand, in such a society opposition to the will of the party is by definition a sign of insanity, or worse. *Tass,* the official newspaper (there being, of course, no other kind), described the dissident "Committee to Establish Trust Between the U.S.S.R. and the U.S.A." as an "act of provocation of Western secret services." According to *The New York Times* report, the protesters were condemned as "anti-Sovieteers, renegades and criminals . . . a handful of swindlers who do not represent anyone in the Soviet Union."

In our society the proponents of the naked public square do not describe themselves as proponents of the naked public square. Some are technocratic liberals, some are secular pragmatists, some are libertarians of either the leftist or rightist sort. Some are socialists who insist that we need to establish "rational control" of political, economic, and cultural forces in order to forge something like a national purpose and plan. Whatever the rationale or intention, however, the presupposition is the naked public square, the exclusion of particularist religious and moral belief from public discourse. And whatever the intention, because the naked square cannot remain naked, the direction is toward the state-as-church, toward totalitarianism. And again, the available form of totalitarianism—an aggressively available form, so to speak—is Marxist-Leninism.

In one of his less felicitous statements, President Carter in a major foreign policy address cautioned against our "inordinate fear of Communism." He did not make clear what measure of fear might be ordinate. Similarly, those who now underscore the dangers of Communism caution us against an inordinate fear of McCarthyism. Presumably, in this respect too there is a measure of fear that is ordinate. The present argument suggests that both fears are legitimate and necessary. Of the two, McCarthyism as a form of what Richard Hofstadter called "the paranoid style" in American politics is the more immediate possibility. We have been through that and the scars are still touchable. In the longer term—say, the next thirty to one hundred years—totalitarianism is the more ominous prospect. This does not mean we should risk "just a little" McCarthyism in order to ward off that prospect. It does mean that we should stop calling a sensible anxiety about that prospect "McCarthyism." It does mean we should stop telling ourselves and others that the choice is between McCarthyism, which truncates liberal democracy, and totalitarianism, which terminates liberal democracy. An open-eyed awareness of the fragility of liberal democracy, and of the alternatives to it, is the best insurance against being reduced to such a dismal choice. As that awareness is heightened, we will as a society be more resistant both to the totalitarian temptation and to the illusion that democracy can be saved by becoming less democratic.

In 1981 the Institute on Religion and Democracy was established in Washington, D.C. Its declared purpose was to lift up the public significance of religion in the democratic process, to promote democratic ideals within the religious communities, and, as a necessary correlate of that, to oppose those dynamics in the churches that seem inclined toward the totalitarian temptation. "Christianity and Democracy" is the Institute's manifesto-like assertion of what it means by democracy:

> Democratic government is limited government. It is limited in the claims it makes and in the power it seeks to exercise. Democratic government understands itself to be accountable to values and to truth which transcend any regime or party. Thus in the United States of America we declare ours to be a nation "under God," which means, first of all, a nation under judgment. In addition, limited government means that a clear distinction is made between the state and the society. The state is not the whole of the society, but is one important actor in the society. Other institutions—notably the family, the Church, educational, economic and cultural enterprises—are at least equally important actors in the society. They do not exist or act by sufferance of the state. Rather, these spheres have their own peculiar sovereignty which must be respected by the state.

The statement goes on to affirm the importance of participation, equality, and fairness in a democratic society. Without dwelling on the point, it notes that "as a matter of historical fact democratic governance exists only where the free market plays a large part in a society's economy." The statement and the Institute received widespread (some would say inordinate) attention in the general media and in the churches. They were the object of a formal debate sponsored by the National Council of Churches and of numerous critiques by theologians and social philosophers on all points of the political spectrum.

The debate produced around groups such as the Institute on Religion and Democracy gives some reason to believe that this decade could be remembered as a time of reinvigorated appreciation of the democratic idea among Christians in America. The intuition of the connection between democracy and religion was until recently part of the foundational consensus supporting what Murray called "the American proposition." It was a constitutive element of the vital center in American thought. The vital center, it will be recalled, was the title Arthur M. Schlesinger, Jr., chose for his 1949 manifesto in favor of democratic freedom. *The Vital Center* is in the tradition of Walter Lippmann's "public philosophy" and John Dewey's "common faith." If one did not know that *The Vital Center* was written thirty-five years ago, she would suspect it was written by one of those who today are called neo-conservative. It is a curiosity of our time that the mainstream liberalism of a few decades ago—and nobody has more assiduously attended to his credentials as a mainstream liberal than Arthur M. Schlesinger, Jr.—is the neo-conservatism of today. The mainstream liberal argument then was, quite rightly, viewed as a radical proposition on the screen of world-historical change. Schlesinger wrote:

> Our problem is not resources or leadership. It is primarily one of faith and time: faith in the value of our own freedoms, and time to do the necessary things to save them. To achieve the fullness of faith, we must renew the traditional sources of American radicalism and seek out ways to maintain our belief at a high pitch of vibration. To achieve a sufficiency of time, we must ward off the totalitarian threat to free society—and do so without permitting ourselves to become the slaves of Stalinism, as any man may become the slave of the things he hates.

Schlesinger and those like him then viewed with approval, indeed the highest hope, the role of the "affirmative" or "positive" state. They knew there were dangers in the self-aggrandizement of the state, but the acknowledgment of the importance of other public actors is almost an aside:

> In the short run, the failure of voluntary initiative invites the spread of state power. In the long run, the disappearance of voluntary association paves the way for the pulverization of the social structure essential to totalitarianism. By the revitalization of voluntary associations, we can

siphon off emotions which might otherwise be driven to the solutions of despair. We can create strong bulwarks against the totalitarianization of society.

But this nod to what we have called the mediating structures of society is almost cancelled out by the emphasis upon state power. To be sure, Schlesinger observed then, "We have strayed too far from the insights of Burke and de Maistre; we have forgotten that constitutions work only as they reflect an actual sense of community." He also warned against "arrogant forms of individualism." "It is only so far as . . . individualism derives freely from community, that democracy will be immune to the virus of totalitarianism." The reiterated "we" in Schlesinger's writing however, is finally the "we" of the total society, the "we" of the state. This is because, in his view, the great domestic threat is the anti-democratic influence of the corporation, of "the business plutocracy." "The corporation began to impersonalize the economic order," wrote Schlesinger.

> Impersonality produced an irresponsibility which was chilling the lifeblood of society. The state consequently had to expand its authority in order to preserve the ties which hold society together. The history of governmental intervention has been the history of the growing ineffectiveness of the private conscience as a means of social control. The only alternative is the growth of the public conscience, whose natural expression is the democratic government.

There, in succinct form, is the nub of the dispute. The choice, we would contend, is not between the private conscience and the public conscience expressed by the state. The private conscience, as Schlesinger also wanted to say in part, is not private in the sense of being deracinated, torn from its roots. It is not "arrogantly" individualistic. Private conscience too is communal; it is shaped by the myriad communities from which we learn to "put the world together" in an order that is responsive to our understanding of right and wrong. As for "the public conscience," it is a categorical fallacy. It harks back to Rousseau's mythology of a "general will" of which the state is the expression. "The Public" does not have a conscience. "The People" does not have a conscience. Only persons and persons-in-community have consciences.

Schlesinger's enthusiasm for the triumph of "the affirmative state" is not widely shared today, neither on the right nor on the left. It is not merely that there is a groundswell of opposition to "big government" or an anti-modernist passion for decentralization in obedience to the axiom that "small is beautiful." It is all that, but it is not merely that. It is rather that there is a growing awareness of the limits of the political, a recognition that most of the things that matter most are attended to in communities that are not government and should not be governmentalized. This awareness is what some critics describe as a "retribalization" or "reprivatization" of American life. But "tribe" used in this way is simply a pejorative for community. And, far from this being a process of reprivatization, it is an expansion of our understanding of what is public. We are no longer content to let "public" be synonymous with "government." Thus, for example, in education the distinction is not between public schools and private schools. It is rather between government schools and voluntary schools, or "schools of choice." All schools that advance a public interest and meet the needs of their relevant publics are public schools.

Jefferson, Jackson, Lippmann, Dewey, Schlesinger, and a host of others strove to articulate democracy as a credal cause. The last chapter of *The Vital Center* is titled "Freedom: A Fighting Faith." But finally it is a faith in which freedom is the end as well as the means. It is a faith devoid of transcendent purpose that can speak to the question of what freedom is *for*. This is, of necessity, a religious question. The truly "positive" state that presumes to address this question becomes the state-as-church. The Marxists are right: the political freedom of liberal democracy is essentially a "negative" freedom (freedom *from*). If we are not to succumb to totalitarianism, the positive meaning of freedom must be addressed in a manner, and through institutions, beyond the competence of what is ordinarily meant by politics or the government. The public square is the stage of many actors, not all of whom are following the same script. It is very confusing. It is democratic.

Historically, the churches in America have been leading actors in voicing the positive side of freedom's question. The purpose of Christianity in America, it is said somewhat scornfully, was to establish "The Righteous Empire." In the nineteenth century there was the hope to construct "a complete Christian commonwealth." The mainline churches, as they are called, have retired such rhetoric in recent decades. Many of their members, joined by today's moral majoritarians, want to pick it up again. Those who retired the idea tended to share the liberal assumption that the tasks of moral definition could and should be taken over by "the public conscience" expressed through the state. In the frequently uncritical affirmation of "the secular city," it was thought a triumph that the churches could step back from what had been a transitional role in the public square. Now it is recognized, however, that man has not "come of age" in the way that many thought. We still need, we more urgently need, the critical tutelage of traditions that refuse to leave "man on his own."

Negative freedom is dangerous to ourselves and others if it is negative freedom alone. As Murray argued, it is not only dangerous but it is "impossible." It is most dangerous *because* it is impossible. That is, its very attempt invites the termination of the democratic freedom in the name of which the attempt is made. The question is not *whether* the questions of positive freedom will be addressed. The question is by *whom*—by what reasonings, what traditions, what institutions, what authorities—they will be addressed. If they are to be addressed democratically in a way that gives reasonable assurance of a democratic future, we must work toward an understanding of the public square that is both more comprehensive and more complex. Along the way to such an understanding, we must listen with critical sympathy to those who are speaking the very new-old language of Christian America.

Are There Any Moral Absolutes?: Finding Black and White in a World of Grays

The word is values. *That's what's hotly urged upon our young people. Moral values. Heaven forbid they should encounter moral laws. They'd probably faint. Or maybe, if they were sitting in Professor Kreeft's philosophy class, they'd sit up straight. He gets your attention: "Suppose Hitler sincerely believed he was doing the world a great good by exterminating the Jews: Why doesn't that make it right?" It's not an exaggeration to say that the future of the world depends on educating men and women capable of explaining how subjective sincerity differs from objective truth.*

Anybody who has spent time in a college classroom in the last fifty years probably knows the whining voice of the sophomore who urgently asserts that his opinion is as good as any other. "A child and a peasant know that right and wrong are not matters of taste or fashion," Professor Kreeft writes. "Only a scholar could miss such an obvious point. . . ."

THIS IS NOT AN ABSTRACT, theoretical question for professors to argue. It is the most concrete, practical question for our civilization. For no civilization has ever survived without moral absolutes.

To disbelieve in all moral absolutes is implicitly to be a snob, to call all cultures fools, and to call that vision folly which has guided the lives of nearly everyone who has ever lived on this planet.

We are snobs if we call people who have been educated by life, tradition, experience, and family "backward" or "primitive." William F. Buckley said, "If I had to choose between being ruled by the first five hundred names in the Harvard faculty directory or the first five hundred names in the Boston Public Telephone Directory, I would unhesitatingly choose the latter."

Buckley's choice is a democratic one, for it prefers the judgments of the majority. It is also democratic because it prefers more traditional opinions, and tradition is simply "the democracy of the dead" (as Chesterton put it), giving the dead a vote too.

Moral Laws or Moral Values?

We can see that we have abandoned belief in moral absolutes by looking at one key change in our language about morality: we no longer talk about moral *laws,* but about moral *values.* This may seem unimportant, but it is momentous. For *laws* are objectively real; they come from above us and command us. The formula for a moral law is "Thou Shalt" or "Thou shalt not." But *values* have no such strong bite, no absolute demand. They suggest something subjective, not objective: "my" values or "your" values or "society's" values. Values come *from* us; laws come *to* us. We *invent* values, but we are *under* laws. Values are nice ideals to aspire to if we wish; laws tell us what we ought to do whether we like it or not.

We no longer like to talk about moral laws, values, and about moral absolutes. But we do like to talk about morality, a morality without absolutes. But a morality without absolutes is not a morality at all. "Do as you please" is not morality, "do what you ought" is morality. "Do whatever you think will have the best consequences" is not morality; it is calculation. "Do what works" is not morality, it is efficiency. Morality *means* something different from doing what we please, or what we calculate will turn out all right, or what works; morality means doing what we ought to do. Morality is not optional, like a "value," but obligatory, like a law. A morality without laws and obligations is simply a confusion, like a triangle without angles.

Why then do people say there are no absolutes? Why do they say morality is a matter of grays, not blacks and whites? Why do they say that making moral choices is so terribly complex and uncertain and difficult? The answer is simple: as Chesterton said, making moral decisions is always a terribly confusing thing—to someone without principles.

This is not about complex moral dilemmas. There are really only a few really complex moral dilemmas for most of us. Ninety-nine out of a hundred of our moral choices are quite simple and clear, if only we stop rationalizing. This essay is practical, not theoretical; therefore it addresses the moral choices we actually make, the ordinary, humdrum choices like whether or not to cheat on your wife or your income tax, not those fascinating academic exercises so cherished by "Values Clarification" like whom do you throw out of the lifeboat when the food runs out, or how to prevent nuclear war. Academic exercises have no bite of guilt in them; ordinary moral choices do. No one is ever *wrong* in Values Clarification. But in real life, everyone has some guilt, some moral wrongness, and some sin. For in real life there are moral laws, but in academic exercises there are only moral "values."

THREE PARTS TO MORALITY

Suppose Hitler sincerely believed he was doing the world a great good by exterminating the Jews: why doesn't that make it right?

Suppose a billionaire gives millions to shelter the homeless, but only to avoid having to pay it in income tax; is that a morally good deed or not?

Suppose a loving husband makes love to his wife, but at a time the doctor warns him is medically dangerous. Is this a good deed or a bad deed?

Thomas Aquinas has a good answer to these questions. He says that there are three parts to morality, and all three parts must be good for any act to be morally good. The three are (1) the objective act itself, (2) the subjective motive, and (3) the situation, or circumstances.

Moral laws can help you with the first part. They define which kinds of acts are good or bad, not because of your motive or intention, but because of the act itself.

The second factor in determining morality is the intention, or motive. The first factor, the nature of the act itself, is objective; the second factor, the intention, is subjective. So when people say morality is subjective, they're partly right. But when they say it's *all* subjective, they're simply wrong. And both the objective and the subjective factors are moral absolutes. We must *always* have good intentions, just as we must always do good things. Hate, greed, lust, envy, sloth, wrath, pride, or despair are absolutely wrong motives, just as murder, theft, etc. are absolutely wrong deeds.

But in addition to these two absolute factors, there is a third factor, which is relative: the situation, or circumstances. These are endlessly changing, and we have to make up our own mind how best to apply the moral absolutes to relative situations. For instance, in one situation, charity to the poor may mean giving a tramp money for food, but in another situation it may mean refusing him money because he'd use it on alcohol. Or charity to the poor may mean contributing to a large charitable organization, or electing a certain political candidate.

This is the factor that is indeed uncertain. For instance, what helps the poor more, Democratic economics of more direct anti-poverty programs, or Republican economics of feeding the economy as a whole? The answer is not certain, as it is certain what acts and what motives are good and bad.

All three factors must be morally right for the act to be right. If you do the wrong thing, it is wrong, even if your motive is sincere. Perhaps Hitler was sincere in his desire to "improve" the world; perhaps Charles Manson or Jim Jones sincerely thought they were doing God's work. But what they did was wrong. You can be sincere and dead wrong. You can be sincere and insane.

If you do the right thing for the wrong reason, it is also wrong, just as wrong as doing the wrong thing for the right reason. Giving money away only to avoid paying taxes, for instance, is dong a morally good thing but not for a morally good reason.

Finally, the circumstances must also be right. Making love to your spouse out of love but when it is medically dangerous is wrong. If any one of these three factors is wrong, the act is wrong; if all three are right, the act is right.

Three popular systems of ethics today emphasize just one of these three factors and ignores the other two. Unthinking *legalism* concentrates on only the first factor, the objective moral law, ignoring the subjective motive and the relative circumstances. Moral *subjectivism* concentrates on only the second factor, the subjective motive, and ignores the other two. (This is probably the most popular morality today: "if only your motive is sincere and loving, nothing else matters.") Finally, *situation ethics* says the situation (or the situation plus the motive) determines everything. This denies factor one, the objective nature of the act itself.

THREE QUESTIONS: ABSOLUTE? OBJECTIVE? UNIVERSAL?

We have been thinking about three related issues, and we should distinguish them: (1) are there any moral *absolutes*? (2) is morality *objective*? and (3) is morality *universal*?

The opposite of *absolute* is *relative*. "Thou shalt not murder" is an absolute. It is true and valid in itself, not relative to anything else, not if and only if you feel like it, or somebody told you, or the weather is nice. The justice of a war, on the other hand, is relative— to whether it is aggressive or defensive, unnecessary or necessary, destructive of innocents or not, and whether more injustice is done than is corrected. (I am here assuming the common-sensical tradition of the "just war theory." Both militarists and pacifists would disagree with it.)

"Honor your father and mother" is a moral absolute. But "support your father and mother" is relative—to their need and your ability.

"Thou shalt not commit adultery" is a moral absolute. It does not depend on your feelings or social mores or consequences. It does not suddenly become right when you feel in love, or when society tolerates it, or if it would make you a million dollars. But "spouses should share their lives together" is relative to their social customs and cultural content.

The opposite of our second term, "objective," is "subjective." Something that's objective is independent of us, our knowledge, our feelings, and our choices. "Trees are green" and "2+3=5" and "Kennedy was shot in 1963" are objective truths. My headache, my feelings for the Boston Red Sox (these two examples are pretty much identical), my opinions about the future, and my liking basset hounds and disliking poodles are subjective: states of consciousness, in me, dependent on me, neither true nor false in themselves.

Moral *intentions* are subjective because *all* intentions are subjective. But the moral law tells me that some intentions are absolutely right (*e.g.,* love and justice) and others absolutely wrong (*e.g.,* hating persons and selfishness).

Moral *laws* are not subjective, but objective. Moral *motives* or intentions are subjective.

The opposite of the third term, "universal," is "particular." "Universal" means always, in all situations, with no exceptions and no change. "Particular" means only in some situations or times, changeable. Situations are particular, laws are universal. You should *never* steal, but in some situations the government should increase taxes and in some situations it should not. Some taxing is stealing, some is not.

Moral laws are absolute, objective, and universal. That is the proposition denied by the modern world. The modern world wants to believe that moral laws are relative, subjective, and particular. That way, we are not under an absolute obligation to obey them. They depend on our subjective belief or unbelief in them, and I can always make particular exceptions when supposedly universal rules would limit my "freedom" too much for my liking.

WHY DO PEOPLE DISBELIEVE IN MORAL ABSOLUTES?

If "why" means "what motives impel them?" the answer is most often *convenience,* I think. All of us know from our own experience that hard, unyielding moral absolutes are often very inconvenient. We would very much like to bend the laws a bit; therefore we bend our *beliefs* about the law. It takes only a little knowledge of modern psychology to reveal how much we all rationalize rather than reason, how often our arguments are supports for our desires rather than honest searches after truth.

A second motive is peer pressure and conformity to fashion. If your college philosophy professor disbelieves in moral absolutes and your parents believe in them (which is the usual situation), you probably want to be "up-to-date" and sophisticated and go with the new-found "wisdom" of your professor.

But these are not good *reasons,* only *motives.* They are not objective logical arguments but subjective psychological causes. What *argu-*

ments do some people (like college philosophy professors) use to try to prove there are no moral absolutes, and how can they be refuted?

The seven most popular arguments are the following:

1. Values are relative to cultures. Different cultues have different values. It is provincial to deny this.

2. Values come from society, by a process now called "conditioning." (It used to be called "education," but "education" is done to free human beings, while "conditioning" is done to rats.)

3. If you want to be free, you must "create your own values." If values are "imposed on you," you are not free.

4. Absolutists and absolutism are intolerant, hard, and uncompassionate. Relativism and relativists are humane and tolerant.

5. Morality is a matter of individual conscience and subjective motive, not of some impersonal objective law of dos and don'ts that is the same for everyone.

6. What's right and wrong varies depending on the situation.

7. Scientific thinking discovers no moral absolutes. They do not appear to the senses, and denying them does not violate any law of logic.

Now here are the refutations of these arguments.

1. **Different cultues have different *opinions* about what is right and wrong.** Nazi Germany thought genocide right. Cannibals think eating humans is right. Americans think fornication is all right. But they're wrong about what's right! Thinking something is so doesn't make it so. *Opinions* are relative to cultures, but *truth* isn't.

   In the second place, even opinions about values are not wholly relative to cultures. No culture thinks courage is bad and cowardice good, honesty bad and dishonesty good, theft and adultery and murder good. Every society has some version of the

Ten Commandments. If a sociologist tells you otherwise, ask him which society has had this totally different set of values. It is true that different societies *apply* these basic values differently. For instance, in some societies suicide is thought to be courageous, in others it is thought to be cowardly. But no society prefers cowardice to courage. Some societies let a man have four wives, others only one, but no society says a man may simply take any woman he wants.

2. **Does society "condition" values in us?** No more than society "conditions" the multiplication table in us. Society "conditions" in us its value opinions, but society does not condition real values themselves.

   Just because we learn something from our society does not mean that thing is socially relative. Some things are (like styles of clothing), some are not (like the rules of good health, and moral health).

3. **Does freedom mean "creating your own values"?** No more than it means creating your own mathematics, or your own history. *Mores* (customs) are created; *morals* (morality) are discovered. We create rules like "drive on the right," and could just as well create other rules, like "drive on the left." But we did not invent the rules of morality, any more than we invented the rules of bodily health, and we cannot change them. We cannot "creatively" make murder and lying and greed and lust good. We are *not* free to "create" values. We are free to choose to obey or disobey them. Similarly, we do not invent the rules of math, or health, but we are free to obey them or disobey them, to say 2+2=4 or 2+2=5, to eat bread or to eat dirt.

4. **Absolutes *are* hard and unyielding, because they are facts.** But absolutists need not be hard and unyielding (though many are) Tolerance is good, indeed; but to admit this is to admit a real, objective value: tolerance!

   Relativism is *not* humane. It is tolerant *only* as long as it feels like being tolerant. Once it feels otherwise, no moral law prevents it from becoming dictatorial. If the only morality is what society dictates, then there is no moral appeal against Nazi genocide or South African racism, if the society approves these things.

5. **Is morality a matter of individual conscience?** Yes indeed. It is *also* a matter of objective fact: the truth of the moral law. Neither one of these two factors substitutes for the other. The law cannot make my decision for me, and I cannot make the moral law by my decisions. Remember, there are three factors in morality, not just one. One of these three factors, the moral law that tells us which acts are good and which are evil, is indeed the same for everyone and not different for different individuals. We are all judged by the same law. Morality is an equal opportunity employer.

6. **What about changing situations?** Just as conscience does not exclude moral law, so changing situations do not exclude moral law. In fact, situational morality presupposes a moral law. The only way to make moral sense of a situation is to apply a moral law to it. Otherwise, it is not a *situation* but a meaningless chaos.

7. **Finally, it is true that scientific thinking does not discover morality.** So what? Neither does poetic thinking, or musical thinking, or awareness of pain and pleasure. There are many ways of thinking, many modes of consciousness. The one that discovers morality is called conscience.

   By what right does the objector assume that *only* the scientific method can prove objective truth? *That* "fact" cannot be proved by the scientific method!

   What do you say to someone who is sincerely puzzled as to how we are supposed to know moral absolutes, since they do not appear to the senses? Tell him that he has inner senses too. Every normal human being discovers right and wrong by the inner eye of conscience. If someone cannot understand even that, what hope is there that he will understand anything else about morality? If a man is color blind, do we expect him to be an artist? Do we trust the tone-deaf to write our music? Then why do we listen to morally tone-deaf philosophers when they teach us that morality is merely relative and subjective? A child and a peasant know that right and wrong are not matters of taste or fashion. Only a scholar could miss such an obvious point, and only a gullible student, more eager to follow fashion than truth, could take the scholar seriously.

THE RELATIVIST'S SELF-CONTRADICTION

The relativist lets the cat out of the bag when you practice what he preaches, when you *act* toward *him* as if his own philosophy of relativism were true. *He* may *preach* relativism, but he expects *you* to *practice* absolutism. For instance, an ethics class of mine told me they thought morality was relative, and what right did I have to "impose my values" of absolutism on them? I replied, "All right. Let's run the class by your values, not mine. There are no absolutes. Moral values are subjective and relative. And my particular set of subjective personal moral values includes this one: all women in my class flunk." They immediately protested in shock: "That's unfair!" "Yes, it is unfair," I agreed. "But what do you mean by 'fair'? If fairness, or justice, is only MY value or YOUR value, then it has no universal authority over both of us. I have no right to impose MY values on you, and you have no right to impose yours on me. But if there is a universal, objective, absolute value called justice, or fairness, then it holds for both of us, and it judges me as wrong when I say all women flunk. And you can appeal to that justice in judging my rule as unfair. But if there is no such thing as absolute objective justice, then all you can mean when you protest my rule is that you don't like it, that your subjective values are different than mine. But that's not what you said. You didn't say merely that you didn't like my rule, but that it was unfair. So you do believe in moral absolutes after all, when it comes down to practice. Why do you believe that silly theory, then? Why are you hypocrites? Why don't you practice what you preach, and stop appealing to justice, or else preach what you practice, and stop denying it?"

Actually, at least one famous moral relativist was consistent even about that. Jean-Paul Sartre, the famous French atheist, protested against the Nuremberg trials of Nazi war criminals on charges of "crimes against humanity," because they were judged not by German law or French law but natural law, universal law. The trial assumed that such a universal moral law really existed. Sartre had always taught that it didn't. So he was consistent. The democracies had no right to judge the Nazis if all values were relative to different cultures or different individuals.

That was consistent. It was also moral bankruptcy—intolerable, unendurable, unlivable. Thank God for consistent moral relativists like Sartre: they show us what relativism really comes to.

PART II

The Social Order

A conservative view from one of this tortured century's most enigmatic souls:

> The first of the soul's needs, the one which touches most nearly its eternal destiny, is order; that is to say, a texture of social relationships such that one is compelled to violate imperative obligations in order to carry out other ones. It is only where this, in fact, occurs that external circumstances have any power to inflict spiritual violence on the soul. For he for whom the threat of death or suffering is the one thing standing in the way of the performance of an obligation, can overcome this disability, and will only suffer in his body. But he who finds that circumstances, in fact, render the various acts necessitated by a series of strict obligations incompatible with one another is, without being able to offer any resistance thereto, made to suffer in his love of good.
>
> At the present time, a very considerable amount of confusion and incompatibility exists between obligations.
>
> SIMONE WEIL, *The Need For Roots: Prelude to a Declaration of Duties Toward Mankind* (1952)

Character and Community: The Problem of Broken Windows

We may sometimes wonder if social scientists can reason at all. So often it seems their conclusions about the "root causes" of antisocial behavior place the blame on society itself. It is, therefore, bracing to read the work of James Q. Wilson, and in it to rediscover the importance—in personal behavior and in social structures—of character.

The article that follows, written with the indomitable George Kelling, who walked a beat with cops on Newark, New Jersey's mean streets, lays bare realities familiar to any urban dweller. The authors quote Nathan Glazer's apt comment concerning subway graffiti: It is a signal that the environment under city streets is "uncontrolled and uncontrollable, and that anyone can invade it to do whatever damage and mischief the mind suggests."

Maintaining the social order has given way to law enforcement. That may seem appropriate, given rising crime rates, but crime arises in part from disorder. Professors Wilson and Kelling make it clear that "broken windows" are more than just a metaphor.

IN THE MID-1970S THE STATE OF NEW JERSEY announced a safe and clean neighborhoods program designed to improve the quality of community life in twenty-eight cities. As part of that program, the state provided money to help cities take police officers out of their patrol cars and assign them to walking beats. The governor and other state officials were enthusiastic about using foot patrol as a way of cutting crime, but many police chiefs were skeptical. Foot patrol in their eyes had been generally discredited. It reduced the mobility of the police, who thus had difficulty responding to citizen calls for service, and it weakened headquarters control over patrol officers.

Many police officers also disliked foot patrol but for different reasons: it was hard work; it kept them outside on cold, rainy nights; and it reduced their chances for making a good pinch. In some departments, assigning officers to foot patrol had been used as a form of punishment. And academic experts on policing doubted that foot patrol would have any impact on crime rates; it was in the opinion of most little more than a sop to public opinion. But since the state was paying for it, the local authorities were willing to go along.

Five years after the program started, the Police Foundation, in Washington, D.C., published an evaluation of the foot patrol project. Based on its analysis of a carefully controlled experiment carried out chiefly in Newark, the foundation concluded, to the surprise of hardly anyone, that foot patrol had not reduced crime rates. But residents of the foot-patrolled neighborhoods seemed to feel more secure than persons in other areas, tended to believe that crime had been reduced, and seemed to take fewer steps to protect themselves from crime (staying at home with the doors locked, for example). Moreover citizens in the foot patrol areas had a more favorable opinion of the police than did those living elsewhere. And officers walking beats had higher morale, greater job satisfaction, and a more favorable attitude toward citizens in their neighborhoods than did officers assigned to patrol cars.

These findings may be taken as evidence that the skeptics were right—foot patrol has no effect on crime; it merely fools the citizens into thinking that they are safer. But in our view, and in the view of the authors of the Police Foundation study (of whom Kelling was one), the citizens of Newark were not fooled at all. They knew what the foot patrol officers were doing, they knew it was different from what motorized officers do, and they knew that having officers walk beats did in fact make their neighborhoods safer.

Disorder and Violent Crime

But how can a neighborhood be safer when the crime rate has not gone down—in fact may have gone up? Finding the answer requires first that we understand what most often frightens people in public places. Many citizens of course are primarily frightened by crime, especially crime involving a sudden, violent attack by a stranger. This risk is real, in Newark as in many large cities. But we tend to overlook or forget another source of fear: the fear of being bothered by disorderly people—not violent people nor necessarily criminals but disreputable or obstreperous or unpredictable people: panhandlers, drunks, addicts, rowdy teenagers, prostitutes, loiterers, the mentally disturbed.

Foot patrol officers elevated, to the extent they could, the level of public order in these neighborhoods. Although the neighborhoods were predominantly black and the foot patrolmen were mostly white, this police function of order maintenance was performed to the general satisfaction of both parties.

One of us (Kelling) spent many hours walking with Newark foot-patrol officers to see how they defined "order" and what they did to maintain it. One beat was typical: a busy but dilapidated area in the heart of Newark, with many abandoned buildings, marginal shops (several of which prominently displayed knives and straight-edged razors in their windows), one large department store, and, most important, a train station and several major bus stops. Although the area was run down, its streets were filled with people because it was a major transportation center. The good order of this area was important not only to those who lived and worked there but also to many others who had to move through it on their way home, to supermarkets, or to factories.

The people on the street were primarily black; the officer who walked the street was white. The people were made up of regulars and strangers. Regulars included both decent folk and some drunks and derelicts who were always there but who "knew their place." Strangers were, well, strangers and viewed suspiciously, sometimes apprehensively. The officer—call him Kelly—knew who the regulars were, and they knew him. As he saw his job, he was to keep an eye on strangers and make certain that the disreputable regulars observed some informal but widely understood rules. Drunks and addicts could sit on the stoops but could not lie down. People could drink on side streets but not at the main intersection. Bottles had to be in paper bags. Talking to, bothering, or begging from people waiting at the bus stop was strictly forbidden. If a dispute erupted between a businessman and a customer, the businessman was assumed to be right, especially if the customer was a stranger. If a stranger loitered, Kelly would ask him if he had any means of support and what his business was; if he gave unsatisfactory answers, he was sent on his way. Persons who broke the informal rules, especially those who bothered people waiting at bus stops, were arrested for vagrancy. Noisy teenagers were told to keep quiet.

These rules were defined and enforced in collaboration with the regulars on the street. Another neighborhood might have different rules, but these, everybody understood, were the rules for this neighborhood. If someone violated them, the regulars not only turned to Kelly for help but also ridiculed the violator. Sometimes what Kelly did could be described as enforcing the law, but just as often it involved taking informal or extralegal steps to help protect what the neighborhood had decided was the appropriate level of public order. Some of the things he did probably would not withstand a legal challenge.

A determined skeptic might acknowledge that a skilled foot patrol officer can maintain order but still insist that this sort of order has little to do with the real sources of community fear, that is, with violent crime. To a degree, that is true. But two things must be borne in mind. First, outside observers should not assume that they know how much of the anxiety now endemic in many big-city neighborhoods stems from a fear of real crime and how much from a sense that the street is disorderly, a source of distasteful, worrisome encounters. The people of Newark, to judge from their behavior and their remarks to interviewers, apparently assign a high value to public order and feel relieved and reassured when the police help them maintain that order.

The Theory of Broken Windows

Second, at the community level, disorder and crime are usually linked in a kind of developmental sequence. Social psychologists and police officers tend to agree that if a window in a building is broken and is left unrepaired, the rest of the windows will soon be broken. This is as true in nice neighborhoods as in run-down ones. Window breaking does not necessarily occur on a large scale because some areas are inhabited by determined window breakers whereas others are populated by window lovers; rather one unrepaired broken window is a signal that no one cares, and so breaking more windows costs nothing. (It has always been fun.)

Philip Zimbardo, a Stanford psychologist, reported in 1969 on some experiments testing the broken window theory. He arranged to have an automobile without license plates parked with its hood up on a street in the Bronx and a comparable automobile on a street in Palo Alto, California. The car in the Bronx was attacked by vandals within ten minutes of its abandonment. The first to arrive were a family—father, mother, and young son—who removed the radiator and battery. Within twenty-four hours virtually everything of value had been removed. Then random destruction began: windows were smashed, parts torn off, upholstery ripped. Children began to use the car as a playground. Most of the adult vandals were well-dressed, apparently clean-cut whites. The car in Palo Alto sat untouched for more than a week. Then Zimbardo smashed part of it with a sledgehammer. Soon passersby were joining in. Within a few hours the car had been turned upside down and utterly destroyed. Again the vandals appeared to be primarily respectable whites.

Untended property becomes fair game for people out for fun or plunder and even for people who ordinarily would not dream of doing such things and who probably consider themselves law-abiding. Because of the nature of community life in the Bronx—its anonymity, the frequency with which cars are abandoned and things are stolen or broken, the past experience of no one caring—vandalism begins much more quickly than it does in staid Palo Alto, where people have come to believe that private possessions are cared for and that mischievous behavior is costly. But vandalism can *occur anywhere once communal barriers—the sense of mutual regard and the obligations of civility—are lowered by actions that seem to signal that no one cares.*

We suggest that untended behavior also leads to the *breakdown of community controls.* A stable neighborhood of families who care for their homes, mind each other's children, and confidently frown on unwanted intruders can change in a few years or even a few months to an inhospitable and frightening jungle. A piece of property is abandoned, weeds grow up, a window is smashed. Adults stop scolding rowdy children; the children, emboldened, become more rowdy. Families move out; unattached adults move in. Teenagers gather in front of the corner store. The merchant asks them to move; they refuse. Fights occur. Litter accumulates. People start drinking in front of the grocery; in time an inebriate slumps to the sidewalk and is allowed to sleep it off. Pedestrians are approached by panhandlers.

At this point it is not inevitable that serious crime will flourish or violent attacks on strangers will occur. But many residents will think that crime, especially violent crime, is on the rise, and they will modify their behavior accordingly. They will use the streets less often and when on the streets will stay apart from their fellows, moving with averted eyes, silent lips, and hurried steps: "don't get involved." For some residents this growing atomization will matter little because the neighborhood is not their home but the place where they live. Their interests are elsewhere; they are cosmopolitans. But it will matter greatly to other people whose lives derive meaning and satisfaction from local attachments rather than worldly involvement; for them the neighborhood will cease to exist except for a few reliable friends whom they arrange to meet.

Such an area is vulnerable to criminal invasion. Although it is not inevitable, it is more likely that here, rather than in places where people are confident they can regulate public behavior by informal controls, drugs will change hands, prostitutes will solicit, and cars will be stripped. The drunks will be robbed by boys who do it as a lark and the prostitutes' customers will be robbed by men who do it purposefully and perhaps violently. Muggings will occur.

Among those who often find it difficult to move away from this are the elderly. Surveys of citizens suggest that the elderly are much less likely to be the victims of crime than younger persons, and some have inferred from this that the well-known fear of crime voiced by the elderly is an exaggeration: perhaps we ought not to design special programs to protect older persons; perhaps we should even try to talk them out of their mistaken fears. This argument misses the point. The prospect of a confrontation with an obstreperous teenager or a drunken panhandler can be as fear inducing for defenseless persons as the prospect of meeting an actual robber; indeed to a defenseless person the two kinds of confrontation are often indistinguishable. Moreover the lower rate at which the elderly are victimized is a measure of the steps they have already taken—chiefly, staying behind locked doors—to minimize the risks they face. Young men are more frequently attacked than older women, not because they are easier or more lucrative targets but because they are on the streets more.

Nor is the connection between disorderliness and fear made only by the elderly. Susan Estrich, of the Harvard Law School, has recently gathered a number of surveys on the sources of public fear. One, done in Portland, Oregon, indicated that three-fourths of the adults interviewed cross to the other side of a street when they see a gang of teenagers; another survey, in Baltimore, discovered that nearly half would cross the street to avoid even a single strange youth. When an interviewer asked people in a housing project where the most dangerous spot was, they mentioned a place where young persons gathered to drink and play music, despite the fact that not a single crime had occurred there. In Boston public housing projects, the greatest fear was expressed by persons living in the buildings where disorderliness and incivility, not crime, were the greatest. Knowing this helps one understand the significance of such otherwise harmless displays as subway graffiti. As Nathan Glazer has written, the proliferation of graffiti, even when not obscene, confronts the subway rider with the "inescapable knowledge that the environment he must endure for an hour or more a day is uncontrolled and uncontrollable, and that anyone can invade it to do whatever damage and mischief the mind suggests."

In response to fear, people avoid one another, weakening controls. Sometimes they call the police. Patrol cars arrive, an occasional arrest occurs, but crime continues and disorder is not abated. Citizens complain to the police chief, but he explains that his department is low on personnel and that the courts do not punish petty or first-time offenders. To the residents the police who arrive in squad cars are either ineffective or uncaring; to the police the residents are animals who deserve each other. The citizens may soon stop calling the police because they cannot do anything.

Changes in Mobility and Policing

The process we call urban decay has occurred for centuries in every city. But what is happening today is different in at least two important respects. First, in the period before, say, World War II, city dwellers—because of money costs, transportation difficulties, familial and church connections—could rarely move away from neighborhood problems. When movement did occur, it tended to be along public transit routes. Now mobility has become exceptionally easy for all but the poorest or those who are blocked by racial prejudice. Earlier crime waves had a kind of built-in self-correcting mechanism: the determination of a neighborhood or community to reassert control over its turf. Areas in Chicago, New York, and Boston would experience crime and gang wars, and then normalcy would return as the families for whom no alternative residences were possible reclaimed their authority over the streets.

Second, the police in this earlier period assisted in that reassertion of authority by acting, sometimes violently, on behalf of the community. Young toughs were roughed up, people were arrested on suspicion or for vagrancy, and prostitutes and petty thieves were routed. Rights were something enjoyed by decent folk, and perhaps also by the serious professional criminal, who avoided violence and could afford a lawyer.

This pattern of policing was not an aberration or the result of occasional excess. From the earliest days of the nation, the police function was seen primarily as that of a night watchman: to maintain order against the chief threats to order—fire, wild animals, and disreputable behavior. Solving crimes was viewed not as a police responsibility but as a private one. In the March 1969 *Atlantic,* one of us (Wilson) wrote a brief account of how the police role had slowly changed from maintaining order to fighting crimes. The change began with the creation of private detectives (often ex-criminals), who worked on a contingency fee basis for individuals who had suffered losses. In time the detectives were absorbed into municipal police agencies and paid a regular salary; simultaneously the responsibility for prosecuting thieves was shifted from the aggrieved private citizen to the professional prosecutor. This process was not complete in most places until the twentieth century.

In the 1960s, when urban riots were a major problem, social scientists began to explore carefully the order maintenance function of the police and to suggest ways of improving it—not to make streets safer (its original function) but to reduce the incidence of mass violence. Order maintenance became to a degree coterminous with community

relations. But as the crime wave that began in the early 1960s continued without abatement throughout the decade and into the 1970s, attention shifted to the role of the police as crime fighters. Studies of
police behavior ceased by and large to be accounts of the order maintenance function and became instead efforts to propose and test ways
whereby the police could solve more crimes, make more arrests, and
gather better evidence. If these things could be done, social scientists
assumed, citizens would be less fearful.

Order and Crime Prevention

A great deal was accomplished during this transition, as both police
chiefs and outside experts emphasized the crime-fighting function in
their plans, in the allocation of resources, and in deployment of personnel. The police may well have become better crime fighters as a result. And doubtless they remained aware of their responsibility for
order. But the link between order maintenance and crime prevention,
so obvious to earlier generations, was forgotten.

That link is similar to the process whereby one broken window becomes many. The citizen who fears the ill-smelling drunk, the rowdy
teenager, or the importuning beggar is not merely expressing his distaste for unseemly behavior; he is also giving voice to a bit of folk wisdom that happens to be a correct generalization: namely, that serious
street crime flourishes in areas in which disorderly behavior goes
unchecked. The unchecked panhandler is in effect the first broken
window. Muggers and robbers, whether opportunistic or professional, believe they reduce their chances of being caught or even identified if they operate on streets where potential victims are already
intimidated by prevailing conditions. If the neighborhood cannot
keep a bothersome panhandler from annoying passersby, the thief
may reason, it is even less likely to call the police to identify a potential mugger or to interfere if the mugging actually takes place.

Some police administrators concede that this process occurs but argue that motorized patrol officers can deal with it as effectively as foot
patrol officers. We are not so sure. In theory an officer in a squad car
can observe as much as an officer on foot; in theory the former can
talk to as many people as the latter. But the reality of police-citizen
encounters is powerfully altered by the automobile. An officer on foot

cannot separate himself from the street people; if he is approached, only his uniform and his personality can help him manage whatever is about to happen. And he can never be certain what that will be: a request for directions, a plea for help, an angry denunciation, a teasing remark, a confused babble, a threatening gesture.

In a car an officer is more likely to deal with street people by rolling down the window and looking at them. The door and the window exclude the approaching citizen; they are a barrier. Some officers take advantage of this barrier, perhaps unconsciously, by acting differently if in the car than than they would on foot. We have seen this countless times. The police car pulls up to a corner where teenagers are gathered. The window is rolled down. The officer stares at the youths. They stare back. The officer says to one, "C'mere." He saunters over, conveying to his friends by his elaborately casual style the idea he is not intimidated by authority. "What's your name?" "Chuck." "Chuck who?" "Chuck Jones." "What'ya doing, Chuck?" "Nothin'." "Got a P.O. [parole officer]?" "Nah." "Sure?" "Yeah." "Stay out of trouble, Chuckie." Meanwhile, the other boys laugh and exchange comments among themselves, probably at the officer's expense. The officer stares harder. He cannot be certain what is being said, nor can he join in and, by displaying his own skill at street banter, prove that he cannot be put down. In the process the officer has learned almost nothing, and the boys have decided the officer is an alien force who can safely be disregarded, even mocked.

Our experience is that most citizens like to talk to a police officer. Such exchanges give them a sense of importance, provide them with the basis for gossip, and allow them to explain to the authorities what is worrying them (whereby they gain a modest but significant sense of having done something about the problem). You approach a person on foot more easily, and talk to him more readily, than you do a person in a car. Moreover you can more easily retain some anonymity if you draw an officer aside for a private chat. Suppose you want to pass on a tip about who is stealing handbags or who offered to sell you a stolen TV. In the inner city the culprit in all likelihood lives nearby. To walk up to a marked patrol car and lean in the window is to convey a visible signal that you are a fink.

The essence of the police role in maintaining order is to reinforce the informal control mechanisms of the community itself. The police cannot, without committing extraordinary resources, provide a substitute for that informal control. Conversely, to reinforce those natural forces the police must accommodate them. And therein lies the problem.

Whose Rules?

Should police activity on the street be shaped in important ways by the standards of the neighborhood rather than by the rules of the state? Over the past two decades the shift of police from order maintenance to law enforcement has brought them increasingly under the influence of legal restrictions, provoked by media complaints and enforced by court decisions and departmental orders. As a consequence the order maintenance functions of the police are now governed by rules developed to control police relations with suspected criminals. This is an entirely new development. For centuries the role of the police as watchmen was judged primarily not in terms of its complying with appropriate procedures but rather in terms of its attaining a desired objective. The objective was order, an inherently ambiguous term but a condition that people in a given community recognized when they saw it. The means were the same as those the community itself would employ, if its members were sufficiently determined, courageous, and authoritative. Detecting and apprehending criminals, by contrast, was a means to an end, not an end in itself; a judicial determination of guilt or innocence was the hoped-for result of the law enforcement mode. From the first, the police were expected to follow rules defining that process, although states differed in how stringent the rules should be. The criminal apprehension process was always understood to involve individual rights, the violation of which was unacceptable because it meant that the violating officer would be acting as a judge and jury—and that was not his job. Guilt or innocence was to be determined by universal standards under special procedures.

Ordinarily no judge or jury ever sees the persons caught up in a dispute over the appropriate level of neighborhood order. That is true not only because most cases are handled informally on the street but also because no universal standards are available to settle arguments over disorder, and thus a judge may not be any wiser or more effective than a police officer. Until quite recently in many states, and even today in some places, the police make arrests on such charges as suspicious person or vagrancy or public drunkenness—charges with scarcely any legal meaning. These charges exist not because society wants judges to punish vagrants or drunks but because it wants an officer to have the legal tools to remove undesirable persons from a neighborhood when informal efforts to preserve order in the streets have failed.

Once we begin to think of all aspects of police work as involving the application of universal rules under special procedures, we inevitably ask what constitutes an undesirable person and why we should criminalize vagrancy or drunkenness. A strong and commendable desire to see that people are treated fairly makes us worry about allowing the police to rout persons who are undesirable by some vague or parochial standard. A growing and not-so-commendable utilitarianism leads us to doubt that any behavior that does not "hurt" another person should be made illegal. And thus many of us who watch over the police are reluctant to allow them to perform, in the only way they can, a function that every neighborhood desperately wants them to perform.

This wish to decriminalize disreputable behavior that "harms no one"—and thus remove the ultimate sanction the police can employ to maintain neighborhood order—is a mistake. Arresting a single drunk or a single vagrant who has harmed no identifiable person seems unjust, and in a sense it is. But failing to do anything about a score of drunks or a hundred vagrants may destroy an entire community. A particular rule that seems to make sense in the individual case makes no sense when it is made a universal rule and applied to all cases. It makes no sense because it fails to take into account the connection between one broken window left untended and a thousand broken windows. Of course agencies other than the police could attend to the problems posed by drunks or the mentally ill, but in most communities—especially where the deinstitutionalization movement has been strong—they do not.

The concern about equity is more serious. We might agree that certain behavior makes one person more undesirable than another, but how do we ensure that age or skin color or national origin or harmless mannerisms will not also become the basis for distinguishing the undesirable from the desirable? How do we ensure in short that the police do not become the agents of neighborhood bigotry?

We can offer no wholly satisfactory answer to this important question. We are not confident that there is a satisfactory answer except to hope that by their selection, training, and supervision, the police will be inculcated with a clear sense of the outer limit of their discretionary authority. That limit roughly is this: the police exist to help regulate behavior, not to maintain the racial or ethnic purity of a neighborhood.

Consider the case of the Robert Taylor Homes in Chicago, one of the largest public housing projects in the country. It is home for nearly 20,000 people, all black, and extends over ninety-two acres along South State Street. It was named after a distinguished black who had been chairman of the Chicago Housing Authority during the 1940s. Not long after it opened, in 1962, relations between project residents and the police deteriorated badly. The citizens felt that the police were insensitive or brutal; the police in turn complained of unprovoked attacks on them. Some Chicago officers tell of times when they were afraid to enter the Homes. Crime rates soared.

Today the atmosphere has changed. Police-citizen relations have improved—apparently both sides learned something from the earlier experience. Recently a boy stole a purse and ran off. Several young persons who saw the theft voluntarily passed along to the police information on the identity and residence of the thief, and they did this publicly, with friends and neighbors looking on. But problems persist, chief among them the presence of youth gangs that terrorize residents and recruit members in the project. The people expect the police to do something about this, and the police are determined to do just that.

But do what? Although the police can obviously make arrests whenever a gang member breaks the law, a gang can form, recruit, and congregate without breaking the law. And only a tiny fraction of gang-related crimes can be solved by an arrest; thus, if an arrest is the only recourse for the police, the residents' fears will go unassuaged. The police will soon feel helpless, and the residents will again believe that the police do nothing. What the police in fact do is to chase known gang members out of the project. In the words of one officer, "We kick ass." Project residents both know and approve of this. The tacit police-citizen alliance in the project is reinforced by the police view that the cops and the gangs are the two rival sources of power in the area and that the gangs are not going to win.

None of this is easily reconciled with any conception of due process or fair treatment. Since both residents and gang members are black, race is not a factor. But it could be. Suppose a white project confronted a black gang or vice versa. We would be apprehensive about the police taking sides. But the substantive problem remains the same: how can the police strengthen the informal social control mechanisms of natural communities in order to minimize fear in public places? Law enforcement per se is no answer. A gang can weaken or destroy a community by standing about in a menacing fashion and speaking rudely to passersby without breaking the law.

The Individual or the Community?

We have difficulty thinking about such matters not simply because the ethical and legal issues are so complex but because we have become accustomed to thinking of the law in essentially individualistic terms. The law defines *my* rights, punishes *his* behavior, and is applied by *that* officer because of *this* harm. We assume in thinking this way that what is good for the individual will be good for the community, and what does not matter when it happens to one person will not matter if it happens to many. Ordinarily those are plausible assumptions. But in cases where behavior that is tolerable to one person is intolerable to many others, the reactions of the others—fear, withdrawal, flight—may ultimately make matters worse for everyone, including the individual who first professed indifference.

It may be their greater sensitivity to communal as opposed to individual needs that helps explain why the residents of small communities are more satisfied with their police than are the residents of similar neighborhoods in big cities. Elinor Ostrom and her co-workers at Indiana University compared the perception of police services in two poor, all-black Illinois towns—Phoenix and East Chicago Heights—with those of three comparable all-black neighborhoods in Chicago. The level of criminal victimization and the quality of police-community relations appeared to be about the same in the town and the Chicago neighborhoods. But the citizens living in villages were much more likely than those living in the Chicago neighborhoods to say that they do not stay at home for fear of crime, to agree that the local police have "the right to take any action necessary" to deal with problems, and to agree that the police "look out for the needs of the average citizen." It is possible that the residents and the police of the small towns saw themselves as engaged in a collaborative effort to maintain a certain standard of communal life, whereas those of the big city felt themselves to be simply requesting and supplying particular services on an individual basis.

If this is true, how should a wise police chief deploy his meager forces? The first answer is that nobody knows for certain, and the most prudent course of action would be to try further variations on the Newark experiment, to see more precisely what works in what kinds of neighborhoods. The second answer is also a hedge—many aspects of order maintenance in neighborhoods can probably best be handled in ways that involve the police minimally, if at all. A busy, bustling shopping center and a quiet, well-tended suburb may need almost no visible police presence. In both cases the ratio of respectable to disreputable people is ordinarily so high as to make informal social control effective.

Even in areas that are in jeopardy from disorderly elements, citizen action without substantial police involvement may be sufficient. Meetings between teenagers who like to hang out on a particular corner and adults who want to use that corner might well lead to amicable agreement on a set of rules about how many people can be allowed to congregate, where, and when.

Where no understanding is possible—or possible, but not observed—citizen patrols may be a sufficient response. There are two traditions of communal involvement in maintaining order. One, that of the community watchmen, is as old as the first settlement of the New World. Until well into the nineteenth century, volunteer watchmen, not policemen, patrolled their communities to keep order. They did so by and large without taking the law into their own hands— without, that is, punishing persons or using force. Their presence deterred disorder or alerted the community to disorder that could not be deterred. There are hundreds of such efforts today in communities all across the nation. Perhaps the best known is that of the Guardian Angels, a group of unarmed young persons in distinctive berets and T-shirts who first came to public attention when they began patrolling the New York City subways but who claim now to have chapters in more than thirty American cities. Unfortunately we have little information about the effect of these groups on crime. It is possible, however, that whatever their effect on crime, citizens find their presence reassuring and that they thus contribute to maintaining a sense of order and civility.

The second tradition is that of the vigilante. Rarely a feature of the settled communities of the East, it was primarily found in those frontier towns that grew up in advance of the reach of government. More than 350 vigilante groups are known to have existed, their distinctive feature was that their members did take the law into their own hands, by acting as judge, jury, and often executioner as well as policeman. Today the vigilante movement is conspicuous by its rarity, despite the great fear expressed by citizens that the older cities are becoming urban frontiers. But some community watchmen groups have skirted the line, and others may cross it in the future. An ambiguous case, reported in the *Wall Street Journal,* involved a citizens' patrol in the Silver Lake area of Belleville, New Jersey. A leader told the reporter, "We look for outsiders." If a few teenagers from outside the neighborhood enter it, "we ask them their business," he said. "If they say they're going down the street to see Mrs. Jones, fine, we let them pass. But then we follow them down the block to make sure they're really going to see Mrs. Jones."

Police as the Key

Although citizens can do a great deal, the police are plainly the key to order maintenance. For one thing, many communities, such as the Robert Taylor Homes, cannot do the job by themselves. For another, no citizen in a neighborhood, even an organized one, is likely to feel the sense of responsibility that wearing a badge confers. Psychologists have done many studies on why people fail to go to the aid of persons being attacked or seeking help, and they have learned that the cause is not apathy or selfishness but the absence of some plausible grounds for feeling that one must personally accept responsibility. Ironically, avoiding responsibility is easier when a lot of people are standing about. On streets and in public places, where order is so important, many people are likely to be around, a fact that reduces the chance of any one person acting as the agent of the community. The police officer's uniform singles him out as a person who must accept responsibility if asked. In addition officers, more easily than their fellow citizens, can be expected to distinguish between what is necessary to protect the safety of the street and what merely protects its ethnic purity.

But the police forces of America are losing, not gaining, members. Some cities have suffered substantial cuts in the number of officers available for duty. These cuts are not likely to be reversed in the near future. Therefore each department must assign its existing officers with great care. Some neighborhoods are so demoralized and crime-ridden as to make foot patrol useless; the best the police can do with limited resources is respond to the enormous number of calls for service. Other neighborhoods are so stable and serene as to make foot patrol unnecessary. The key is to identify neighborhoods at the tipping point: where the public order is deteriorating but not unreclaimable, where the streets are used frequently but by apprehensive people, where a window is likely to be broken at any time and must quickly be fixed if all are not to be shattered.

Most police departments do not have ways of systematically identifying such areas and assigning officers to them. Officers are assigned on the basis of crime rates (meaning that marginally threatened areas are often stripped so that police can investigate crimes in areas where the situation is hopeless) or on the basis of calls for service (despite the fact that most citizens do not call the police when they are merely frightened or annoyed). To allocate patrol wisely, the department must look at the neighborhoods and decide, from firsthand evidence, where an additional officer will make the greatest difference in promoting a sense of safety.

One way to stretch limited police resources is being tried in some public housing projects. Tenant organizations hire off-duty police officers for patrol work in their buildings. The costs are not high (at least not per resident), the officer likes the additional income, and the residents feel safer. Such arrangements are probably more successful than hiring private watchmen, and the Newark experiment helps us understand why. A private security guard may deter crime or misconduct by his presence, and he may go to the aid of persons needing help, but he may well not intervene—that is, control or drive away—someone challenging community standards. Being a sworn officer—a real cop—seems to give one the confidence, the sense of duty, and the aura of authority necessary to perform this difficult task.

Patrol officers might be encouraged to go to and from duty stations on public transportation and, while on the bus or subway car, to enforce rules about smoking, drinking, disorderly conduct, and the like.

The enforcement need involve nothing more than ejecting the offender (the offense after all is not one with which a booking officer or a judge wishes to be bothered). Perhaps the random but relentless maintenance of standards on buses would lead to conditions on buses that approximate the level of civility we now take for granted on airplanes.

But the most important requirement is to think that maintaining order in precarious situations is a vital job. The police know this is one of their functions, and they also believe correctly that it cannot be done to the exclusion of criminal investigation and responding to calls. We may have encouraged them to suppose, however, on the basis of our oft-repeated concerns about serious, violent crime, that they will be judged exclusively on their capacity as crime fighters. To the extent that this is the case, police administrators will continue to concentrate police personnel in the highest crime areas (though not necessarily in the areas most vulnerable to criminal invasion), emphasize their training in the law and criminal apprehension (and not their training in managing street life), and join too quickly in campaigns to decriminalize harmless behavior (although public drunkenness, street prostitution, and pornographic displays can destroy a community more quickly than any team of professional burglars).

Above all, we must return to our long-abandoned view that the police ought to protect communities as well as individuals. Our crime statistics and victimization surveys measure personal losses, but they do not measure communal losses. Just as physicians now recognize the importance of fostering health rather than simply treating illness, so the police—and the rest of us—ought to recognize the importance of maintaining, intact, communities without broken windows.

The Hole in the Theory

Compassion. It's the impetus behind much of our social policy, and, as Myron Magnet suggests, a reason why it is so difficult to change such policies when they've failed. This kind of concern is hot.

And yet the compassion behind our welfare programs is strangely cool, oddly detached. It sees its clients as passive, as victims, as helpless. In the minds of policy makers, poor equals weak. This is, of course, a lie.

It's not the economy, stupid. It's the social structure, dummy.

OF THE... MAJOR EXPLANATIONS for the rise of the underclass [none has received more notice than] that put forward by Charles Murray's brilliant *Losing Ground*. The most dazzling part of Murray's powerful argument is his analysis of how changes in the nation's welfare system in the 1960s inflamed the epidemic of illegitimacy central to underclass pathology.

Since the mid-sixties, Murray shows, welfare has been a particularly insidious snare. Since then, a combination of AFDC, food stamps, Medicaid, and other benefits has provided welfare mothers in the big urban states where the underclass is concentrated with more purchasing power than they'd get from a minimum-wage job. Even in less free-spending states, the benefit package is enough to support these mothers and their children fully if meanly.

If an income they can get by on is the consequence of having a baby, observes Murray, why should poor women worry about getting pregnant? Since welfare fosters the kind of passivity that makes it hard to see alternatives to the admittedly marginal existence it provides, what would impel them to seek work instead of having another illegitimate baby? And why should these women get married? A welfare mother's child, says Murray, "provides her with the economic insurance that a husband used to represent."

There is no need to invoke a breakdown of the work ethic or the development of a culture of poverty among the underclass, says Murray, though these may operate also. The welfare system by itself is enough to account for the nonmarriage, bastardy, and some of the nonwork that make up the pathology ailing the underclass. It even explains the casual attachment to work that these women's boyfriends usually have: they need work only fitfully to supplement the women's welfare payments. Welfare provides an utterly perverse set of "incentives to fail," in Murray's somber phrase.

Murray notes that other incentives changed at the same time and in the same direction. Crime was met so much less often with punishment that its benefits generally came to outweigh its cost to the criminal. Discipline and educational standards collapsed catastrophically in the public schools, subverting incentives to work hard and sanctions against disruptive behavior. Increasingly, mainstream society withdrew "status rewards" from hardworking poor people who resisted the "incentives to fail." Mainstream society did this by erasing the distinction between the respectable poor and the irresponsible, disorderly, dependent poor. Once society began to see the poor who didn't work and who neglected their families as "victims" of "the system" rather than as personally responsible for their fate and actions, then how could these poor be seen as morally inferior to the industrious poor? These simultaneous changes in the incentive structure of American society reinforced each other powerfully, Murray says, and they fostered the social pathology out of which, mushroomlike, the underclass sprang.

Following a direction set by the path-breaking sociologist of crime James Q. Wilson, Murray focuses quite narrowly on social policy and the power its incentives and disincentives have to shape the behavior of individuals. Whereas the deeper social influences on human action, the "root causes," are resistant to change, Wilson had argued, specific policies can be altered readily, and so they provide a real handle for regulating behavior. In this policy-making spirit, Murray couches his argument in the language of economic calculation, of an individual's rational balancing of costs and benefits within the altered structure of incentives and disincentives that any policy change produces. With extraordinary wisdom and originality, however, Murray demonstrates how the powerful effects policymakers achieve are often dismayingly different from those they intended. Modifying human behavior, it turns out, is a highly inexact science, given the perversely protean elasticity of people in chasing after their own goals.

Though Murray is the profoundest of all commentators on the underclass, his economic language finally pulls him up short. His discussion of "status rewards" reveals most clearly the limitations his language imposes upon him. The very term "status rewards" transforms the deepest issues of how we judge and value each other, of what we take to be the sources of dignity and of meaning in human life, into the jargon of social science, and thereby blunts and trivializes them. *Losing Ground,* a reader feels, wants to break through into the large realm of values, and Murray's subsequent work has tried to do so. But *Losing Ground* is held back by language that can only calculate the value of this or that incentive weighed against this or that disincentive, a paltrier matter altogether.

In the end, the world Murray paints, with its heartlessly mechanical interplay of incentives, seems aridly devoid of values. Its inhabitants seem mere passive responders to external incentives, not free moral agents with lives and fates that have moral significance. In this value-free universe, what else can you expect these women to do? Wouldn't any choice other than this rational one be incorrect?

So when Murray asks why, given the welfare system, an unmarried underclass girl should regret getting pregnant, or why she should marry the child's father and so lose the financial autonomy welfare gives her, one wants to cry out, "Because it is right!" What used to prevent such behavior were deeply rooted community standards and values, in terms of which people who made such choices met with condemnation not just from others but also from themselves. Before an individual could dream of engaging in such calculations as Murray imagines, a momentous sea change in values must first have occurred. Before one can focus so exclusively on the question of what the reward or penalty of this act will be, one must no longer be interested in, or troubled by, the larger question of what kind of person will I be—who will I become—if I do this.

Behavior is influenced not just by considerations of outside sanctions or rewards like jail or money, but also by what others do and think, by what is customary and accepted in terms of the culture of the community. The rational-calculation school gives short shrift to such forces, or to the vast power of conscience, in which the values of our culture are internalized and made a part of ourselves. The truth is that when underclass women decide to have illegitimate children, they don't sit down and do a cost-benefit analysis of the welfare package. What they say to themselves is what one typical young welfare mother told *The Washington Post:* "Everybody else I knew was having babies, so I just went along."

Nothing tells these young women that getting pregnant without being married and having illegitimate babies they can't support and aren't equipped to nurture well is wrong. The culture they live in, both the larger culture and the culture of the underclass, tells them that a life on welfare is perfectly acceptable and, arguably, just as good as any other kind of life. Under those circumstances, who can wonder that no inner voice condemns them for choosing such a fate? With such an outlook on the world and on themselves, it's a short step to embracing welfare.

The puzzling—and crucial—question is how they got that outlook in the first place, not where it led them once they had it. After all, by the start of the sixties, reports were already beginning to circulate of families that had been on welfare for two and sometimes even three generations, indicating that such dependency was economically feasible even before the War on Poverty made its dramatic changes in the economics of AFDC. Those reports are only anecdotal evidence, but they do suggest that the key ingredient necessary to ignite the ensuing explosion in welfare dependency was not so much the enrichment of welfare's economic lure—a lure that already existed—as it was the cultural changes that made swallowing the lure acceptable.

In fact, the policy changes that sweetened the welfare package or lessened the criminal's odds of being punished were themselves emanations of the vast cultural change the sixties accomplished. The policy changes couldn't have occurred if the cultural changes hadn't happened first. Made and applied with moral fervor by people whom a new set of cultural values had deeply persuaded of their rightness, as Murray himself notes in *Losing Ground,* these new policies emphatically conveyed to those whose lives they affected the cultural values that gave rise to the policies. And though James Q. Wilson may be right in general that policies are easier to change than root causes, that's hardly the case with policies forged, as antipoverty policy was forged, with crusading, almost religious zeal and venerated as testaments to the moral excellence of the culture.

The idea that moral choices are made primarily by economic rationality is itself an expression of the cultural unraveling that this book is talking about. That notion is a distant cousin of the idea that only the economic realm is real, while the cultural realm floats insubstantially above it, passively reflecting it. Both these ideas embody a mechanistic materialism that allows no room for the human spirit and the realm of value and meaning it creates.

Unquestionably valuable in its proper sphere, cost-benefit thinking nevertheless often turns a blind eye to that realm, sometimes producing absurd distortions. For example, such thinking led the nineteenth-century utilitarian philosopher Jeremy Bentham to the conclusion that the child's game of pushpin, since it produced an equivalent quantity of pleasure, was as valuable as poetry. Some of *Losing Ground*'s critics, who take this sort of economic calculation much further than Murray himself, end up at conclusions as absurd as Bentham's. If changes in the level of welfare benefits really did figure large in the creation of the underclass, they say, why don't the differences in welfare enrollment among states exactly mirror the variations in benefits? Why don't enrollments change precisely in line with changes in the real value of benefits, adjusted for inflation? Since they don't, these critics sum up with a flourish, *Losing Ground* is all wrong.

It's hard to imagine a more mechanical, even robotic, conception of human nature than these rigidly statistical critics seem to hold. For in truth, though I have highlighted the flaws of *Losing Ground* to show how Murray's focus on policy leads him, mistakenly, into giving primacy to economic rationality, his superb book surely is resoundingly right in its fundamental insight that raising welfare benefits above the purchasing power of the lowest-level job powerfully furthered the growth of the underclass.

The other major explanation for the underclass phenomenon, which University of Chicago sociologist William Julius Wilson expounds in his influential work, *The Truly Disadvantaged,* is a more problematic matter, less compelling than Murray's argument. Journalists love to cite Wilson, so much so that his argument routinely appears in the national newsweeklies and newspapers as the universally accepted explanation of the origin of the underclass. Part of his argument, at least: for to Wilson's annoyance, reporters are prone to getting him wrong or giving only a partial account of his thought. That may happen as regularly as it does, I suspect, because journalists are instinctively trying to separate the kernels of real insight in Wilson's work from the chaff in which they are embedded. His prose may account for the problem too; by contrast with the elegant precision of Murray's writing, Wilson's style is academically flatfooted, clotted with statistics, endlessly repetitious in assertion rather than finely spun and coherently persuasive in argument.

Wilson is a principal exponent of the view that economic change caused the formation of what he calls the "ghetto underclass." Combed free of its knots and tangles, his basic argument looks like this. In the seventies and eighties, a structural shift occurred in the economies of the old northern cities, where blacks were concentrated. Well-paid factory jobs that required few skills sharply declined, to be replaced by jobs in the service industries, such as the financial services business or the health care business. Because these jobs required higher educational attainment, they left low-skill blacks out in the cold.

At the same time, racism waned, partially but nonetheless significantly. Opportunity in education, employment, and housing opened to blacks. The black middle class vigorously expanded, and middle- and solid working-class blacks streamed into suburbs and formerly all-white urban neighborhoods. Left behind in the old, central-city ghettos after the industrious and the upwardly mobile had fled was a residue of the unskilled—the truly disadvantaged—who faced the stark reality of a transformed, "deindustrialized" urban economy offering no employment for which they were qualified. So they didn't work.

Moreover, those who had left the ghettos were the stable people who formerly breathed vitality into the institutions—churches, schools, community centers—that knit a collection of separate individuals into a community. As those institutions languished, they lost their power to enforce standards of conduct. In addition, the citizens who left took with them their personal moral authority: these were the kind of people who uphold community norms by a sharp word or censorious look at the unruly young when necessary. They were the people who exemplified the connection between prosperity and education, marriage, and work. Plugged into the world of work, they also used to help young people find jobs. Now these young people have no connection to the informal networks through which people get wind of job openings and get recommended for them.

Without economic opportunity, driven by a desperate economic rationale to the only choices that existed for them, inner-city dwellers understandably turned to welfare dependency, crime, and the familiar brew of underclass disorder. As already mentioned, Wilson attributes illegitimacy to the chronic joblessness that allegedly made inner-city men economically "unmarriageable"; inner-city women accordingly didn't marry them. The pathological behavior economic disadvantage bred was intensified by the "social isolation," as Wilson calls it, that resulted from the rapid decampment of the stable and stabilizing members of ghetto communities. It was intensified further by the "concentration effects" inevitable when so much disadvantage and pathology is squeezed together and left to fester on its own, like mold and mildew in the dark, beyond the bounds of the normal community.

The result is a quite distinctive underclass culture. But it would be incorrect to call it a "culture of poverty," says Wilson, because that would imply that culture has an autonomous power to shape lives and determine circumstances. It has no such power, Wilson vigorously asserts. On the contrary, "Cultural values emerge from specific circumstances and life chances and reflect an individual's position in the class structure," he writes in *The Truly Disadvantaged*. "They therefore do not ultimately determine behavior. If ghetto underclass minorities have limited aspirations, a hedonistic orientation toward life, or lack of plans for the future, such outlooks ultimately are the result of restricted opportunities and feelings of resignation originating from bitter personal experiences and a bleak future."

Therefore, even though the pathology may *appear* to come out of the cultural realm, one can't try to cure it by looking to that realm. Rather, one must ameliorate the economic circumstances that produce the pathology, and in response the values will regain their health, albeit with a lag in time. And so Wilson puts forth a vast program of centralized economic planning aimed at energizing the economies of the central cities—a program that, at a time when even Russia and Eastern Europe have confessed the bankruptcy of central planning and command economies, looks as quaintly antique as the Copernican cosmology.

Though in the end Wilson's argument is deeply mistaken, it contains much of real value. To begin with, he exhaustively documents that there *is* an underclass, that it is defined by its pathological behavior, that most of its members are black. At a time when so many blacks and liberals deny even the existence of a definable underclass, it makes a difference that Wilson, a widely respected black who describes his politics as social democratic, authoritatively upholds the opposite view. It matters, too, that Wilson roundly confutes the idea that racism caused the underclass. How can discrimination be a cause, he asks, when the underclass arose *after* racism had abated enough to permit a surge of blacks into the middle class? Indeed, the recent opening of the American economy and society to blacks in a sense created the underclass by allowing so many to escape from the ghetto, leaving behind the least skilled to congeal into the underclass. And Wilson is right to observe that underclass behavior comes out of the realm of culture, even though he surely is wrong in seeing culture as no more than the passive reflection of economic circumstances. He is right, too, in seeing that the concentration and homogeneity of underclass communities only intensify the cultural disturbance.

But he is wrong in ascribing the underclass phenomenon to lack of economic opportunity. I won't rehash the arguments already set forth against the economic explanation for the birth of the underclass—that plenty of low-skill jobs exist, that despite the low wages immigrants are finding those jobs an adequate first step up the ladder, that no economic reason can explain why generation after generation of the underclass fails to get the skills needed to take the higher-skill jobs that are plentiful. (Generations are short when mothers can be fifteen and grandmothers thirty-two.) The point, I hope, is amply made; and if it is true that economic opportunity does exist, then Wilson's fundamental argument crumbles.

So does some of his logic. For example, following his argument that cultural values merely reflect economic reality but do not create it, you would expect to see a hunger for education and a blossoming of ambitious self-discipline among the young in underclass neighborhoods, "reflecting" the same plentiful availability of higher-skill jobs that has permitted so many of the motivated to escape the ghetto. And putting aside the debatable question of whether unemployment makes underclass men unmarriageable, how can unemployment explain the epidemic of illegitimacy that is at the core of underclass pathology? Even if unemployment makes people unable to marry, in an age of ubiquitous birth control it surely doesn't force them to have children.

It seems an additional inconsistency that Wilson should propose his vast program of central economic planning to bring the economic reality into line with the culture of the ghetto, rather than wait for ghetto culture to adjust to the economic opportunities that exist, as his theory contends it will. Such a program, almost certainly, would succeed in radically slowing the engine of economic expansion and job creation that helped propel the exodus from the ghetto into the middle class. For if one incontestable lesson is to be learned from the experience of the eighties from Peru to Poland to the Soviet Union, it is that free, flexible economies work vastly better in every respect than centrally planned ones.

At the bottom of Wilson's theory is the erroneous assumption that people are basically passive. To take the largest example, his idea that culture merely reflects economic circumstances is a passive conception of man's relation to the material world. And as I've said, it isn't true only that circumstances make people; people in turn rework and transform the circumstances that are given to them. Within Wilson's conception of economic opportunity is a similarly troubling streak of passivity. For Wilson, opportunity is something that the ghetto population passively awaits, utterly dependent on outside circumstances either to present or withhold it. But in the same way that the real roots of wealth are less in material resources than in people—in their skill and imaginativeness and daring in deploying those resources—opportunity too can be found, or created, in the most apparently barren circumstances.

That is the lesson of Korean economic success in ghetto neighborhoods. No opportunity? Then why do Korean greengrocers flourish in Harlem and Bedford-Stuyvesant, where no such business has flourished for years? Why do newly opened Korean-owned liquor stores prosper in the Los Angeles ghettos? It doesn't take arcane skills to run a vegetable stand, only hard work, long hours, determination, rudimentary entrepreneurialism, and family cooperation. These are skills that you learn from home and community; they are skills that are nothing but the reflection of cultural values.

What limits economic opportunity for the underclass above all is the lack of such skills—skills like being able to show up on time dependably, to be conscientious and have manners, to treat customers well enough so they'll come back, to stick to something unpleasant and arduous, to attend to details. So when William Julius Wilson says that a lack of skills debars the underclass from economic opportunity, he is inadvertently describing—despite his protestations to the contrary—a cultural, not an economic, problem. You couldn't make the lesson more luminously clear if you inscribed it in big letters upon every Korean vegetable stand: in today's America, cultural values make economic opportunities.

Film director Spike Lee ruminates upon that lesson in *Do the Right Thing,* in which a Korean greengrocery in the heart of an underclass neighborhood is a sphinxlike mystery, the subject of endless puzzlement and speculation. Maybe the greengrocers succeed because the Reverend Sun Myung Moon secretly bankrolls them, one nonworking ghetto dweller theorizes, voicing a view widely held in such neighborhoods. The grain of truth behind this zany hypothesis is that Korean greengrocers do have a mechanism—a rotating credit association called the *gae*—for raising capital without collateral from friends or relatives. The twenty or thirty members of such a club each contribute three hundred or five hundred dollars or more to a monthly pot, and every month the total pot is loaned to a different member, beginning with the neediest. So that makes enough to pay a landlord his rent and to buy and stock the shelves and refrigerated cases.

But capital isn't what makes the difference—and in fact enterprising black or Hispanic ghetto dwellers aren't barred from access to capital, since they are eligible for start-up loans from an array of state-run programs or from the Small Business Administration's direct loan and loan guarantee programs. Culture, not capital, is the key ingredient in Korean business success in the ghettos. Indeed the *gae* itself, a traditional way of organizing people for mutual self-help, is nothing but a manifestation of culture. The same can be said of the sense of cooperation, loyalty, and obligation that makes such an institution of mutual trust viable. It can be said yet again of the tradition of close-knit families whose members willingly defer gratification, toil at menial jobs, and save fervidly to raise the monthly payments required for membership in a *gae.* No external bar prevents members of the underclass from doing the same thing. The economic opportunity that Koreans have taken in the ghetto was there for anyone to take, as Spike Lee's movie ruefully concludes.

But by no means all blacks who have commented publicly on this subject have agreed with Lee. Resentment of Asian economic success in underclass neighborhoods runs high, as evidenced by the widespread destruction of Korean-owned businesses in the 1992 Los Angeles riots and by ugly boycotts and threats of boycott across the nation. The public statement of a black local legislator representing Washington's Anacostia ghetto typifies the tone: "The day of the Asian community occupying or getting the majority of business in a [black] neighborhood is over. . . . We are not going to burn down our community. . . . We are going to use our clout in city hall."

The anger is understandable as well as deplorable: Asian business success in urban ghettos tears away the myth that the underclass is imprisoned in its penurious, pathological idleness by an utter absence of economic opportunity. Asian entrepreneurs have uncovered robust economic opportunity and decent livings right in the blighted and supposedly barren heart of the ghettos. Instead of allowing the underclass the solace of seeing themselves as victims, their fate not their own responsibility but forced upon them, Asian success contains an implicit reproach: *What's the matter with the underclass that they couldn't do what immigrant Asians, starting at the bottom and scarcely able to speak English, have so swiftly accomplished?* The answer is to be found in underclass culture—not, as William Julius Wilson and many others claim with increasing hollowness, in the economy.

However striking Wilson's concepts of "social isolation" and "concentration effects," the experience of Washington, D.C., suggests that neither of these forces, much less a lack of economic opportunity, is essential for the formation of the underclass. As described by sociologist James Q. Wilson, Washington's underclass emerged in the absence of virtually every condition that William Julius Wilson (no relation) deems necessary. When you look at what happened in Washington, the conclusion seems hard to avoid that forces other than those *The Truly Disadvantaged* posits are responsible for bringing the underclass into existence.

Throughout the 1960s, Washington's large black population showed strong progress by many statistical measures. Its educational level rose; its family income soared. In the high-unemployment year of 1970, the unemployment rate for Washington blacks was relatively low. Far from being a vast slum, a compressed mass of the skill-less and jobless, black Washington remained a vital middle- or lower-middle-class community. Yet within this intact community, rich in re-spectable role models and thriving institutions, an epidemic of drugs, crime, and welfare dependency broke out, raging through the sixties and on into the seventies.

A major reason for this explosion lies in the demographics, James Q. Wilson suggests. The growing up of the postwar baby boom chil-dren meant that Washington's sixteen- to twenty-one-year-old popu-lation increased by almost a third during the sixties. You can trace this singular generation's progress through the decade by the flood-marks of self-destructive behavior it left on a succession of institu-tions. In 1962, dropouts from junior high schools began to increase. In 1968, the rise in the number of senior high school dropouts reached its peak. By 1970, the unemployment rate for blacks aged sixteen to twenty-one hit 16 percent for men and 20 percent for women, while for blacks aged twenty to fifty-nine it remained a modest 4.5 percent for men and 3.6 percent for women. During the sixties, heroin addic-tion soared among the young; of the six thousand men who'd been born in Washington in 1953, addiction claimed over 13 percent. The number of women on AFDC tripled during the decade, with so many baby boomers added to the rolls that the average age of welfare moth-ers fell from thirty to twenty-three. Crime increased, with a signifi-cant but unmeasurable quantum contributed by baby boom thugs.

The young have always gotten into a disproportionate share of trouble—and with more young, more trouble was bound to ensue. But as the baby boom went through its troublemaking years, it went wrong at a startlingly higher rate than the young usually do. The rise in welfare dependency in Washington was 600 percent greater than experts would have predicted from the change in the population's age profile, for example; the rise in crime, over 1200 percent greater.

Clearly the baby boom generation made so decisive an impact not just because it was so large, but more especially because it was so dif-ferent. A huge cohort grew up formed by a new culture—a new set of values, beliefs, and institutions—that was only just cooling and solid-ifying as the baby boom was coming to consciousness. That culture came out of the larger American community, not out of the inner city; and, as it got its distinctive twist in ghetto neighborhoods, it disposed many inner-city baby boomers to grow up underclass. The problem wasn't that the underclass was isolated from mainstream culture, but rather that it was all too powerfully influenced by it.

As the underclass version of the new culture took shape in response to the inexorable pressure of cultural forces operating in the society as a whole, it acquired an immeasurable power for ill. So potent did it grow that, far from being formed by economic circumstances, it instead often rode roughshod over them as it asserted its sway. The fact that culture, regardless of economics, is the true crucible of underclass identity is one of the key lessons of the Central Park "wilding" of 1989.

Look back for a moment on that chilling event. On the night of April 19, about a dozen and a half Harlem teenage boys, black and Hispanic, went into the northern end of Central Park, looking for trouble. Their term for this evidently familiar activity was "wilding"—pronounced, as the papers reported with punctilious respect for the niceties of underclass slang, "wil'ing." They unsuccessfully tried to mug a couple of cyclists, yelling, "Fucking white people." They beat up a drunk and attacked several male joggers, knocking one unconscious with a length of pipe and sending him to the hospital with a concussion. Then one teenager reportedly cried, "Let's get a woman jogger."

Around nine-thirty, a slim, twenty-eight-year-old woman who worked as an investment banker at Salomon Bros. had the misfortune of jogging across their path. They chased her and knocked her down, kicking and punching her as she tried to fight them off. They smashed her head and face with the pipe and a brick. They pulled off her jogging tights, and several boys held her down. Laughing, between two and four of the others took turns raping her. One sodomized her. One of the boys may have used a knife to make the deep gashes later found in her thighs.

The assailants left her for dead, bleeding and unconscious at the bottom of a muddy ravine, where she was found at one-thirty in the morning, with three quarters of her blood drained out of her and her body temperature sunk to 80 degrees. Though at first she was expected not to live, and then to live but remain badly brain-damaged, she made an extraordinary recovery and seven months after the assault returned to work part-time. "It was something to do," one of her attackers reportedly said about these events. "It was fun."

A note of puzzlement blended into the public outrage over this crime when the newspapers reported that most of the alleged assailants—the "wolf pack," as journalists called them—weren't typical underclass kids. Instead of being the offspring of teenage welfare mothers, some came from intact families, most had working parents, and around half lived in a building reported to have a doorman. One attended a private school. Could they be *middle* class? the papers fretted. But then how could they have committed such a crime, an outbreak of the anarchy and racial animosity they believed was percolating in urban ghettos? Who *were* these boys?

The six youths sentenced for the "wilding" were borderline characters in many senses of the word. Four of them lived on the very margin of Harlem, right at the corner of Central Park, overlooking but utterly separate from the world of affluence that lines most of the park's perimeter. Their building was relatively new and well kept, but its doorman, universally invoked by the newspapers as a totem of middle-classness, was only a security guard, and most of its apartments, though occupied by working people, were government-subsidized. The private school student? He'd recently enrolled in a $1,100-a-year Harlem parochial school after he'd been suspended from the public school he'd previously attended for carrying weapons.

The families of the youths ranged from a hairbreadth out of the underclass, with many underclass cultural characteristics, to full-fledged working class. Toward the underclass end of the spectrum was a fourteen-year-old living with his father and grandmother. The father, though regularly employed, paid little attention to his son. Yet he was arguably a better parent than the mother, who formerly had had charge of the boy; she reportedly had found him less interesting than drugs, drink, and sex. Another family, having the superficial appearance of stability, lacked the reality of it. The mother, described by a community center director as a "strong, caring woman," had feared when her son was twelve that she would seriously hurt him; he was placed temporarily in a group home. The father and one brother have criminal records for drugs; another brother is a transvestite. The boy failed ninth grade and, with two of the other youths involved in the rape, was suspected of being part of a gang that specialized in vandalizing a nearby housing project and beating up its residents.

Two families were intact, stable, and industrious. Yet one, headed by a postal worker who imposed a nightly curfew on his children, had produced a son who, before he was charged in the attack upon the jogger, had been the suspected leader of the housing project vandals. The other family honorably embodies the very thing that William

Julius Wilson says underclass communities lack. The mother is a day-care worker, the father a parking attendant who coaches a neighborhood baseball team and is looked up to as a role model. Reportedly, their only son had started getting wild in school not long before the attack on the jogger.

Of the somber lessons in all this, the one I want to underscore is the power underclass culture has to mark even those who from an economic point of view are outside that class, albeit not far from its brink. Like a collapsing star sucking a rush of matter into its dense, dying mass, underclass culture exerts a vast gravitational force that not only sways those within it but radiates even beyond.

It wasn't the welfare system that made these six indicted youths what they turned out to be—or poverty or drugs or school-leaving. It was that they lived all their lives in an underclass community and continually drank in its values.

When they went wrong, they went wrong with a characteristic underclass ferocity and lack of restraint. Mischief for them wasn't hooky or beer drinking but, if the allegations are true, terrorizing their neighbors and vandalizing their homes. "Wilding" played a big enough part in their lives, and in their culture, to require a special name. When, doubtless following a leader gripped by a psychopathology beyond class or culture, they went crazily, catastrophically wrong, nothing in their culture pulled them up short at some intermediate atrocity instead of letting them go all the way to gang rape and—but for the timely finding of the battered jogger by unexpected passersby—murder.

Talk to any social worker or educator who deals with the poor and sooner or later you'll hear about how hard it is to "compete with the streets." This hoary cliché is a monument to the practical, gut knowledge, widespread among frontline professionals, that culture really is crucial in shaping underclass fates, that peer pressure—a key way by which culture comes to bear on individuals—carries almost all before it. Even those driven by that pressure are at least dimly conscious of what's impelling them. How else to understand the bizarre claim of one of those indicted in the attack on the jogger that he didn't really rape her but only feigned intercourse so as not to be shamed before the other thugs? Whether true or not, that claim indicates his accurate awareness of how preeminent a place the worldview of his peers holds in his imagination.

Finally, if culture rather than economics is what fundamentally makes people underclass, as I am arguing, you would expect that changes in the cultural circumstances, without any alteration in the economic ones, would successfully raise people out of that condition. Let me conclude this chapter with three dramatic examples of exactly that transformation.

The first began with a millionaire's whim. In 1981, technology entrepreneur Eugene M. Lang agreed to give the commencement speech at his old grammar school in East Harlem. Things had sure changed since he graduated in 1928, when the neighborhood was mostly Jewish and Italian. How hollow these platitudes must sound, he thought as he looked down from the podium at the bored faces eyeing him as he spoke. You need to have a dream, he exhorted. You must go to college to achieve it.

Yeah sure, these sixth graders must be thinking; fat chance. After all, in this neighborhood around three quarters of the students don't graduate from high school, and almost no one goes to college.

You *can* go, he told them; and on the spur of the moment he made them a promise that hadn't entered his mind when he first walked onstage. Finish high school, he said; get into college—and I promise I'll give you scholarships. It took a moment of stunned silence before pandemonium erupted, with bewildered mothers calling out in Spanish from the back of the auditorium: What did he say?

By June 1988 almost three quarters of the students had earned their high school diplomas; almost 90 percent had them (or the equivalent GED certificate) by June 1992. So far, almost 70 percent of the students have enrolled in post–high school education, the majority part-time. Six of the original fifty-four have earned bachelor's degrees, including B.A.'s from such elite institutions as Barnard and Swarthmore. Lang expects that ultimately around fifteen of his students will earn B.A.'s, and ten more will get community college certificates.

But note: Lang didn't spend a dime of the promised scholarship money until after he'd worked the minor miracle of getting over half his kids to graduate from high school. And by the end of the 1992 school year, Lang will have spent not much more than $200,000 keeping his promise—around $340 per kid per year, or $6.54 a week. Compared to the magnitude of the achievement, the expenditure is tiny.

For money isn't what accomplished this success. What these kids needed—what underclass kids need most—is an authoritative link to traditional values of work, study, and self-improvement, and the assurance that these values can permit them to claim full membership in the larger community. "It's important that they grow up to recognize that they are not perpetuating a life of the pariah," Lang says, "but that the resources of the community are legitimately theirs to take advantage of and contribute to and be a part of. It's a question of outlook, of self-expectations, of knowing alternatives that are available to them."

To show them what the world offered, Lang took them to restaurants, the opera, the theater. To strengthen the outlook and self-expectations part of the equation, he got involved in their lives. He made time for them to visit his midtown office, where his sober, formal manner—expressive of an old-fashioned, even antique, bourgeois ethic—conveyed its message that the work ethic pays off, even for those who started from so poor a neighborhood as he had. He hired a full-time social worker to watch over them, to help them sort out problems with school and to keep them together as a mutually supportive group, a community of shared values that endowed them all with a feeling of specialness.

The lesson took. After a men's clothing manufacturer offered to donate four suits to Lang's program as prizes to the most outstanding boys, the four winners arrived at a meeting of all the kids in the suits they had chosen. "I looked for the bright colors, the signs of youth," Lang says, "and here these four boys came in, each wearing blue or charcoal pinstripes, as though they were walking out of the training program at Morgan Stanley. I can't tell you how good I felt, because one could see what had happened *inside* these youngsters. Just that one thing alone to me was a silent justification of the program."

Programs like Lang's unfortunately can't be cloned on a grand, government-sponsored, national scale, because their success depends on intimate personal connection and intense, nonbureaucratic commitment. As Lang says: "These kids have a substitute—not an ideal substitute—for what every reasonably affluent middle-class child has. I'm to these kids the same person I was to my own children." But however particular its application, Lang's success is real; and it eloquently testifies that cultural deformation is the worst affliction underclass kids suffer. That deformation prevents them from getting what is already available for them to get. Plenty of scholarship money and lots of low-cost public institutions, after all, are already available to qualified low-income applicants.

If Lang worked his magic from outside the underclass community, the same magic gets worked from within the nation's ghettos every day. Principal Jeffrey Litt works it at the Mohegan School in a drug-ridden Bronx neighborhood, where all his students are minority, mostly from welfare-dependent, single-parent homes. In this public elementary school, Litt instituted a core curriculum based on educator E. D. Hirsch's theory that poor and marginal pupils need, even more than other kids, to be put in touch with a body of mainstream culture's common knowledge, which their family life fails to provide to them.

Accordingly, Mohegan teaches its pupils about Beethoven and Monet, *Treasure Island* and the Industrial Revolution, ancient Egypt and classical Greece. They act out what they learn: a mock trial of Long John Silver, a play about mummification, a dramatization of the life of Mozart. Litt and his teachers keep the expectations high. "Make your parents proud; make your teachers proud; make yourselves proud" is Litt's continual exhortation. When students misbehave, Litt doesn't punish them but rather tells them, "If you want to fight, you're in the wrong place: this is a place for winners." The result: four years after Litt took over, attendance is way up, no student has had to be suspended for disciplinary reasons, reading scores have risen significantly, and Mohegan students have begun winning prizes in citywide academic competitions.

Kimi Gray worked the magic on a bigger scale at the 464-unit Kenilworth-Parkside housing project in Washington. Fed up with dirt, crime, no heat, no hot water, Gray got herself elected head of the project's residents' council in 1972 as a twenty-five-year-old welfare mother with five kids. She and her council immediately organized tenants into committees, started cleanup brigades, and appointed safety officers to keep front doors locked and hall lights on. Whereas Kenilworth residents once had displayed their feelings about the police by turning over their cars, Gray and her supporters fostered cooperation and got residents and officers to view themselves as allies against criminals. After she persuaded tenants not to buy stolen goods, housebreaking plummeted, since you can only lug a hot TV so far. When drug pushers infested the neighborhood, she organized tenant marches to drive them out and told resident pushers and addicts that if they didn't quit in thirty days she'd have them evicted. "Crime is down seventy-five percent since we started," says Gray. Drug killings, formerly a more than once-a-month occurrence, have stopped entirely for the last four years.

Gray encouraged residents to take over the neighborhood PTA. As parental interest and involvement grew, the children's test scores gradually rose, and Kenilworth kids increasingly began to enroll in college. She threatened to take some residents to court for neglecting their children. Coming out of her mouth—the mouth of an impressive, Sumo-wrestler-size neighbor—ordinary standards of respectable behavior took on new force. They became the standards of one's own community, rather than alien impositions, tainted with the suspicion of racism.

From this grass roots beginning, Gray and her committee took over management of the entire project in 1982, thereby arming their efforts with the economic power of the management fee the committee received. Gray used the money to organize an employment agency to get tenants jobs outside the housing project and to start small businesses, such as a window-screen repair shop and a day-care center, which gave employment to tenants. After living on welfare, residents found themselves earning a $10,000 annual salary by working for Gray, perhaps supplemented by the $4,000 wage of their teenage child, whom Gray had encouraged to work at McDonald's. In real life, *that's* how people get out of poverty, as legions of immigrants know. One usually doesn't go straight from poverty to pinstripes.

Since 1972, welfare dependency in Kenilworth has dropped 60 percent, and some of the project's households now earn over $30,000 a year. Gray's management corporation is in the process of buying the entire project from the government, with the hope of selling individual units to tenants in the future. This amounts to a revolution in the lives of the residents, but it is a revolution that took place in the hearts of individuals and in the communal standards they set for each other. All the economic consequences flowed from that source.

At this point, my argument must seem almost self-contradictory. On one hand I hold that an infusion of mainstream, conventional respectability in outlook and actions auspiciously transforms the underclass. On the other, I argue that the culture of the Haves mightily contributed to the formation of the underclass. Am I not ascribing two diametrically opposed effects to mainstream culture?

But the paradox isn't in my argument. It is, instead, in mainstream culture, which over the last thirty years has transmitted to those at the bottom of society anything but conventional respectability.

The Feminist Perversion

If conservatives are attached to traditional structures in society (and they are), then it is only natural that contemporary feminism should find little sympathy on the right.

But the end of patriarchy isn't what worries us. Why sweat the demise of a thing that never existed? No, it's the shrill, ideological tone of feminist discourse. It's as much a question of aesthetics as it is of philosophy.

Men have been making way for women for quite some time, not always without resentment. But it's unique to our time to hear that women have been, indeed still are, oppressed. Miss Iannone here takes up the case of one such victim: Anita Hill.

IT'S PRETTY EMBARRASSING TO HAVE TO ADMIT now that I was first seriously drawn to feminism by its messianic dimension. I was never a hands-on, political, activist feminist and I've never owned a pair of red stockings. But I was first introduced to feminism in graduate school in the mid-Seventies as it was making its long march through the institutions. Soon I was teaching it in the context of women in literature classes and shaping my intellectual life by its tenets. I enjoyed, reveled in the utterly systematic property feminism takes on when used as a tool of analysis, especially when to the exclusion of all others. Like Marxism, feminism can explain everything from advertising to religion by following its single thread, the oppression of women. How comprehensible everything became! All injustice and evil were caused by patriarchy; dismantle patriarchy and we would have the brave new world of feminism: humane, generous, peaceful, good. Women had been defined by men; let women define themselves and then we'll change the world.

When I defected from the feminist philosophy some years later, it was largely out of simple, gut-level, personal disillusionment. As time went by, however, I began to see more clearly the extent of the damage feminism has done to women and to our culture. I would like to focus first on the damage feminism as a way of thinking has done to women, and then move more directly into consideration of its effect on the culture, although each category contains implications for the other.

First of all, feminism is a series of self-indulgent contradictions and anyone following it for a while is going to find her thought coarsened. Women are the same as men, women are different from men, according to the ideological need. Women are strong and capable. And yet have been the slaves and victims of men throughout history. Women are angry, rebellious, even murderous in patriarchy, but also superior to men because loving and tender. Women are the humane and nurturing sex, but can put their children in child care centers for ten hours a day. Feminism sponsors choices for women, unless the choice is the domestic role. Feminism is for the social good, even though it openly advocates dismantling the entire social order. Feminism is a legitimate academic and intellectual approach, but it cannot be judged by ordinary academic and intellectual standards. Women writers have been wrongfully excluded from the mainstream tradition, but they have also been wrongfully seen outside their separate "female tradition."

Second, feminism encourages women to look at their experience only within narrow feminist terms. Consciousness raising inflames the discontent that is bound to be in every woman's life and then in the ensuing disarray invites her to see it as the result of oppression—of being seen as a sex object—or whatever, and to look to alleviate it in political terms. To the extent that the personal becomes political, the woman loses contact with herself. She is constrained from seeing how many "feminine" problems are more moral and characterological than social or political, and that, regardless of origin, can only be overcome by the individual—vanity, self-centeredness, the tendency to want to idealize men, even the tendency to surrender to emotional weakness.

Then there is the hidden destructiveness and the various female poses and postures of helplessness and dependency which women have always been loath to acknowledge, and which feminism has helped them avoid acknowledging too. When Susan Brownmiller argues that "while the extremes of masculinity can harm others (rape, wife-beating, street-crime, warfare . . .) the extremes of femininity are harmful only to women themselves in the form of self-imposed masochism," she is revealing a terrible ignorance about the ways of human nature. How apt seems the Saturday Night Live parody of the Phil Donahue Show in which a woman sociologist comes on to discuss her new book titled *Women: Good; Men: Bad.*

The preliminary result of the politicization of the internal life may seem liberating but the end result is enslavement, since it diminishes the individual's sense of control over her own destiny and weakens her self-discipline by encouraging her to blame others. Much New Left thought began with the demand for greater individual freedom, but the subsequent fear of the real demands of freedom led to a rush into collective, pre-fabricated identities, with feelings, thoughts, and ideas dictated by ideology. Thus feminism has enabled women to behave childishly, demanding equality and independence, but also preferential treatment and special protection as a group.

Third, feminism has made many things worse by preventing women from seeing their experience clearly, as in the unspeakably dishonest comparison of women with blacks, or in the pretense that female biological needs are the result of male indoctrination. Feminism refuses to see how much of a hand women have had in creating the despised system, and how much it has served not only men's but women's needs as well. Feminism also joins the rest of the New Left in disdain for the Western tradition for its purported oppression of women, although it is only on the basis of this tradition that a campaign for greater freedom for women could ever have been mounted. With all its faulty but rigidly held convictions about certain matters, however, feminism is utterly and foolishly amoral about a whole host of issues, unable, for example, to decide if prostitution is exploitation of women, or a praiseworthy example of women controlling their own sexuality in patriarchy. Similar debates go on over pornography, surrogate motherhood, etc.

After its original insistence that women are the same as men, much feminist thought now derives from differences. In literature, for example, feminists have managed to make headway by insisting that the canon of great works was founded by white males and that therefore they can discard the standards upon which this canon is based and single out works for study based on female standards which thus far have eluded clear articulation. Academic feminism is even able to influence some of the work being produced by women writers today and it is not uncommon for a poet or a novelist to appear at conferences and on panels, reading some creative adaptation of the feminist vision. For example, I recently heard a poem extolling the decision of Lot's wife to disobey God's directives and to turn and look at the city of Sodom while it was being destroyed because as a woman, she felt the pull of communal identity. Recently, too, I heard a prominent feminist scholar denounce Eudora Welty's memoir, *One Writer's Beginnings,* for presenting too sunny a version of its author's life. Welty does a disservice to women, the feminist critic insisted, by hiding her anger at patriarchy. Again, I can't resist pointing out the contradiction between the two versions of women's experiences—they have special, loving, communal female values, they are full of anger at patriarchy. If one argues that patriarchy creates their anger, might it not also be argued that patriarchy creates their nurturing and communal female values?

A recent study by feminist psychologist Carol Gilligan of Harvard which posits separate male and female moral sensibilities has aroused a lot of positive commentary, some even from conservative critics, who are happy to see differences asserted. Gilligan argues that women tend to see moral choices more in terms of responsibilities and men more in terms of rights: women tend to be concerned with who else will be affected by their choices, not only with the absolute rights and wrongs of the case. Gilligan does argue for an eventual integration of both types of morality, but, as more than one commentator has noted, the emphasis in her works falls on difference and she implicitly glorifies the more relational, caring, selfless qualities of the female over what comes to look like the emotional deficiencies of the male.

Such thinking, when codified into an intellectual approach, can serve to encourage self-flattery and self-righteousness among women, in the retrograde manner of a 19th century American female sentimental writer documented by Ann Douglas in *The Feminization of American Culture.* These writers created and peddled a false, fulsome, meretricious view of redemptive womanhood that was a caricature and that cheapened the terms of cultural life. To the extent to which such formulations have been adopted by feminism in our time—and it is to a considerable extent—intellectual life has suffered, with reality split into artificial dichotomies.

Recently, I sat in on a Columbia graduate fellowship seminar and heard a young woman state that women's poetry must be taught to offset the "male values" advanced in poetry by men. Homer, for example, sponsors martial values which must be balanced by the more nurturing values of female writers. This dichotomization leads to a terrible flattening on both sides, but one in which female writers especially are seen to be mainly talking from, and about, the gender or gender-related experiences which supposedly give rise to their female experiences such as menstruation, child-bearing, sex, motherhood, courtship, etc.

All of this emphasis on spurious differences—so there is a refusal of genuine difference and an elevation of spurious difference—brings me to my last point, which is how feminism has hurt women: it has denied to them any possibility of transcendence or universality. The modern thinking female lives and moves and breathes in a world more gender inflected, to use the current jargon, than that of the most benighted and reactionary Fifties housewife. Academic feminism has created separate disciplines through women's studies—we have women's language, literature, forms, traditions, history, philosophy, theology, science, morality and art. The only activity that miraculously is allowed to be neuter is child-rearing.

In popular culture too, in movies, television shows, magazines, fiction, it seems that if a woman is asked to take any view at all on the meaning of her existence, it is on the basis of her problematic position as a female in patriarchal culture. One almost begins to feel that the reason some women worked feverishly to get into men's clubs is to have a respite from the womanized world feminists have created. A generation of women has sacrificed real intellectual growth to this parochialism, until it is actually incapable, it seems, of understanding that ancient Greek philosophy, for example, is not a white male view of the world.

The extent of the feminist depredation on the intellectual life of women was graphically illuminated for me some time ago when I heard Allan Bloom participate in a panel discussion. In the general

course of an attack on Bloom, a woman professor defended the relativism of the universities, insisting that different modes of thought
had a right to be heard, since there are no absolutes. Later in her remarks, she said she hoped her own students would come to renounce
racism and sexism in their own lives. Professor Bloom set aside a lot
of other questions she had posed and probed this weak spot. "Do you
consider sexism an evil," he asked. She said she did. "Then," he said,
"you cannot be a relativist, since you believe that there is something
which is absolutely evil. Unless, of course, you consider sexism being
evil only your opinion, and consider another view—that sexism is not
evil—just as good an opinion. You see, you can't have it both ways."
The woman professor was completely at a loss. Having shot this ar-
row, Bloom went in for the kill: "When you have spoken in contradictions like that you have said *nothing*," he declared. At that moment, a
distinctly uneasy panel moderator stopped Bloom by insisting that it
was time to move on to the next speaker. Later the room was filled
with bristling women denouncing Bloom for his sexist treatment of
the woman professor. And, it seems, there were a number of men who
agreed with them.

This leads more directly into consideration of my second major
category, the damage feminism has done to our culture. The Anita
Hill–Clarence Thomas episode is the most graphic illustration of this
phenomenon, proof positive that ideas have consequences, and that
the half-baked, unsifted, unweighed, unsubstantiated theories of academic and literary feminism have actually taken hold in the real
world. Feminist Naomi Wolf, among the heirs apparent to the mantle
of Gloria Steinem, asserts proudly that on the day that the Hill-
Thomas hearings opened, "the meaning of being a woman was
changed forever." Indeed, it can well be said that it was—changed,
that is, from women's being generally expected within broad and perhaps disputed limits to behave like moral beings to an official exemption from any obligation to do so.

To begin with, the sexual harassment charges against Thomas were
brought at the eleventh hour when the proceedings over his nomination to the Supreme Court were almost over, and, moreover, they
were brought by a person who wished her identity kept secret. The
Senate Judiciary Committee investigated the matter as far as possible
within these restrictions and quite rightly concluded that it could not
properly be pursued further, especially if the confidentiality of the

plaintiff was to be preserved. But when the female members of the House got wind of this decision, through leaks from the Senate itself, they stormed the steps of the Senate building in protest, and are now memorialized in an ignominious photograph that gives modern witness to the idea behind mythological creations like the Bacchae and the maenads. In addition, Capitol Hill switchboards were flooded with calls from outraged women who could hardly have been in possession of all the facts, but who nevertheless also demanded, like the congresswomen, a public airing of the charges.

Suddenly, all normal modes of procedure had to be suspended, and the Committee members had to prove that they "got it," i.e., that they understood "female rage" enough to forgo all deliberation. It was like watching the *Oresteia* in reverse (with the exception that the Furies at least knew for a certainty that Orestes had committed a crime). Centuries of jurisprudence evaporated in a few moments—the ideas behind due process, statutes of limitations, rules of evidence, presumption of innocence. All the civil liberties liberals have always insisted upon in the most outrageous criminal cases dissolved completely in face of the possibility that a single woman might have been subjected to unwanted sexual banter years before.

The excuse given for the suspension of due process and the public smearing of a nominee with unproved and finally unprovable ten-year-old charges of verbal transgression was that the standards for a Supreme Court Justice must be higher than those for the common man. That may well be, but it does not follow therefrom that there exists any way beyond due process to uncover misconduct without committing greater wrong, something that certainly happened in this case. Thomas underwent a Kafkaesque humiliation before the entire world—a punishment that would not have fit the crime even if he were guilty, and he was made to endure it without even the establishment of guilt. It was the first pure show trial in American history, and it came courtesy of feminism.

At the time of the alleged harassment, Anita Hill had been unable to make clear to Thomas that his remarks bothered her. In fact, she followed him from job to job, "harassment" notwithstanding. Even after she left his employ, she kept in telephone contact with him, congratulated him on his marriage, was seen conversing with him in a friendly manner, and on one occasion offered to drive him to the airport after he spoke at her former law school. In all this time, even when she was long out of his sphere of influence, she never indicated to him that she was upset over his alleged ill-treatment of her years before. Then, at the height of his public exposure, she was coaxed out of the dark to destroy him, revealing herself only when it was no longer avoidable. For all this she is made a feminist heroine, and indeed, it may well be said that she is, a perfectly fitting heroine for the moral inversion that is the feminist universe.

Hill's inability to make Thomas see that she was offended by his alleged remarks was not to be taken as regrettable weakness and passivity, but rather, according to the feminist spin, as typical of the long-suffering harassment victim, choked with powerlessness and shame. Furthermore, her tolerance of the alleged offenses out of supposed (but, as it turned out, entirely unfounded) fear for her career was not to be seen as a rather sorry willingness to go along with tawdry treatment for the sake of advancement or security, but justified behavior for women finally making their way up the ladders of the working world. Likewise, keeping in touch with him after she no longer worked for him was also understandable, inasmuch as he was in a position to help her.

And can we even begin to touch upon the question of one's moral obligation to inform a fellow human being when he is being obnoxious or hurtful? Jesus says to tell a man his fault, and to make it more widely known only after he has turned a deaf ear. Are we not our brother's keeper, at least to some extent? No. Our brothers, i.e., men, are the enemy, the oppressors, the victimizers, and women are their victims. If there are those who imagine that this model of male-female interaction was just a rhetorical abstraction made for the sake of intellectual argument around certain points, they should now be disabused. "Hill's situation" as a victim of sexual oppression "was readily identifiable," writes feminist Christine Stansell suggestively, and perhaps somewhat ominously, "her choices entirely plausible, and her dilemmas were well known to feminist scholarship and contemporary women's writing." Clearly many women really believe the oppressor-oppressed model and apply it across the board, feeling no obligation to observe any behavioral strictures that are to them only patriarchal constructs meant to perpetuate male dominance. Thus Hill cannot be faulted, in fact is to be congratulated, for trying to destroy Thomas anonymously, when our tradition has always demanded that a man be able to face his accuser; for centuries women's voices have been stifled and silenced; she had no obligation to observe rules of fairness that women have had no part in making.

And, indeed, look what happened when she was finally forced into public view. The committee of "white males," having suspended all the rules to allow these unsubstantiated charges to ruin a man's good name before millions of people, showed that they still didn't "get it," had not really grasped the total and systematic moral inversion of feminism. Some of them actually professed to doubt Anita Hill's story, tried to poke holes in it, offered alternative scenarios, and attempted to discredit her. Indeed, a lot of Thomas's "defense" on the part of his Senate supporters was crude and outlandish, and Hill herself was subject to innuendo, but his defenders were after all faced with the impossible task of proving a negative in a case of "her word against his."

Feminists have their McCarthyesque answer to this dilemma, however: *The accusations should have been enough* to sink the nomination; Hill should have been believed without proof. It began to be clear that Thomas was guilty in the minds of many women, not by virtue of the evidence in his individual case, but *by virtue of their own experiences with men.* "Hill's story," Stansell writes, "was immediately familiar to thousands of women," hence, apparently, their willingness to believe Thomas guilty before any corroborating evidence had even been presented. It turns out that the whole affair was not just about Anita Hill and Clarence Thomas, but about the fury of thousands of women who had endured abuse of the kind she described from thousands of men. The departure in the Thomas hearings was not only from due process, then, but from the entire Western tradition of individual as opposed to collective responsibility. Thomas became, in effect, the scapegoat whose atrocious punishment arose from bottomless wells of female anger and grievance against his sex.

Perhaps vaguely conscious of how far off the chart they went, feminists and their supporters must now indulge in the dehumanization of Thomas. Left sitting in their own filth, they perhaps feel they have no choice but to continue to sling it. Ronald Dworkin writes of him, hyperbolically, as "someone who abused power and enjoyed other people's suffering." Or sometimes the tactic is simply to prohibit debate. Wendy Kaminer, herself a feminist, reveals that the Thomas-Hill episode is one of those subjects feminists simply cannot discuss freely.

"A prominent feminist journalist who expressed misgivings to me about the iconization of Anita Hill chooses not to be identified," reports Kaminer.

Hill herself has found refuge, according to *The New York Times*, "in the arcane language of the academic doctrines currently fashionable in legal and literary criticism." The *Times* reported Hill's graceless, cumbersome, and oddly detached interpretation of the hearings, which she gave at a gathering some time after the events:

> Not only did the Senate fail to understand my lack of attachment to certain institutions, like marriage and patronage, they failed to relate to my race, my gender, my race and gender combined, and, in combination with my education, my career choice and my demeanor. . . . Because I and my reality did not comport with what they accepted as their reality, I and my reality had to be reconstructed by the Senate committee members with assistance from the press and others.

But of the horror she inflicted, even if unintentionally, on Clarence Thomas, and on the country as a whole, not a word.

Have feminists and their supporters truly lost their moral compass? Perhaps not so utterly, so universally, so damnedly as it might seem. What we are witnessing may in some cases just be cynical partisan politics played in a totally unprincipled way in order to win at any cost. This would be the "good news."

For example, Carol Moseley Braun rode to her Senate seat largely on the strength of the notion that had gained currency during the Thomas-Hill hearings: More women are needed in politics to prevent the abuse Hill suffered at the hands of a committee of "white males" who supposedly ignored her confidentially registered charges and generally just "didn't get it." But when Braun was confronted with an internal report on charges of sexual harassment against her campaign treasurer (and boyfriend), she refused to take the matter any further, explaining: "The people who were interviewed were interviewed in confidence. I see no choice but to honor their desire that their comments be confidential."

And then there is the case of Florynce Kennedy. Kennedy was one of the feminist leaders who opposed Thomas from the very beginning, declaring soon after the announcement of his nomination, "We're going to bork him. We have to bork Thomas. We don't wait—

we don't wait for questions, we don't wait for the senators, and we kick ass and take names.... We're going to kill him politically. This little creep, where did he come from." And during the period of Hill's testimony, Kennedy was certainly not heard coming to Thomas's defense in any way. But her response was very different in a later case of sexual harassment.

When a black man named Randy Daniels was appointed to a position by New York's liberal Democrat Mayor David Dinkins in 1992, just about a year after the Thomas-Hill episode, he was accused by a black woman, Barbara Wood, of having sexually harassed her some years before when they worked together in the office of then City Council President Andrew Stein. Unlike Anita Hill, Barbara Wood had made her specific complaints known at the time of the events to Stein and to her uncle, Bob Teague, a television newsman. When this matter erupted, liberal feminist writer Amy Pagnozzi, then a columnist for the *New York Post,* had a most interesting interview with Florynce Kennedy.

"What kind of politics must Barbara Wood have in order to let a thing like this explode?" Kennedy fumed to Pagnozzi. "Is she going to bring down Randy Daniels and possibly even David Dinkins to protect her five-year-old besmirched virtue? Was she a virgin? The average businesswoman in this century does not make a big deal about sexual harassment. Any man can make a pass."

Pagnozzi reminds Kennedy at this point that "Wood's uncle, Bob Teague, claimed Daniels repeatedly asked Wood to perform oral sex on him, then harassed her on the job when she refused." Kennedy retorts, "So what? [Oral sex is] a very popular thing to do these days. For $15 you can have one." And she continues, "I would think that she would have more dignity, especially racially, than to complain that a black man asked her for a _____. What did she say? 'Uncle Bob, somebody asked me for a _____'?...I think her politics should come first—as a feminist and as a black person."

Anita Hill, call your office, that is, if Florynce Kennedy is saying anything you hadn't realized.

Irony aside, on the *truly* "good news" side, we know that many women supported Thomas at the hearings and some even in print. It is important to maintain the distinction between feminists and women, so to speak. The inestimable Camille Paglia argued that, "For feminists to make a heroine out of Hill is to insult all those other women who have taken a bolder, more confrontational course and forfeited career advantage." Such women are unlike Hill, who, even if she were telling the truth, "went along to get along." In his excellent, detailed study of the whole affair, *The Real Anita Hill,* David Brock reports that "Billie Wright Dziech, a professor at the University of Cincinnati and the author of *The Lecherous Professor: Sexual Harassment on Campus,* took her fellow sexual harassment experts to task for exhibiting professional irresponsibility by unequivocally embracing Hill's case as paradigmatic, despite the lack of any corroborative evidence or any pattern of harassment by the accused." (Ironically, however, the idea of Hill's as the "typical case" of sexual harassment persists.)

But "good news" notwithstanding, the Anita Hill episode has inflicted traumatic damage on our body politic. A great many Americans no doubt shared the pain Thomas felt when he said at one point in his testimony that being accused as he was "means losing the belief in our system, in this system, in this process, losing a belief in a sense of fairness and honesty and decency." It is no accident that he felt this, since feminism aims precisely to destroy our system, and to subvert all standards of fairness, honesty, and decency; and the confusions and contradictions that beset its theory have not prevented it from succeeding to a great extent. Since, according to feminism, men through history only did what they did to get and keep power, invoking ideals only to further their rule, feminists are exempt from any principles but for those that will advance their cause. Guilt mongering, hatred, hysteria, irrationality, vengeance, spite, unfairness, and intellectual perversity are all elevated to acceptable methods of procedure on the grounds of women's historic oppression (which of course has never been proved or established to the extent that it is routinely invoked). Every stereotype that men have ever held about women has turned out to be true of feminists. Naomi Wolf triumphantly declares that Hill's testimony "set in motion a train of events that led American women into becoming the political ruling class." By women, she of course means feminist women; alas, she may be right, and God save us if she is.

PART III

The Economic Order

The last word from the man himself:

> The rich only select from the heap what is most precious and agreeable.
> They consume little more than the poor, and in spite of their natural
> selfishness and rapacity . . . they divide with the poor the produce of all
> their improvements. They are led by an invisible hand to make nearly
> the same distribution of the necessaries of life which would have been
> made, had the earth been divided into equal portions among its inhabi-
> tants.
>
> —ADAM SMITH, *The Theory of Moral Sentiments* (1759)

The Last Metaphysical Right

It is often assumed that conservatives are naturally allied with capitalists; with Wall Street, big business, and multinational corporations. Not really. The modern economy is so complicated, and is so wedded to government policies that there are probably fewer and fewer laissez-faire capitalists.

When Richard Weaver's Ideas Have Consequences was published just after World War II, it seemed appropriate to worry that "when properties are vast and integrated . . . it requires but a slight step to transfer them to state control." In wartime, the line between state and private holdings becomes thin indeed. But I doubt that Microsoft is leading us closer to some new form of state socialism. My guess is the opposite is true.

But the state still wants to grow, and the one surest obstacle to its utter immenseness is private property.

BEGINNING WITH MAN'S first yielding to materialism, we have seen a train of consequences proceeding, in the same way that conclusions come from premises, to the egotism and social anarchy of the present world. The topic now changes, for the fact of one's writing signifies that he admits no necessity for these things.

At the outset of proposing any reform we must ask for two postulates, that man both can know and can will. Some may think they are too doubtful to be assumed, but without them there is no hope of recovery. In the confidence that those who have considered these questions most deeply will agree that there is a presumption in their favor, I shall proceed to outline the task of healing.

I have endeavored to make plain in every way that I regard all the evils in our now extensive catalogue as flowing from a falsified picture of the world which, for our immediate concern, results in an inability to interpret current happenings. Hysterical optimism is a sin against knowledge, and the conviction has been here expressed that nothing substantial can be done until we have brought sinners to repentance. Such phrases echo the language of a world thought past reviving, but the statement means simply that those who are in a quandary must be made to see that quandary. Complacency does not look before and after. It has been said with probable truth that the Roman Empire was in decline four hundred years before the situation was generally realized. The Whig theory of history, teaching that the most advanced point in time is the most advanced in development, is total abandonment of discrimination. Once man has regained sufficient humility to confess that ideals have been dishonored and that his condition is a reproach, one obstruction has been removed.

We must avoid, however, the temptation of trying to teach virtue directly, a dubious proceeding at any time and one under special handicaps in our age. It is necessary rather to seek out those "incalculably subtle powers" of which Ortega y Gasset speaks. This means that the beginning must not be less hardheaded and sophisticated than dozens of competing doctrines which would lure people into paths of materialism and pragmatism. Good will alone fails in the same way as does sentiment without the underpinning of metaphysic.

The first positive step must be a driving afresh of the wedge between the material and the transcendental. This is fundamental: without a dualism we should never find purchase for the pull upward, and all idealistic designs might as well be scuttled. That there is a world of ought, that the apparent does not exhaust the real—these are so essential to the very conception of improvement that it should be superfluous to mention them. The opening made by our wedge is simply a denial that whatever is, is right, which takes the form of an insistence upon the rightness of right. Upon this rock of metaphysical right we shall build our house. That the thing is not true and the act is not just unless these conform to a conceptual ideal—if we can make this plain again, utilitarianism and pragmatism will have been defeated. For such are the ultimates which determine value, significance, and even definition. Since knowledge finally depends on criteria of truth, we can even restore belief in the educative power of experience—which relativism and skepticism both deny. The prospect of living again in a world of metaphysical certitude—what relief will this not bring to those made seasick by the truth-denying doctrines of the relativists! To bring dualism back into the world and to rebuke the moral impotence fathered by empiricism is then the broad character of our objective.

Because we are now committed to a program which has practical applications, we must look for some rallying-point about which to organize. We face the fact that our side has been in retreat for four hundred years without, however, having been entirely driven from the field. One corner is yet left. When we survey the scene to find something which the rancorous leveling wind of utilitarianism has not brought down, we discover one institution, shaken somewhat, but still strong and perfectly clear in its implications. This is the right of private property, which is, in fact, the last metaphysical right remaining to us. The ordinances of religion, the prerogatives of sex and of vocation, all have been swept away by materialism, but the relationship of a man to his own has until the present largely escaped attack. The metaphysical right of religion went out at the time of the Reformation. Others have been gradually eroded by the rising rule of appetite. But the very circumstance that the middle class rose to power on property led it to consecrate property rights at the same time that it was liquidating others. Accordingly, private property was made one of the absolute rights of man by the middle-class French Revolution, and it was firmly guaranteed by all the "free" constitutions of the early nineteenth century. Its recognition by the American constitution was unequivocal. Now that the middle class itself is threatened, the concept of private property loses defenders, but it is still with us, and, though we may not be happy about its provenance, here is a tool at hand. Its survival may be an accident, yet it expresses an idea. It is the sole thing left among us to illustrate what right, independent of service or utility, means.

We say the right of private property is metaphysical because it does not depend on any test of social usefulness. Property rests upon the idea of the *hisness* of *his: proprietas, Eigentum,* the very words assert an identification of owner and owned. Now the great value of this is that the fact of something's being private property removes it from the area of contention. In the *business* of property we have dogma; there discussion ends. Relativists from the social sciences, who wish to bring everyone under secular group control, find this an annoying impediment. But is it not, in truth, quite comforting to feel that we can enjoy one right which does not have to answer the sophistries of the world or rise and fall with the tide of opinion? The right to use property as something private is, as I shall show more fully later, a sanctuary. It is a self-justifying right, which until lately was not called upon to show in the forum how its "services" warranted its continuance in a state dedicated to collective well-being.

At this point I would make abundantly clear that the last metaphysical right offers nothing in defense of that kind of property brought into being by finance capitalism. Such property is, on the contrary, a violation of the very notion of *proprietas*. This amendment of the institution to suit the uses of commerce and technology has done more to threaten property than anything else yet conceived. For the abstract property of stocks and bonds, the legal ownership of enterprises never seen, actually destroy the connection between man and his substance without which metaphysical right becomes meaningless. Property in this sense becomes a fiction useful for exploitation and makes impossible the sanctification of work. The property which we defend as an anchorage keeps its identity with the individual.

Not only is this true, but the aggregation of vast properties under anonymous ownership is a constant invitation to further state direction of our lives and fortunes. For, when properties are vast and integrated, on a scale now frequently seen, it requires but a slight step to transfer them to state control. Indeed, it is a commonplace that the trend toward monopoly is a trend toward state ownership; and, if we continued the analysis further, we should discover that business develops a bureaucracy which can be quite easily merged with that of government. Large business organizations, moreover, have seldom been backward about petitioning government for assistance, since their claim to independence rests upon desire for profit rather than upon principle or the sense of honor. Big business and the rationalization of industry thus abet the evils we seek to overcome. Ownership through stock makes the property an autonomous unit, devoted to abstract ends, and the stockholder's area of responsibility is narrowed in the same way as is that of the specialized worker. Respecters of private property are really obligated to oppose much that is done today in the name of private enterprise, for corporate organization and monopoly are the very means whereby property is casting aside its privacy.

The moral solution is the distributive ownership of small properties. These take the form of independent farms, of local businesses, of homes owned by the occupants, where individual responsibility gives significance to prerogative over property. Such ownership provides a range of volition through which one can be a complete person, and it is the abridgment of this volition for which monopoly capitalism must be condemned along with communism.

The assertion is tantamount to saying that man has a birthright of responsibility. That responsibility cannot exist when this essential right can be invaded in the name of temporary social usefulness and extraneous compulsion can be substituted. Therefore we are bound to maintain that some rights begin with the beginning and that some sort of private connection with substance is one of them. Others, too, we hope to see recognized, but our present concern is to find one ultimate protection for what is done in the name of the private person.

It is not a little disquieting to realize that in private property there survives the last domain of privacy of any kind. Every other wall has been overthrown. Here a unique privacy remains because property has not been compelled to give a justification of the kind demanded by rationalists and calculators. It must be maintained that property rests on the prerational sentiments in that we desire it not merely because it "keeps the man up"—this would reduce to utilitarianism—but because somehow it is needed to help him express his being, his true or personal being. By some mystery of imprint and assimilation man becomes identified with his things, so that a forcible separation of the two seems like a breach in nature.

But as we lay our plans for restoration, we find practical advantages in its preservation, and, while these are not to be pleaded as its ultimate justification, they are of legitimate use. To combat the swirling forces of social collapse, we must have some form of entrenchment, and especially do we need sanctuary against pagan statism. For it is evident that, as society gravitates toward a monstrous functionalism, the very basis of recovery may be destroyed before counterforces can be deployed. Almost every trend of the day points to an identification of right with the purpose of the state and that, in turn, with the utilitarian greatest material happiness for the greatest number. In states which have unreservedly embraced this ideal, we have seen the very sources of protest extirpated. A functional unit operates best when it has the machine's one degree of freedom, and governors of the modern kind will not be so restrained by sentiment as to tolerate less than the maximum efficiency. The day of respect for the "loyal opposition" has gone with the day of the gentleman class. The plain truth is that believers in value are on the point of being engulfed completely, so that they cannot find means of continuance on any condition. In the past, revolutionary movements have frequently drawn strength from elements in the very society that they proposed to overthrow. Such opportunity came through the existence of a measure of liberty. In the monolithic police state which is the invention of our age, assisted as it is by technology, surveillance becomes complete. And when we add to these political fanaticism, which seems an outgrowth of our level of development, the picture grows terrifying.

Shall we not declare that the thinking people of our day, who see the suicide in massness and who individually reprobate the crimes of parties and of states, must be spared their private areas as the early Christians were the catacombs? In seeking protection against an otherwise omnipotent state, the opposition must now fall back upon the metaphysical right of private property. Actually something of this kind is a custom of long standing in the West. We have not regarded our political leaders as playing for their heads. If they meet failure through sponsoring some unpopular measure, they return home to their bit of the world, and there they plant, or they sell their professional services, or they write for publication in a market not entirely dominated by politics. So Abraham Lincoln, after losing the voters' favor by opposing the Mexican War, returned to the practice of law.

Private right defending noble preference is what we wish to make possible by insisting that not all shall be dependents of the state. Thoreau, finding his freedom at Walden Pond, could speak boldly against government without suffering economic excommunication. Walt Whitman, having become a hireling of government in Washington, discovered that unorthodox utterance, even in poetry, led to severance from income. Even political parties, driven from power by demagoguery, can subsist and work in the hope that a return to reason will enable men of principle to make themselves felt again. Private property cannot without considerable perversion of present laws be taken from the dissenter, and here lies a barrier to *Gleichschaltung*.

Nothing is more certain than that whatever has to court public favor for its support will sooner or later be prostituted to utilitarian ends. The educational institutions of the United States afford a striking demonstration of this truth. Virtually without exception, liberal education, that is to say, education centered about ideas and ideals, has fared best in those institutions which draw their income from private sources. They have been able, despite limitations which donors have sought to lay upon them, to insist that education be not entirely a means of breadwinning. This means that they have been relatively free to promote pure knowledge and the training of the mind; they have afforded a last stand for "antisocial" studies like Latin and Greek. In state institutions, always at the mercy of elected bodies and of the public generally, and under obligation to show practical fruits for their expenditure of money, the movement toward specialism and vocationalism has been irresistible. They have never been able to say that they will do what they will with their own because their own is not private. It seems fair to say that the opposite of the private is the prostitute.

Not only does the citadel of private property make existence physically possible for the protestant; it also provides indispensable opportunity for training in virtue. Because virtue is a state of character concerned with choice, it flourishes only in the area of volition. Not until lately has this fundamental connection between private property and liberty been stressed; here in the domain of private property, rational freedom may prove the man; here he makes his virtue an active principle, breathing and exercising it, as Milton recommended. Without freedom, how is anyone to pass his probation? Consider Thoreau, or any hard-bitten New England farmer of Thoreau's day, beside the pitiful puling creature which statism promises to create. The comparison points to this: a great virtue is realizable here, but we must be willing to meet its price.

It may indeed appear before the struggle is over that the attack upon private property is but a further expression of the distrust of reason with which our age seems fatally stricken. When it is no longer believed that there is a restraining reason in accordance with which men may act, it follows that the state cannot permit individual centers of control. The repudiation of transcendentalism compels the state to believe that individual centers of control will be governed by pure egotism, as indeed they largely are at present. At the same time, this

repudiation pushes aside the concept of inviolability. The modern
state does not comprehend how anyone can be guided by something
other than itself. In its eyes pluralism is treason. Once you credit man
with the power of reason and with inviolable rights, you set bounds
beyond which the will of majorities may not go. Therefore it is highly
probable that, subconsciously or not, the current determination to diminish the area of inviolable freedom masks an attempt to treat man
as a mere biological unit. For liberty and right reason go hand in
hand, and it is impossible to impugn one without casting reflection
on the other.

These are some benefits of property in our time of crisis. But in ordinary times, too, property shows itself a benevolent institution by
encouraging certain virtues, notable among which is providence. I
tread gingerly here, observing how close I have come to a subject of
bourgeois veneration, yet I am inclined to think that there is something philosophic in the practice of providence; certainly there is in
the theory. Providence requires just that awareness of past and future
that our provincial in time, eager to limit everything to present sen-
sory experience, is seeking to destroy. It is precisely because providence takes into account the nonpresent that it calls for the exercise
of reason and imagination. That I reap now the reward of my past industry or sloth, that what I do today will be felt in that future now potential—these require a play of mind. The notion that the state
somehow bears responsibility for the indigence of the aged is not far
removed from that demoralizing supposition that the state is somehow responsible for the criminality of the criminal. I will not deny
that the dislocations of capitalism afford some ground for the former.
But that is another argument; the point here is that no society is
healthful which tells its members to take no thought of the morrow
because the state underwrites their future. The ability to cultivate
providence, which I would interpret literally as foresight, is an opportunity to develop personal worth. A conviction that those who perform the prayer of labor may store up a compensation which cannot
be appropriated by the improvident is the soundest incentive to virtuous industry. Where the opposite conviction prevails, where popular
majorities may, on a plea of present need, override these rights earned
by past effort, the tendency is for all persons to become politicians. In
other words, they come to feel that manipulation is a greater source
of reward than is production. This is the essence of corruption.

While we are looking at the moral influence of real property, let us observe, too, that it is the individual's surest protection against that form of dishonor called adulteration. If one surveys the economic history of the West for the past several centuries, he discovers not only a decline of craftsmanshp but also a related phenomenon, a steady shrinkage in the value of money. This is a fact of gravest implication, for it indicates that nations do not live up to their bargains. Their promises to pay are simply not kept. What happens is something like this: The nation gets into a difficulty, perhaps through war; then, instead of getting out by means of sacrifice and self-denial, it chooses the easier way and dishonors its obligations. Popular governments, whose disrespect for points of reference we have underscored, are especially prone to these solutions. A familiar term for the process is inflation, but, whatever it may be called, it represents the payment of pledges with depreciated media. France has afforded some of the most instructive lessons in this evil. During the course of the Great Revolution, for example, it was determined to issue paper money based on the nation's vast holding in expropriated land. Despite this guaranty, the assignats declined at a dizzy rate. In August, 1795, the record shows, a gold louis bought 36 of them; in September, 48; in November, 104; in December, 152; in February of 1796 it bought 288, and eventually the issue was repudiated. But in the meantime, according to one historian, there came upon the nation "the *obliteration of the idea of thrift.* In this mania for yielding to present enjoyment rather than providing for future comfort were the seeds of new growths of wretchedness; and luxury, senseless and extravagant, set in: this, too, spread as a fashion. To feed it, there came cheatery in the nation at large, and corruption among officials and persons holding trusts: while the men set such fashions in business, private and official, women like Madame Tallien set fashions of extravagance in dress and living that added to the incentives to corruption. Faith in moral considerations, or even in good impulses, yielded to general distrust. National honor was thought a fiction cherished only by enthusiasts. Patriotism was eaten out by cynicism." In our own day we have seen the franc decline to a minor fraction of its former value after the first World War and to a minor fraction of that after the second.

Adulteration can, of course, be a useful political weapon, and one of the first steps taken by a recent reform administration in the United States was the inflation of currency. However much this may be defended as a means of meeting the particular contingency, the essential character of the act is not altered: values determined politically by governments under shortsighted popular control tend to depreciate. There is perhaps a sort of economic royalism in maintaining that the standard of value of today shall not be different from that of yesterday.

Now productive private property represents a kind of sanctuary against robbery through adulteration, for the individual getting his sustenance from property which bears his imprint and assimilation has a more real measure of value. And this enables him to predict with some degree of assurance or, in the broadest sense, to examine his life. It is important to distinguish between the security which means being taken care of, or freedom from want and fear—which would reduce man to an invertebrate—and stability, which gives nothing for nothing but which maintains a constant between effort and reward.

There is, moreover, a natural connection between the sense of honor and the personal relationship to property. As property becomes increasingly an abstraction and the sense of affinity fades, there sets in a strong temptation to adulterate behind a screen of anonymity. A Spanish proverb tells us with unhappy truthfulness that money and honor are seldom found in the same pocket. Under present conditions money becomes the anonymous cloak for wealth; telling us how much a man has no longer tells us what he has. In former times, when the honor of work had some hold upon us, it was the practice of a market to give his name to the product, and pride of family was linked up with maintenance of quality. Whether it was New England ships or Pennsylvania iron or Virginia tobacco, the name of an individual usually stood behind what was offered publicly as a tacit assumption of responsibility. But, as finance capitalism grew and men and property separated, a significant change occurred in names: the new designations shed all connection with the individual and became "General," "Standard," "International," "American," which are, of course, masks. Behind these every sort of adulteration can be practiced, and no one is shamed, because no one is identified; and, in fact, no single person may be responsible. Having a real name might require having character, and character stands in the way of profit. The invented names have a kinship with the dishonest hyperboles of advertising.

Accordingly, one of the most common tricks of the masters of modern commerce is to buy up an honored name and then to cheapen the quality of the merchandise for which it stands. The names have been detached from the things and can be bought and sold. They were established by individuals who saw an ideal of perfection in the tasks they undertook, and they were willing to be judged by their fidelity. In this way does utility drive out the old-fashioned virtue of loyalty to an ideal, which is honor.

Accordingly, if we take into account all reasonable factors, it is by no means clear whether the world is growing richer or poorer. The idea that it could be growing poorer will of course be scouted by those fascinated by a multiplicity of gadgets, but we should ponder carefully what is meant by this steady withdrawal of quality. We who have just passed through a great war are familiar with the feeling that no matter how much we improve our wage, we never seem able to buy what we want; we pay and pay, and yet the essential quality that we seek eludes us. Such depreciation has occurred to a marked extent over the last thirty years and to a lesser extent for far longer. The world is being starved for value. We are being told bigger lies and we are being fed less—this is the substantial fact flowing from the degradation of the ideal. A genuine article of fine material, put together by that craftsmanship which is oblivious of time, is almost certain today to be in the superluxury class, if indeed it is not already a museum exhibit. The genius of value seems to have taken wings along with the other essences which nominalists would deny.

A most eloquent example may be seen in the story of housing. A hundred years ago, more or less, when men built houses to live in themselves, they were constructing private property. The purpose was one to be honored, and they worked well, with an eye at least to the third generation. This is a simple instance of providence. One can see those dwellings today in quiet villages of New England and in remote places of the South, the honesty of the work that went into them reflected even in a grace of form. A century or a century and a half goes by, and they are both habitable and attractive. Let us look next at the modern age, in which houses are erected by anonymous builders for anonymous buyers with an eye to profit margins. A certain trickiness of design they often have, a few obeisances to the god comfort; but after twenty years they are falling apart. They were never private except in a specious sense; no one was really identified with them. Thus our spiritual impoverishment is followed by material impoverishment, in that we are increasingly deceived by surfaces. We lose in the most practical manner conceivable when we allow intension to be replaced by extension.

We must now get back to some general aspects of our problem and inquire whether the distributive ownership of real property might not correct a subversion of values which has been a scandal of the last century. I refer here simply to economic determinism. The fact that property broke away from this metaphysical relationship gave it a presumptive autonomy which played havoc with our thinking about the whole world. A consequence evident to everybody was the enthronement of economic man. The tendency of property under captialism to aggregate lent powerful support to the notion that economic factors are ultimate determinants. Perhaps this was only an interpretation of surface phenomena; yet so many men became the pawns of corporate economic bodies that it seemed plausible to explain all human activity as product or by-product of the search for economic satisfactions. (We must not forget, too, that Darwinism was lurking in the background.) Politics, arts, everything, came under the rule; man was primarily a food- and shelter-finding animal, and whoever wished the final explanation of political organizations and cultural differences was advised to seek it in what really counted—the struggle for material accommodation. It came to be assumed that politics was a mere handmaiden of economics, and books describing the ancillary role of political belief were received as revelations. This was the supreme falsification by the bourgeois mentality.

People who live according to a falsified picture of the world sooner or later receive sharp blows, and the first of these came in the Great Depression. It is interesting to note the reversal of roles which this disruptive experience effected. For everywhere the crisis was met by putting economic activity under stern political direction or, in other words, by setting political authority over supposedly unchangeable economic law. Such action, incidentally, occurred in the United States and in Germany at almost the identical moment. This corrected the fallacy by which economics had broken loose from the metaphysical hierarchy and presumed an exclusiveness. It will stand as a true observation that this episode marked the end of economic man. The principle re-emerged that what is done with economic goods must be somehow related to man's destiny. And so the world picture as final determinant was partially re-established.

The idea of metaphysical right subsumes property, and it is this idea that was lost to view in man's orientation away from transcendence. If material goods had been seen as something with a fixed place in the order of creation rather than as the ocean of being, on which man bobs about like a cork, the laws of economics would never have been postulated as the ordinances of all human life. But this again requires belief in nonmaterial existence.

It would be naïve to take an unmixed delight in the thought that politics has at length dethroned economics. The simplest meaning of the event, together with that of many others we have detailed, is that the world of 1789 has come to an end. There is a degree of comfort in knowing that we are not at the mercy of iron economic laws and that we can will the character of our wealth-getting activities. This could, in fact, be an important step toward rational freedom. But, under the present dispensation, the prospect of making politics the final arbiter is not without its terror. No thoughtful person can feel that we have found means of getting our political authority regularly into the hands of the wise. We have here something like the fallacy of humanism carried over into politics; our magistrates are, alas, human, all too human. Can we admire, or even trust a man who is merely the common denominator of all men? We have escaped one form of irrational domination only to be threatened by another which may prove more irresponsible—domination by the propertyless bureaucrat. I emphasize this in order to keep before us the question of how to preserve the spirit of obedience in a purely secular society.

It is by now reasonably plain that the frantic peoples of Europe thought their solution was to turn over their lives to unrestricted political control. By doing this, they found temporary amelioration and the illusion of future security. But the people into whose hands they allowed authority to fall were so selfish and so irrational that they exemplified power without wisdom. They did demonstrate that political dictation can end economic chaos; but this, after all, was technique. The question of what to do after the power of political control had been sensed found no reasonable answer. The leaders cultivated a political fanaticism, which had the result, as Emil Lederer has shown, of institutionalizing massness. We have already pointed to the antithesis of mass and society. A primary object of those who wish to restore society is the demassing of the masses, and in this the role of property is paramount.

Private property, in the sense we have defined it, is substance; in fact, it is something very much like the philosophic concept of substance. Now when we envision a society of responsible persons, we see them enjoying a range of free choice which is always expressed in relation to substance. I certainly concur with Péguy that the relationship between spirit and matter is one of the great mysteries, but I do not think that the mystery calls for the annihilation of matter. It is, on the contrary, important to keep substance in life, for a man's character emerges in the building and ordering of his house; it does not emerge in complaisance with state arrangement, and it is likely to be totally effaced by communistic organization. Substance has a part in bringing out that distinction which we have admitted to be good; it is somehow instrumental in man's probation.

The issue involves, finally, the question of freedom of the will, for private property is essential in any scheme which assumes that man has choice between better and worse. It is given him like the Garden of Eden, and up to now he seems guilty of a second forfeit of happiness. An abuse, however, does not stigmatize the thing abused. And, underlying all, there is for us in this critical battle against chaos the concept of inviolable right. We prize this instance because it is the opening for other transcendental conceptions. So long as there is a single breach in monism or pragmatism, the cause of values is not lost. It is likely—though this is not a question to be resolved by babes and sucklings—that human society cannot exist without some resource of sacredness. Those states which have sought openly to remove it have tended in the end to assume divinity themselves.

Therefore one inviolable right there must be to validate all other rights. Unless something exists from which we can start with moral certitude, we cannot depend on those deductions which are the framework of coherent behavior. I have read recently that a liberal is one who doubts his premises even when he is proceeding on them. This seems the very prescription for demoralization if not for insanity. And I think it true that the sort of metaphysical moral right we have outlined bears comparison with the a priori principles which we cannot doubt when we do our thinking.

The Greeks identified god with mind, and it will be found that every attack upon religion, or upon characteristic ideas inherited from religion, when its assumptions are laid bare, turns out to be an attack upon mind. Moral certitude gives the prior assurance of right sentiment. Intellectual integrity gives clarity to practice. There is some ultimate identification of goodness and truth, so that he who ignores or loses faith in the former can by no possible means save the latter.

For centuries now opportunism has encroached upon essential right until certitude has all but vanished. We are looking for a place where a successful stand may be made for the logos against modern barbarism. It seems that small-scale private property offers such an entrenchment, which is, of course, a place of defense. Yet offensive operations too must be undertaken.

The Kinetic Economy

The ongoing debates over NAFTA and GATT have had the effect of obscuring rather than clarifying the reasons why open borders are preferable to barriers. This may be because the proponents of free trade avoid vigorous acknowledgment of the inevitable consequences of economic freedom: winners and losers.

Facing the truth about economics takes vision and guts, and few have both qualities in quite the abundance that George Gilder has. All one needs to know about the reasons why we ought to oppose excessive government intervention in the economy and be in favor of free trade are captured in Mr. Gilder's brief meditation on Sir Henry Bessemer.

Here is one instance where conservative principle places us four-square against . . . the status quo.

IN EVERY ECONOMY, as Jane Jacobs has said, there is one crucial and definitive conflict. This is not the split between capitalists and workers, technocrats and humanists, government and business, liberals and conservatives, or rich and poor. All these divisions are partial and distorted reflections of the deeper conflict: the struggle between past and future, between the existing configuration of industries and the industries that will someday replace them. It is a conflict between established factories, technologies, formations of capital, and the ventures that may soon make them worthless—ventures that today may not even exist; that today may flicker only as ideas, or tiny companies, or obscure research projects, or fierce but penniless ambitions; that today are unidentifiable and incalculable from above, but which, in time, in a progressing economy, must rise up if growth is to occur.

Except in the very short run, growth does not consist of the kind of booming demand and rising productivity—the sale of more soap and Chevrolets—that the president discusses with the Business Roundtable when they gather to consider how to stimulate the American economy. Growth may not even spring from what most of the business establishment calls investment: the repair, duplication, and expansion of existing capital plant and equipment. Existing systems become more expensive and less appropriate as time passes and conditions change. Their reproduction is often a burden on growth, a diversion from always necessary investment in new technology. Long-term growth can be virtually defined as the replacement of existing plants, equipment, and products with new and better ones.

Sir Henry Bessemer, the creator of the Bessemer method of large-scale steel production, vividly described such a nineteenth-century moment of discovery and displacement. In 1854, after his first breakthrough in tests for making steel, he wrote:

> I could now see in my mind's eye, at a glance, the great iron industry of the world crumbling away under the irresistible force of the facts so recently elicited. In that one result the sentence had gone forth, and not all the talent accumulated in the last 150 years . . . no, nor all the millions that had been invested in carrying out the existing system of manufacture, with all its accompanying great resistance, could reverse that one great fact.

Bessemer was right. Although the adaptation and diffusion of his method took far longer than he expected, Bessemer's invention indeed ended by wreaking ghost towns and bleak motionless factories from the British Midlands to eastern Pennsylvania. By the last decades of the nineteenth century the Bessemer system was producing some 85 percent of America's steel output, replacing wrought iron everywhere in the vast extension of railroads. But the Bessemer technique also was to succumb to change. By 1910 the open hearth process, with its radically different capital plant, had usurped Bessemer and had taken over some two-thirds of the steel market in the United States.

As Schumpeter so memorably wrote, "Creative destruction is the essential fact about capitalism . . . it is by nature a form or method of economic change, and not only never is, but never can be stationary. . . . The fundamental impulse that sets and keeps the capitalist engine in motion comes from the new consumer goods, the new methods of production or transportation, the new markets, the new forms of industrial organization that capitalist enterprise creates."

In the struggles of creative destruction neither large nor small companies have a decisive advantage. In general large companies are most valuable in making incremental (though cumulatively very large) productivity improvements and in extending their markets into the world economy, where political and financial clout are often more important than innovation. Small companies are collectively far less efficient. But they are also more likely to create totally new items. Large firms can sometimes succeed in buying or forming subsidiaries, such as Exxon's Zilog and Vydec, that display much resourcefulness in imitating and improving the innovations of others. What large firms lack is the fertility of numbers and the flexibility of uncommitment. Although any particular small firm may be less creative than a large corporation, the millions of small businesses together are the prime source of creative destruction—the chief initiators of valuable change.

The very virtues of size—the economies of scale they offer—are the corollary of their vices: their huge and settled investments in particular capital and management practices. Without expressing any hostility toward the large corporations, one can maintain that the struggle between past and future is in part a struggle between David and Goliath, and this struggle will never end. Although Schumpeter himself came to underestimate the changeless implications of the imperative of change—and many contemporary economists astonishingly imagine that we are now entering a stationary or stagnant technological age—creative destruction is always the essence of growth.

From this fact arises the central question about any system of political economy, any platform of a political party, any inspiring scheme of leadership: will it allow the future to prevail? Will it favor the promise of the unknown against the comforts and passions of the threatened past? Little else matters. As at every other point in the harrowing course of human history, current technologies and productivities are inadequate to a rapidly growing and, above all, increasingly demanding world population. As at every other historical epoch, faithless and shortsighted men attempt to halt the increase of knowledge and the advance of technology; they dream of "stationary states," "economic equilibria," "alternative lifestyles," "diminishing technological returns," "ecological stasis," and "a return to nature," all the while mumbling of "the threat of scientific progress." Such fantasies, endlessly refuted and endlessly recurrent, are the prime obstacle to the survival of civilization.

The problem emerges with ever more insistent urgency in every modern state. Governments everywhere are torn between the clamor of troubled obsolescence and the claims of unmet opportunity; between the sufferers of aging pains and the sufferers of growing pains; between enterprises shrinking from competition or asking subsidies for their errors and companies seeking human and capital resources to create new products and markets for them.

Socialist and totalitarian governments are doomed to support the past. Because creativity is unpredictable, it is also uncontrollable. If the politicians want to have central planning and command, they cannot have dynamism and life. A managed economy is almost by definition a barren one, which can progress only by borrowing or stealing from abroad.

After a trip to the Soviet Union Luigi Barzini described the results of "progressive" leadership in that vastly endowed land. Many operating Russian factories, Barzini said, resemble nothing so much as beautifully maintained and managed industrial museums for nineteenth-century machinery, all oiled, buffed, and polished like an old Packard ready for presentation at a rally of antique cars. Except in the vital realm of national defense, where Soviet businesses must compete with the United States, communism in general is a purely reactionary system, a kind of dream come true at a conference of industrial archaeologists. This creative sterility can in theory be overcome by socialist countries that "plan" for freedom and change (that is, become partly capitalist). But as a practical matter it is on capitalism we must rely to unleash the forces of creative destruction that can save the world in its perpetual crisis of population and scarcity.

Nonetheless, as capitalist governments weave themselves ever more deeply into the economic fabric, capitalist and democratic political systems enlist themselves more and more on the side of the established order—on the side of stagnation and against creative growth. A democratic legislator normally supports the most powerful businesses and cultural influences in his constituency. Labor unions, deeply important in the politics of all non-Communist countries, normally back the interests of the large companies they have already organized. Bureaucracies often are closely allied with the industries they regulate, particularly when the regulations—together with excessive taxation—so damage the industry that, like the American railroad and utility corporations, they finally fall helplessly into the arms of the state.

Detailed systems of regulation understandably tend to favor the products and patterns of behavior that have been adjusted to the rules—the "good" companies that can be easily understood and supervised by the existing expertise of the incumbent regulators. Innovation always has unpredictable and possibly dangerous results. In early stages, it is always uncertain, inefficient, and if it is based on new scientific findings, even inscrutable. Any fail-safe system of regulation to prevent environmental damage, work-place hazards, and every possible peril to consumers would never have permitted the launching of an airplane, let alone an industrial revolution. Regulators must always rely on existing knowledge, commanded by existing scientific disciplines and their leading proponents.

Yet scientific expertise is nearly always as narrow as it is deep, and established scientists resist change as doggedly as any other establishment. William Shockley was one of the inventors of the transistor, one of the heroic innovators of the modern age. But in the early 1960s he was as blind to the potentialities of the semiconductor as he is now to the genetics of intelligence. Most scientific breakthroughs are made by men in their twenties or early thirties. The National Laboratories, the Food and Drug Administration (FDA), the Environmental Protection Agency (EPA)—all used by government to appraise the products of civilian science—are full of men who are past their prime, emotionally and intellectually committed to earlier technologies, and deeply resistant to progress. Asking them to judge the implications of new breakthroughs in fusion energy or microbiology is like using railroad technicians in the nineteenth century to appraise the plans of the Wright brothers.

These realities do not preclude regulation. But they suggest its inevitable pitfalls and grave unaccountable costs. The more comprehensive the regulatory systems, the more surely they will be dominated by

mediocrities, and the more surely mediocre will be the growth of the
U.S. economy. Excessive regulation to save us from risks will create
the greatest danger of all: a stagnant society in a changing world. The
choice is not between comfortable equilibrium and reckless progress.
It is between random deterioration by time and change and creative
destruction by human genius. Our current regulatory apparatus is in
danger of becoming an enemy of creative destruction.

Thus the EPA has for nearly a decade relentlessly obstructed the use
of new biological insecticides—pheromones, pesticidal bacteria, and
other organic pest controllers of the sort celebrated by Rachel Carson
as potential replacements for DDT. This stance has led to continued
use of chemicals such as parathion, which is far more poisonous and
destructive than DDT, although most of the new biological substances pose no environmental threat at all. The cause of the paraly-
sis, William Tucker of *Harper's* concluded in a prize-winning analysis
of the situation, is not any deliberate or conspiratorial opposition to
the new devices, but a characteristic ineptitude in the face of novelty.

As the manufacturers saw it, the chief technical problem of the new
pesticides was how to keep them in the environment long enough to
affect insects, not to mention humans. And the chief commercial
problem has been that their narrow effectiveness, usually against just
one pest, restricts their market and thus the amount of money that
can be profitably invested in testing them.

Yet EPA applies to these exotic microbial substances, designed to
confuse the mating patterns or otherwise disrupt the lives of specific
species of bugs, exactly the same testing requirements developed for
toxic chemicals that kill a wide range of insects, are used in large
quantities, and persist tenaciously in the earth. EPA did not anticipate the organic pest controllers and thus was bureaucratically mal-
adapted to approve them. Businesses arose and went bankrupt year
after year, scientists achieved spectacular breakthroughs and then
turned in frustration to other fields, while EPA ruminated endlessly
over what to do with the new inventions, prescribed testing programs
costing hundreds of millions of dollars, and shifted personnel so often
that the companies could never determine the locus of responsibility for their plight. The result was to block progress in its tracks, and
to promote regression to pesticides far worse than the DDT that
prompted the initial regulations.

Similarly, the Food and Drug Administration is dominated by

doctors who cannot really understand the new developments in pharmacology but who cling to a Frances Kelsey complex, obstinately obstructing anything new on the grounds that it might turn out to be thalidomide. The fact is that a system that prevented testing of any drug with possible side effects as bad as thalidomide would preclude almost all progress in pharmacology and cost far more lives than it saved. Today the FDA is the chief obstacle to U.S. medical progress, foolishly blocking the deterring innovation in drugs, including a whole new generation of antiviral agents, which cannot be proven safe and effective without the very decades of use by humans that the FDA forbids.

In 1974, through the Toxic Substances Control Act Congress threatened to extend this kind of snarl to the entire compass of American industry, involving thousands of chemicals in myriad combinations, most of them toxic in varying degrees and applications. This assignment is essentially impossible, entailing a recall demand for the entire economy. Like the Occupational Safety and Health Administration, this law constitutes a license to the government to harass any company that offends it, for whatever reason. The most likely reason, however, is that a company persists in creating new products. The best way to avoid trouble is to avoid innovation. Under this law the more conscientious EPA becomes, the more destructive the effect will be. In this instance, the only hope is incompetence.

The frequent perversity of such interventions in the marketplace has been often shown. But despite all problems, regulation is sometimes needed, and should be adopted, as all agree, "whenever the benefits exceed the costs." But the calculation is by no means simple. Many of the costs are impossible to measure, for they consist of the benefits of a more open and competitive economy that allows the ready exploitation of new technologies. The most serious damage inflicted by excessive controls is the discouragement of innovation and entrepreneurship and the perpetuation of slightly laundered and government-approved obsolescence. Government, for all its seductive uses and virtues, is almost always an obstacle to change. Since, throughout the world, people live longest in the most industrialized, dynamic, and polluted countries—and longevity continues to rise in industrial societies—the burden of proof should normally fall on those who wish to halt progress in the name of saving lives.

One reason for government resistance to change is that the process of creative destruction can attack not only an existing industry, but also the regulatory apparatus that subsists on it; and it is much more difficult to retrench a bureaucracy than it is to bankrupt a company. A regulatory apparatus is a parasite that can grow larger than its host industry and become in turn a host itself, with the industry reduced to parasitism, dependent on the subsidies and protections of the very government body that initially sapped its strength. Such industries exist all over Europe today, firms feeding on the societies they once amply fed. Not one of the nationalized manufacturing companies in Europe has made a consistent profit; all are burdens on the economies they seemingly dominate but actually subvert.

In Great Britain the discovery of North Sea oil is sometimes called a "curse in disguise" because it allowed that country to continue financing its parasite leviathans throughout the 1970s and even to endow new nationalized firms such as Inmos, a hopeless laggard in the computer industry, as well as virtual government creatures like De-Lorean Autos. This firm will probably never pay back the immense subsidies by which Britain outbid lucky Puerto Rico for the right to deplete the national economy in order to "create" a few jobs and destroy many more.

Even when governments give more modest help to independent business, they often act in ways that favor established firms against potential rivals. Tariffs, import quotas, accelerated depreciation, and other tax and trade policies all are most useful to settled firms with long established product lines to protect, equipment to depreciate, and profits to offset. These policies, often hailed for being targeted to achieve specific social benefits, generally promote the enlargement and reproduction of the existing capital stock: the factories and machines used to build and sell more automobiles, color televisions, dishwashers, hairdryers, chemical fertilizers, and insecticides—all estimable products but all also items of declining relevance to the rising problems of a changing national predicament. As our circumstances change, our capital stock must be transformed, and this will inevitably mean the decline in the fortunes of all the least foresighted owners of existing capital, all the unions that depend on them, and the localities and bureaucracies that the businesses support.

These government tendencies toward regression are reinforced by the media. Every report of a defective new product, a possibly poisonous industrial waste, a vaguely carcinogenic chemical, produces headlines in the newspapers and somber commentary on television news. But the valuable products and services that are never created or marketed because of regulatory excess have no voice. When a corporate leviathan suffers a setback or retrenches its payroll—whether because of import competition or simple obsolescence or even government policy—cameras and microphones are wheeled forward to record every whimper and complaint. But hundreds of thousands of small businesses involving millions of jobs expire annually without notice. Again the image of the economy as a conglomeration of big businesses and governmental bureaucracies is propagated for the public and the true sources of long-term growth are obscured. Imports are seen as a threat, progress is depicted as a peril, and governmental leaching of the economy to finance mismanagement and failure is presented as a way of "saving jobs," although in fact many more jobs are eventually lost when the disciplines of competition are allowed to decay.

Labor unions and politicians join the press in pretending that the bankruptcy of a Penn Central, a Chrysler, or a Lockheed would be a dead loss for the economy rather than a means of reorganizing the companies' assets in a more profitable way. Indeed, the greatest problem of the railroads is the idea that the present pattern of train service is indispensable in all its parts and must ultimately be supported by government if the private sector fails. This notion, demonstrable nonsense, becomes a self-fulfilling prophecy because no industry (or city) can successfully negotiate with its unions if workers believe that the firm has ultimate access to the federal treasury.

Similarly, the field of energy is full of self-fulfilling prophecies as the media spread technophobic propaganda about nearly all forms of fuel production and transport. Power plants, oil and gas refineries, and all new energy development is invariably obstructed and delayed in the name of saving lives or protecting the environment. Yet the blackouts, power shortages, increased energy costs, and industrial stagnation of coming decades will cause far more death and destruction later, when the society resorts to desperate measures: nationalizes utilities, returns to coal, and heightens the risk of environmentally pollutant wars. In celebrating decay and cringing before technology, the media promote the emergence of truly dangerous crises in the future.

The phenomenon of government support for mismanagement, inefficiency, and reaction reaches far beyond business. Comfortable failure will always and inevitably turn to politics to protect it from change. Just as declining businesses turn to the state, people and groups that shun the burdens of productive work and family life will proclaim themselves a social crisis and a national responsibility—and sure enough, they become one. The more federal aid that is rendered to the unemployed, the divorced, the deviant, and the prodigal, the more common will their ills become, the more alarming will be the graphs of social breakdown. A government preoccupied with the statistics of crisis will often find itself subsidizing problems, shoring up essentially morbid forms of economic and social activity, creating incentives for unemployment, inflation, family disorder, housing decay, and municipal deficits, making problems worse by making them profitable. As government grows, there all too quickly comes a time when solutions are less profitable than problems.

Throughout the Washington of the seventies, behind the inevitable rhetoric of innovation and progress, the facades of futurity, the forces of obstruction gathered: an energy department imposing counterproductive new taxes and price controls; a department of housing promoting rent controls; even a National Center for Productivity forced to celebrate the least productive of all unions per man hour—the American Federation of State, County, and Municipal Employees.

Despite his best intentions, the government planner will tend to live in the past, for only the past is sure and calculable. In response to the inevitable crisis of scarcity, he will prescribe, as progress, a series of faintly disguised anachronisms: a revival of bicycles, a renaissance of consumer cooperatives, a new federal scheme of price controls, a massive return to coal, or a recrudescence of small-lot farming and windmills.

The entire range of current government programs can be seen as a far-reaching and resourceful defense of the status quo against all emerging competitors. Economic policy focuses on stimulating aggregate demand for existing products rather than on fostering the supply of new ones. Investment credits and rapid depreciation, allowances—although better than no tax cuts at all—tend to favor the re-creation of current capital stock rather than the creation of new forms of capital and modes of production. Antitrust suits are directed chiefly against successful competitors (such as IBM) and ignore the government policies at the root of most American monopoly. The system of floating exchange rates deals with lapses in international trade by depreciating the dollar rather than by forcing a competitive response of greater productivity and new products. Our taxation and subsidy systems excessively cushion failure (of businesses, individuals, and local governments), reward the creativity and resourcefulness chiefly of corporate lawyers and accountants, and wait hungrily in ambush for all unexpected, and thus unsheltered, business success.

There is a similar bias in our social and employment programs. Under current affirmative-action rules and perennial threats of litigation, civil service now passes out jobs and promotions on the basis of nearly immutable credentials such as test scores, diplomas, race, and sex rather than on a competitive performance of work. The nation's employment policies are increasingly based on new forms of tenure and entitlement rather than on expanding opportunities and new kinds of jobs.

Most of these policies are ostensibly designed to shield the poor and vulnerable from the costs of change, but regardless of the cosmetics of egalitarian policy, the chief effect is to deny to the lower classes the benefits of a progressing economy. Risk and competition, death and change are the very essence of the human condition. The effort to escape inflation by indexing the incomes of favored groups and to fight unemployment by subsidizing outmoded jobs merely makes these problems worse and foists them onto the unorganized majority: onto small businesses, onto nonunion workers, and onto the public at large in a stagnant economy.

Even voluntary wage-and-price controls mostly penalize the rapidly growing and changing companies in competitive industries, which need to pay their personnel highly to prevent them from moving to other companies or which need to charge heavily for rare services and products in which the company commands a brief monopoly. In addition, the controls shift the largest burdens to the uncontrollable sectors. To the extent the government can artificially repress the prices of automobiles and television sets, it will increase the pressure on prices for food, fuel, and housing. Since government will usually be able to influence the prices of luxuries more than of necessities, with a given money supply controls will always tend to raise the prices of necessities dominant in the budgets of the poor. This effect was evident under both the Nixon and Carter efforts for price stabilization.

In general the most important effect of the government attempt to shield itself and its clients from uncertainty and risk is to place the entire system in peril. It becomes at once too rigid and too soft to react resourcefully to the new shocks and sudden challenges that are inevitable in a dangerous world.

Supporting the future, though theoretically simple, provides plenty of challenges for human governance. Government can bring forth miracles of creativity and growth merely by enforcing the laws equally; protecting patents and property rights; promoting educational excellence—above all, in science and technology; restricting public powers to create and sustain monopoly; removing barriers to trade; lifting wherever possible the dumb hand of bureaucracy; imposing sensible penalties and incentives on industries that endanger the environment; fostering an atmosphere of stability and security both in domestic and international affairs.

Such assignments offer ample responsibilities for the Washington bureaucracy. To fulfill them will require heroic efforts. The more ambitious agenda of contemporary liberalism simply ensures that government will do nothing well, except to expand itself as an obstacle to growth and innovation. Government best supports the future by refraining as much as possible from trying unduly to shape it, for the impact of government policy nearly always conforms with the current incidence of political power, which derives from the configuration of existing capital and labor.

Perhaps the supreme symbol of the struggle between past and future is the continuing battle over tax policy, particularly on capital gains. The stakes are relatively simple. Although large companies naturally will benefit most in absolute terms, cuts in the tax on capital gains are a redemptive boon to companies that expect to grow fast, that is, new and innovating companies. Capital gains are the chief source of new wealth in a capitalist economy. It is the way people get rich. With a rate of inflation over 8 percent, a 20 percent tax on capital gains quickly rises above 100 percent in its average impact on assets held more than a few years. One still can make money, if one is wise or lucky, by speculating in stocks and bonds, commodities and collectibles, and trying to outguess the market or the Fed. But an early purchase of shares in a pioneering firm—if held through the span required to launch a new product—will often be taxed at confiscatory levels when sold.

This tax constitutes a big business protection act—a defense of large companies against small, old wealth against new, the past against the future. But so-called progressive politicians bitterly resist its removal from stocks. Although most liberals now acknowledge the need to promote investment, they all favor, in the words of Senator Kennedy, Treasury Secretary Blumenthal, and President Carter, a "targeted approach" of bonuses and subsidies for the kinds of investment they prefer, rather than the general cuts that will create new wealth and multiply the numbers of rich entrepreneurs.

Liberals seem to want wealth without the rich. Yet most real wealth originates in individual minds in unpredictable and uncontrollable ways. A successful economy depends on the proliferation of the rich, on creating a large class of risk-taking men who are willing to shun the easy channels of a comfortable life in order to create new enterprise, win huge profits, and invest them again. It will be said that their earnings are "unearned" and "undeserved." But, in fact, most successful entrepreneurs contribute far more to society than they ever recover, and most of them win no riches at all. They are the heroes of economic life, and those who begrudge them their rewards demonstrate a failure to understand their role and their promise.

The attitudes of politicians—at least about wealth—are quite understandable. To a great degree politicians are American aristocrats. They attained their eminence by submitting to competition as intense, taking risks as great, and making sacrifices as large as any entrepreneur. Winning politicians are at the very pinnacle of their profession. Yet they are paid less than a professional such as a doctor or a lawyer, who is assured a lifetime of risk-free income and prestige, and they have incomes vastly smaller than the fortunes of comparably successful and risk-taking entrepreneurs. It is understandable that politicians resent the mode of distribution of American wealth. Senators, governors, mayors, and congressmen should be paid at least four or five times their current salaries. The only reason they are not is their irrepressible populist demogoguery, for which they are themselves to blame, and the inherited wealth that many of them hold, cherish, and resent, which relieved them of the usual economic risks of political contest.

Understandable or not, however, the hostility of politicians toward the chief sources of wealth in America makes most of them—regardless of their professed beliefs in progress and equality—reactionary defenders of the old plutocracy against the forces of innovation and progress. Politicians who have prevailed in ruthless rivalries of wit and risk become natural allies of bureaucracy and privilege and diehard opponents of economic growth and vitality. Yet politicians, through their lives of ambition and adventure, are spiritual kin of entrepreneurs. Politicians, if they consider their own careers, and their final attainment of a fortune in prestige, should be able to comprehend the dynamics of capitalism and the necessity of great rewards for triumph against great odds.

The future of American capitalism depends on this shift of the political order from a reactionary defense of the past to a progressive embrace of the future. In the anomalous world of American politics, this change almost necessarily entails overcoming the "progressive" trends in the society.

PART IV

The Political Order

As close to Utopia as we're liable to come:

> Racial integration has worked better in baseball than in any other area of American life. The game has an unforced racial and ethnic balance. It succeeds because the rules are really impartial. Baseball is a refuge from "social justice." What it offers instead is simple fairness. There are no "racist" balls and strikes, no "affirmative action" balls and strikes, only balls and strikes.
>
> The umpires don't care who deserves to win on moral, progressive, or demographic grounds. Their role is modest but crucial, and would be corrupted if they brought any supposed Higher Purpose to their work. They care only about the rules. The Supreme Court could learn from them.

—JOSEPH SOBRAN, "The Republic of Baseball," in *National Review* (1990)

Little Platoons

Charles Murray's Losing Ground *is as influential a book as has been published since the end of World War II. It has made rational discussions about poverty in America possible, and is the impetus behind much of the welfare reform that has been gathering steam during the last decade.*

But Mr. Murray's concerns go beyond the "underclass" and touch upon every aspect of American social and political life. He is especially concerned about what government can, cannot, and must not do for people.

Living in New York City, I often had to remind myself that the key to survival there is "making the big city small." Gotham is not just five boroughs; it's five thousand neighborhoods. You have to know the Irish cop on the beat, the Italian butcher on the corner, and the Korean greengrocer across the street. Affiliations are what make politics work.

STRONGLY BOUND COMMUNITIES, fulfilling complex public functions, are not creations of the state. They form because they must. Human beings have needs as individuals (never mind the "moral sense" or lack of it) that cannot be met except by cooperation with other human beings. To this degree, the often-lamented conflict between "individualism" and "community" is misleading. The pursuit of individual happiness cannot be an atomistic process; it will naturally and always occur in the context of communities. The state's role in enabling the pursuit of happiness depends ultimately on nurturing *not* individuals, but the associations they form.

The text for this discussion is one of Burke's best-known passages: "To be attached to the subdivision, to love the little platoon we belong to in society, is the first principle (the germ as it were) of public affections. It is the first link in the series by which we proceed towards a love to our country, and to mankind." I will be using the image of the "little platoon" to represent the essential relationship of social organization to the pursuit of happiness and, by extension, the relationship of the state's social policy to the pursuit of happiness. We each belong to a few "little platoons." The great joys and sorrows, satisfactions and preoccupations, of our daily life are defined in terms of them. This observation, I will assert, applies to everyone, wherever his little platoons fall within the larger social framework.

Using a central government to enable people to pursue happiness becomes in this perspective a process of making sure that the little platoons work. The enabling conditions have to be met—in a properly constructed society, people must have access to material resources, safety, self-respect, and intrinsic rewards. But the little platoons of work, family, and community are the nexus within which these conditions are worked out and through which the satisfactions that happiness represents are obtained. That being the case, "good" social policy can be defined only after we have answered the questions:

> How do little platoons form?
> How are they sustained?
> What makes them nourishing?

AFFILIATION AS THE MECHANISM FOR FORMING LITTLE PLATOONS

[Among the enabling conditions of Abraham Maslow's famous hierarchy is the need] for intimacy and belongingness . . . in effect, it is the master resource whereby human beings in society go about seeing that the other needs are met. The label I will give to this mechanism is "affiliation." Here, too, Burke has distilled the essence of what I mean: "Men are not tied to one another by papers and seals. They are led to associate by resemblances, by conformities, by sympathies."

Parents, teachers, and (in their turn) children are engaged in a tacit, complex process. Each parent has certain individual interest. So does each prospective teacher. The result is not just the meeting of those particular interests, but something more. The little platoon called "community" had been enriched, with positive results that are more than the sum of the educational and professional outcomes. This is no accident, but a characteristic result when small groups of people have individual problems that can best be solved by gaining the voluntary cooperation of others—or in other words, when small groups engage in voluntary affiliations through the force of individual circumstance. We are now in a position to talk about affiliation more systematically.

Affiliations as Small Steps

An affiliation behavior may be one whereby one person forms new relationships with others (by marrying or moving to a particular town or neighborhood). It may consist of an effort to alter an existing environment (circulating a petition, or forming a neighborhood block watch). Sometimes it means leaving relationships that are unsatisfactory (getting a divorce or quitting a club). But the word "affiliation" probably tends to evoke too many of these formal types of affiliation and not enough of the small acts of affiliation that make up the larger ones. The places you shop, the friends you choose to see a lot of, the relationships you have with coworkers, the ways you spend your leisure time, all bespeak and define affiliations.

Affiliation behaviors, as I am using the term, are not contractual. I have a favorite delicatessen up the street. The prices sometimes aren't the best I could find, but I like the place for many little reasons. I can joke with the people behind the counter. They recognize my children when they come in. They let me buy a sandwich on credit when I have forgotten my wallet. And the food's pretty good. If once in a while my expectations are not met, I do not immediately start considering other options. If they were consistently not met, then sooner or later I would drift off. Technically, what I am doing could be construed and analyzed as a series of market decisions about where to shop (just as affiliations in the aggregate bear many similarities to the way that free markets work, through analogous dynamics). But in reality, the formation and sustenance of my affiliation with the delicatessen are much closer in their characteristics to the way that friendships form and are sustained.

I use this homely example to emphasize that people very rarely wake up one morning and "decide" to form a particular affiliation. They only rarely decide all at once to leave them. Most commonly, the interactions embraced under the heading of affiliation are small steps, taken for reasons having nothing to do with any conscious interest in forming affiliations, that have cumulative effects over time. As people go about their daily life, affiliation behaviors occur.

Or fail to occur. For a second important point about affiliations is that they do not have to exist. It is possible to live in a neighborhood, isolated and alone, and have no affiliations. It is possible to have a job that consists of a purely contractual outlook ("I agree to be at this place, doing these tasks, for this many hours per week, for this amount of money"), devoid of affiliations. Affiliations may be many or few, strong or weak, rich or bland. One of the chief determinants of their existence and their nature is the extent to which they are used to live out beliefs.

Affiliations as a Way of Living According to Beliefs

The affiliation involving the delicatessen is one of many that constitute my larger affiliation with a neighborhood, which in turn is one component of the affiliations that constitute my still larger affiliation with a community. Trivial as it is in itself, the affiliation with the deli serves to illustrate a feature of affiliations that has tended to be lost in the recent and often romanticized rhetoric about people "relating" to other people. People affiliate with other people because of *something about* other people—in this case, the qualities of being friendly, helpful, and amusing.

It may seem a distinction too obvious to mention. Of course one is attracted to "something about" someone else, since there is no such thing as being attracted to someone as an abstract entity. But however obvious, the distinction is essential to understanding why little platoons are rewarding or unrewarding, why they sustain themselves or fall apart: *Affiliation is a means whereby people of common values are enabled to live by those values.* "Values" in this case means your views about how the world works or ought to work, ranging from religion to childrearing to politics to table manners to standards of public civility.

The reason why affiliation is so intimately linked to values is that, to have much use—or, in fact, to be truly held—values must be acted on. Furthermore, they are typically expressed not in a one-shot action but as patterned behaviors over a period of time. Still further, values can seldom be acted upon in isolation; to live by them requires that your standards be shared by a consensus of your neighbors. Unless most of your neighbors believe in calling the police when something suspicious is happening to a neighbor's house, you are not going to be able to practice community crime control. Unless most of your neighbors believe that stealing is wrong and that sex for fourteen-year-olds is bad, you are going to have a tough time making your norms stick with your own children. If you conduct your business on the assumption that one's word is one's bond, you are going to go broke unless the other businessmen you deal with operate by the same principle. In other words, to live according to many of your most important beliefs, it is essential that you be free to affiliate with fellow believers and that, together, you enjoy some control over that environment. To the extent that you are satisfied that you are "living according to your beliefs"—that anciently honored right of Americans—it is because of affiliations.

So far, presumably, no surprises: All I have done is impose some nomenclature on a familiar process. But it also remains true that in the everyday world some affiliations work much better than others. Some marriages are much richer affiliations than others, some neighborhoods are much more closely knit than others, and so on. Even a commonality of beliefs is obviously not enough—some local churches are much more vital than others. The question therefore becomes not only how affiliation occurs, but how it becomes infused with satisfying content.

RESPONSIBILITY AND EFFORT AS THE MECHANISMS FOR ACHIEVING SATISFACTION

Put aside the concept of affiliation for a moment (we shall return to it) and consider self-respect, locus of control, intrinsic rewards, autotelic activities, competence, and self-determination. In different ways, from different perspectives, they argue for the reality of this relationship: The satisfaction one takes from any activity is a complicated product of the degree of effort one puts into it, the degree of responsibility one has for the outcome, and the function it serves.

Effort. The importance of effort is perhaps self-evident—try to think of something from which you take great satisfaction (not just momentary pleasure) that involved no effort on your part. I need not belabor this. Any number of aphorisms make the same point: "Nothing worth having comes easily," for example, or "You take out of something what you put into it." The technical literature provides scientifically respectable language for very old common wisdom.

Responsibility. It is the importance of responsibility that needs emphasis. To achieve satisfaction, there must be an element of "It was because of me!" in the accomplishment. Effort alone is not enough. Underlying this sense of responsibility are three crucial conditions: the sense of having made a choice (it was possible that you would *not* have done it); of following through, consummating an identifiable effect; and of having done this in the face of the possibility of failure. It is not necessary to be fully responsible for every aspect of an achievement, but it is necessary to be responsible for some identifiable and meaningful corner of it. Thus construction workers commonly report that one of the satisfactions of their job is to return to the completed skyscraper or bridge and say to themselves that they helped build it. They had an extremely high degree of what might be called "local responsibility" for their component of the effort.

The brunt of these remarks is that the relationship of effort and responsibility to satisfaction is not simply additive. If I were putting the relationship in the form of an equation, I would say that effort and responsibility have both an additive and a multiplicative effect. If either is zero, the multiplicative component of the effect is zero as well.*

Function. The assertion here (and it is an assertion) is that the degree of satisfaction produced by the effort and responsibility depends on the function being served. Generally speaking, functions can be arrayed on a continuum in importance from "trivial" (e.g., passing the time) to "profound" (e.g., saving someone's life). In the absence of some highly unusual circumstances, it can be generalized that spending a great deal of effort and assuming great responsibility on a trivial function is not as satisfying as spending the same amount of effort

---

*The relationship is still more complicated when the behaviors are not voluntary. For example, being *forced* to put forth great effort with no responsibility typically produces dissatisfaction (a negative score, as it were). The main point in the text is that effort and responsibility interact in producing satisfactions.

and assuming equally great responsibility on a profound function.*
This is an assertion, but not such an implausible one.

The point I wish to stress is that *the same conditions that shape individual satisfactions apply to the satisfactions gained from affiliations.* The affiliation called a friendship is decisively affected by the effort, responsibility, and functions it serves as well as by the personal attractiveness that the two friends see in each other. The affiliations that make up a community are much different if they are formed by dinner parties and encounters at the supermarket than if they are formed by barn-raisings and fighting off the locusts. Or to put it in terms of the little platoons through which we work out the pursuit of happiness: To exist and to be vital, little platoons must have something to do.

Let me now begin to put these considerations alongside the problem of making good social policy. I am no longer trying to formulate effective policies to deal with discrete social problems, but trying to characterize more broadly the shape that good social policy will take. The proposition is that the importance of affiliation—of *rich* affiliations, imbued with responsibility and effort, used as a way of living according to one's beliefs—transcends any of these discrete social goods. Much of what we observe as rootlessness, emptiness, and plain unhappiness in contemporary life may ultimately be traced to the many ways, occasionally blatant, more often indirect and subtle, in which social policy has excised the option of taking responsibility, the need to make an effort, or both—the ways in which social policy has, in a phrase, taken the trouble out of things.

THE GENERAL RELATIONSHIP OF SOCIAL POLICY TO SATISFACTIONS

"Taking the trouble out of things" is the theme song of modernity. The very process of technological progress may be seen as an unending attempt to take the trouble out of things. Certainly "taking the trouble out of things" has driven the consumer economy. Electric can

---

*It is important not to confuse *activity* with *function*. The same superficial activity can serve quite different functions. Tennis, for example, "just a game" in itself, has escalating levels of potential satisfaction for the casual player, for whom tennis is a way to pass the time pleasurably; for the dedicated amateur, for whom tennis is a principal means of "expressing his realized capacities"; and for the professional, for whom tennis is both a principal means of self-expression and a way of making a living.

openers take the trouble out of opening cans. Garbage disposals take the trouble out of getting rid of the garbage. Automobiles take the trouble out of getting from one place to another. Such changes are, by and large, welcome. People naturally try to make life better, and "better" not unnaturally has tended to be identified with "easier."

"Taking the Trouble Out of Things" as the De Facto Goal of Social Policy

Most changes in social policy over the last half century may be viewed as having served the same function. Social Security took some of the trouble out of preparing for retirement. Unemployment insurance took some of the trouble out of being unemployed. Aid to Families with Dependent Children (AFDC) took some of the trouble out of having a baby without a father. Alterations in the bankruptcy laws took some of the trouble out of failing at business.

A problem with such reforms, quite apart from anything having to do with their immediate effects, is that in every instance in which "taking the trouble out of things" works, there is a corresponding diminution in the potential satisfaction that might be obtained from the activity that has been affected. To be employed is not quite as satisfying if being unemployed doesn't cause hardship. To be a businessman who scrupulously pays his bills is not quite as satisfying if not-paying-bills is made less painful.

The carrots and sticks act at second hand. Theoretically, for the businessman to continue to take as much satisfaction in paying his bills, it is necessary only that his fellow businessmen continue to consider it disgraceful not to pay bills. In reality, to soften the tangible penalties of bankruptcy also, over a period of time, softens the degree of disgrace. To soften the tangible penalties for being unemployed also, over a period of time, diminishes the status associated with holding a job. To return to the running example of education, the reforms in education during the 1960s and 1970s may be seen as a series of steps that "took some of the trouble" out of educating one's child and to that degree attenuated this important source of satisfaction. Responsibility for decisions about nearly everything—curricula, textbooks, disciplinary standards, rules of attendance and suspension, selection of teachers, testing requirements, the amounts of money to be spent, guidelines for lunch menus—moved outward from the neighborhood to the state or federal government. The argument here is not about whether these changes were substantively good or bad; rather, it is that *even* if they had been good educationally, they were still bad for parents in that they constrained and depressed the ways in which a parent with a child in public school could take satisfaction from that component of life called "overseeing the education of one's child."

Adopting this viewpoint, one may also make the case that what really happened for any given reform was that some enrichment of satisfactions occurred further down the line. The United States has always avoided truly Draconian penalties for bankruptcy, to enable people to make a fresh start—certainly a plus in enabling people to pursue happiness. Social Security takes some of the trouble out of preparing for retirement, yes; but the existence of Social Security makes it possible for large numbers of people who otherwise would be destitute to have enough material resources—a critical enabling condition—to pursue happiness in their old age. The actual net of each trade-off has to be calculated on its merits.

The Need for a Stopping Point

The problem is not deciding whether good social policy ever means taking the trouble out of things, but rather finding where to stop. Almost everyone thinks it is good that the police take the trouble out of having to catch burglars. A large majority of Americans seem to be content with the more extensive transfer of burdens that has occurred. Judging from international experience, the process will continue. No democracy has yet said to its government, "Stop doing this for us." If we look to Western Europe for a picture of our future, and if in Europe the Scandinavian countries represent the cutting edge of social progress, then we may look forward to more and more trouble being taken out of more and more things.

The psychological reasons why people seem endlessly willing to accept such measures is no more complicated than the reason why any of us, given a choice, will often take the easy way out even when we know that we will derive more satisfaction from the more troublesome choice. It is the all-too-familiar problem of knowing that one "will have enjoyed" doing something (reading a fine novel) but lacking the will to get started on it (therefore picking up a magazine instead). This is not reprehensible, but it does raise two important points.

The first is that the process cannot ultimately be a healthy one. Taking the trouble out of things must eventually go too far. Somehow the mixture of things with which we fill up our time must give us long-term satisfaction with life as a whole. And satisfaction depends crucially on being left important things over which we take trouble.

The second observation is that we cannot expect legislatures to define a stopping point. If the decisions about what government may not do on our behalf is left to a majority vote of elected representatives, logrolling and shifting coalitions will mean a perpetually expanding domain of benefits.

Programs that provide benefits are triply vulnerable to this form of perpetual expansion. First and most obviously, perception of the benefit tends to dominate perception of the cost, for the same reason that the offer of a free lunch used to attract business to saloons. Second, a majority can easily be put together to vote for a wide variety of benefits if only a minority is taxed to pay for them. Third, even a *minority* can often pass a benefit because of the asymmetry in the incentives to support and oppose any given benefit. Specifically, when a minority within the population stands to benefit greatly from a particular good and the individuals who constitute the majority suffer only a minor cost, the highly motivated minority can get the "public good" that it wants. In defining a proper stopping point for government services and benefits, trusting to the vote-by-vote behavior of the members of the United States Congress is a mistake. They will never define a stopping point on their own.

So the problem is set. Somehow the mix of somethings with which we fill up our time must give us happiness. And happiness depends crucially on taking trouble over things that matter. *There must be a stopping point, some rule by which governments limit what they do for people*—not just because of budget constraints, not just because of infringements on freedom (though either of these might be a sufficient reason in itself), but because happiness is impossible unless people are left alone to take trouble over important things.

Furthermore, the stopping point must leave untouched certain possibilities of failures, of losses, of pains. Recall Csikszentmihalyi's formulation: Enjoyment follows from the balance of challenge and skills. The word "challenge" has embedded in its meaning the element of "possibility of failure"; take away that possibility, and the possibility of enjoyment goes with it. Take away the possibility of failure, and the concept of "measuring up" that underpins self-respect is meaningless.

So we dare not make life as hazardless for ourselves as we have it in our power to do. The pursuit of happiness means making life deliberately difficult in certain ways—not so difficult that we *cannot* cope, but difficult enough, in certain important ways, that coping is an authentic accomplishment.

The Current Stopping Point: A Safety Net

The current stopping point for social welfare policy is supposed to be based on *who* is helped, not on the functions to be performed—the rationale of the safety net.* The statement of the stopping point goes something like this: "A good social policy leaves individuals free to do as they wish. The government steps in only when an individual demonstrates that he is *not* able to cope, that the challenges have overmatched his skills. Any form of help may be provided, but only to those who need it." The underlying premise—the central government should act to help those who need help—is accepted by mainstream conservatives and liberals alike. Their differences lie in definitions of who needs help and what constitutes an appropriate level of help.

But social policy affects not only individuals. It also takes away functions from the little platoons, and therein lies a much more difficult set of trade-offs to be assessed. If it is true that most of the important satisfactions in life are rooted in, processed through, or enhanced by little platoons, we are left with the general (if still not very specific) conclusion that it is extremely important for social policy to leave the little platoons with the "somethings to do" that keep them vital.

An Alternative Stopping Point: Proscribing Functions

The alternative is to establish the stopping point according to functions. This might be defined in various ways. Curiously, those out of the political mainstream—libertarians and democratic socialists, for example—share this principle in common, just as conservatives and liberals share the safety-net rationale in common. Their differences lie in the lists of functions that are forbidden to government. The demo-

*In reality, a very large proportion of income transfers violates the rationale of the safety net. The rationale for farm subsidies has nothing to do with helping people in need. The Social Security system embraces everyone, not just those in need. But the rationale of the safety net nonetheless pervades the debate and is treated as if it were a self-limiting stopping point, even if it has not been in practice.

cratic socialists see the government as the provider of basic services, setting aside a few areas of noneconomic personal behavior as areas in which government may not intrude. Libertarians want a government forbidden from all except the most limited functions (national defense and the police function being the main ones). For purposes of discussion here, I propose a loosely stated stopping point: "Functions that people as individuals and as communities are *able* to carry out on their own should be left to them to do as individuals and communities." That the federal government thinks it could do a *better* job of carrying out those functions is not a sufficient justification for intervention.

The motivation for the rule is the logic of the teacher shortage writ large: Just as it is *odd* that too few people want to do something as satisfying as teach, it is above all else *odd* that satisfying affiliations fail to occur in other sectors of life, for everyone. For individuals of all classes and abilities, the activities associated with getting and holding a job, finding and holding a spouse, and raising a family are all, in the natural course of things, chock-full of challenge and satisfaction, and cause rich affiliations to occur. They are the stuff of which life is made. It is odd that so many people should see themselves as living lives in which they go through meaningless motions.

The same applies even more emphatically to community activities. There is no shortage of important tasks, requiring people to take responsibility and effort, everywhere that human beings congregate. There are hungry to be fed, children to be taught, the uncivil to be civilized, the sick to be cared for, failures to be commiserated with and success to be celebrated. All the raw material is always there, in every collection of human beings. Modernity has not done away with a bit of it.

On the contrary, one of the virtues of modernity is that it has given larger and larger proportions of people the wherewithal to extend more and more help. When a society is living on the margins of subsistence, Maslow's formulation sets in and competition for limited goods can sweep away all other considerations.* But given contemporary American wealth, under what conditions does a person of ordinary goodwill—not a saint, just average—*not* feed a hungry

---

*Elsewhere, I have elaborated on this thought by comparing village cultures in what I call "subsistence" vs. "sufficiency" environments. My generalization is that behaviors associated with Edward Banfield's "amoral familism" and Oscar Lewis's "image of the limited good" are found in cultures where no one is far from the possibility of starvation. In cultures where subsistence can be taken for granted and with loose social structures (the anthropologist's phrase for substantial personal freedom), generosity and community cooperation are taken for granted.

neighbor? Under what conditions does a sick person go untended? Under what conditions do adults not keep a benevolent watch over children playing nearby? Everybody doesn't always behave in helpful ways, true, but how is it that an average collection of human beings there is not a sufficient quantity of such responses? In short, how is it that we have managed in recent decades to *prevent* vital little platoons called "communities" from forming?

Allow me to anticipate here one big question that my own questions will have raised: What about the inner cities? Hasn't recent history demonstrated that poor urban neighborhoods in America are too alienating and impersonal to permit community, that in places where people are so poor and victimized by discrimination, human affiliations of the type I have described break down? I am not so pessimistic, and can call upon considerable historical evidence in support (urban ethnic communities, including black urban communities, being the main source). Still, it is fair to say that under such circumstances affiliations are more difficult to sustain and more vulnerable to disruption—especially including disruption by government policy. Let me suggest two responses. First, to argue that such neighborhoods are lacking in community at this moment in history is not to prove that community is an irrelevant issue, or that anything else can take its place. The second response is that something less than 4 percent of Americans live in those most battered neighborhoods. If it should be decided (over my objections) that some different system is needed for that 4 percent, so be it. But as we try to develop a social policy that enables people to pursue satisfying lives, it must be a system that first of all works for 96 percent, then deals with the other 4 percent—not the other way around.

THE TENDRILS OF COMMUNITY

Now, to repeat the question: Why, in a nation with the wealth of the United States, would there not be enough people to attend naturally and fully to the functions of community that I have been describing?

The answer I am proposing is indicated by the image in the title, "tendrils" of community. To occur in the first place, then to develop, certain kinds of affiliations must have something to attach themselves to. Communities exist because they have a reason to exist, some core of functions around which the affiliations that constitute a vital community can form and grow. When the government takes away a core function, it depletes not only the source of vitality pertaining to that particular function, but also the vitality of a much larger family of responses. By hiring professional social workers to care for those most in need, it cuts off nourishment to secondary and tertiary behaviors that have nothing to do with formal social work. An illustration: In the logic of the social engineer, there is no causal connection between such apparently disparate events as (1) the establishment of a welfare bureaucracy and (2) the reduced likelihood (after a passage of some years) that, when someone dies, a neighbor will prepare a casserole for the bereaved family's dinner. In the logic I am using, there *is* a causal connection, and one of great importance.

I am arguing ultimately from two premises. One is again straight from Aristotle, that the practice of a virtue has the characteristics of a habit and of a skill. People may be born with the capacity of being generous, but become generous only by practicing generosity. People have the capacity for honesty, but become honest only by practicing honesty. The second, for which I do not have a specific source, is the human response to which I have referred several times: People tend not to do a chore when someone else will do it for them. At the micro-level, the dialogue between the government and the citizen goes roughly like this:

"Do you want to go out and feed the hungry or are you going to sit here and watch television?"
"I'm tired. What'll happen if I don't go?"
"Well, if you don't go I guess I'll just have to do it myself."
"In that case, you go."

It shows up in the aggregate as well. In the normal course of events, the personal income that people and corporations contribute to philanthropies "ought" to increase not only in raw dollar amounts, but as a proportion of income, as wealth itself increases: If I can afford to give away 5 percent of my income when I make $10,000, then (ceteris paribus, as always) when I make $11,000 I can afford to give away a higher percentage and still have more money for my personal use than I had before. From the beginning of the 1940s through 1964, this expectation held true: the richer the United States got, the greater the proportion of its wealth that was given to philanthropy. Then, suddenly, sometime during 1964–65, in the middle of an economic boom, this consistent trend was reversed. The proportion of wealth being given away began to fall even though wealth continued to increase. This new and disturbing trend continued through the rest of the 1960s, throughout the 1970s, and then suddenly reversed itself again in 1981 (during a period of hard times), when a new administration came to office that once more seemed to be saying "If you don't do it, nobody will." The following graph shows this intriguing history from 1950 through 1985.

A Coincidence of Policy Rhetoric and Private Philanthropy . . .

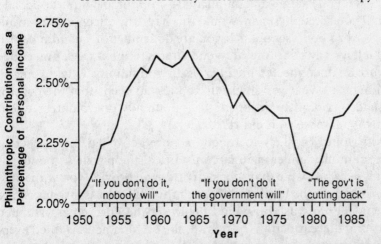

SOURCES: Bureau of the Census, *Historical Statistics of the United States* (Washington, D.C.: Government Printing Office, 1975), Series F297–348 (for personal income), Series 398–411 (for philanthropic contributions), and Bureau of the Census, *Statistical Abstract of the United States 1987* (Washington, D.C.: Government Printing Office, 1987), table 713 and comparables in other volumes (for personal income), table 630 and comparables (for philanthropic contributions).

I use the graph to illustrate, not as proof. But the causal relationship—government spending crowds out private philanthropy—has been demonstrated in a number of technical analyses.* The causal

---

*The displacement effect is both exaggerated and understated by the illustrative case shown in the figure. It is exaggerated in that comparatively little philanthropy during the period shown in the graph (1950–85) went to services for poor people—the trend line reflects changes in a more generalized "propensity to contribute income to public causes." It is understated in that the technical analyses demonstrate dramatically how efficiently government funding for the poor drives out private money: Whatever money is contributed is shifted from the poor to other causes. In other words, it is not just that people stopped increasing the proportion of income given to philanthropy, much more of the money they *did* give would have gone to helping the poor in the absence of governmental action.

explanation needn't be much more complicated than the private dialogue ("What'll happen if I don't do it?") played out on a national
scale.*

It seems to be inevitable. If the message is that if people don't do
these things themselves then the state will hire people to do these
things for them, that knowledge affects behavior. You may once again
use yourself as a source of evidence.† Suppose, for example, that tomorrow you were told that every bit of government assistance to poor
people—federal, state, and municipal—in your neighborhood had
ended. If you are a physician, would this have any effect on your availability for pro bono services? If you are a member of a church board,
would it have any effect on the agenda items for next week's meeting?
If you are an unconnected member of the community, would you give
any thought to what you might do to pick up needs that the government had so callously dropped? If you already do volunteer work,
would you increase your efforts?

If you would be likely to function more actively as a member of
your community under such circumstances, the puzzle to ponder is
this: It is very probable that such activities will provide you with satisfactions. You can be fairly confident of this—so why is it that you are
not behaving *now* as you would behave if the government stopped
performing these functions? After all, the evening news is filled every
night with stories of people who have fallen between the cracks of the
existing social service system. Why not go out and take for yourself
these satisfactions in the same full measure that you would take them
if the government were no longer involved?

The correct answer is that "It just wouldn't be the same." If a child
in the neighborhood will not be fed unless the neighborhood church
feeds it, the church will feed that child. But if the church is merely a

*For those who are curious how much more money would be donated today if the trend of the
1950s had continued: If the relationship between real personal income and percentage given
away had persisted, we would in 1985 have been donating 5.1 percent of personal income, or
$88.2 billion dollars more than we actually donated. To get an idea of the comparative size of
such numbers, the cost of the entire federal "public aid" effort in 1985—comprising AFDC,
Medicaid, social services, Supplemental Security Income, training programs, low-income energy assistance, surplus food for the needy, work-experience programs, refugee assistance, and
a miscellany of other programs—came to $60 billion. The point is not a specific prediction, but
a general statement. There is a whole lot of money that private individuals can, do, and would
donate to public uses, depending on what the reality test tells them about who else will do what
if they watch TV instead.
† At the extremes are people who will be involved in community activities no matter what and
misanthropes who will never be involved. I am referring to a wide middle range of people who
can tip in either direction depending on circumstances.

distribution point, if it is simply a choice of whether the church feeds the child or a Generous Outside Agency does it, the urgency is gone, and so is some of the response by the church members. And so is some of the vitality of that church.

Recall the formulation: Satisfactions are a product of responsibility, effort, and function. When the Generous Outside Agency has the action, the reality is that your level of responsibility is small and nebulous. Thus voluntary agencies are faced with the problem of either finding something to do that does not have a government program competing with it, or of convincing prospective volunteers that they are doing something that is falling between the cracks. As government responsibilities expand, each of these cases becomes harder to make persuasively. Why donate $500 of your money (which represents a lot, to you) to a local agency when there is a bureaucracy in your city spending $20 million on the same function? Why give up an evening a week, when you're working a full day at your job, to do something for which the city has a full-time paid staff of several hundred people? If the job's not getting done, make them do what they're being paid to do.

None of this is meant to ignore the voluntary and philanthropic programs that exist; rather, I am suggesting that what we observe is the tip of what would exist otherwise, the behavior of a comparative few who are highly motivated. Nor am I at this particular moment making a case for the best way to feed hungry children. The welfare of the fed child is not the issue here; the issue is the vitality of the church as a community institution.* The church will be a satisfying institution of community life (not just religious life) to the extent that the members have something important to do; that institutional role will atrophy to the extent that it does not. Similarly for schools, clubs,

---

*Another approach to such issues was developed by a research project at the American Enterprise Institute initiated by Peter L. Berger and Richard John Neuhaus. They explored the uses of what they termed "mediating structures," defined as "those institutions standing between the individual in his private life and the large institutions of public life"—local churches, for example. Their arguments anticipate many of the points made here, with the more sanguine conclusion that large-scale federal assistance can continue if channeled through the mediating structures. I am not optimistic because of what happens when the GOA provides the hundred parents with more money to pay teachers. It is quite possible that the use of mediating structures would result in more efficient and effective delivery of services than now exists, which is not a trivial benefit. But it is in my view unlikely that the benefits that I am most concerned with in this chapter will occur. It is not possible to get the benefits of a vital community on the cheap; the price *must* be authentic reliance on the community to do its job, because it is only authentic responsibility that will energize the response. Nonetheless, mediating structures is an intriguing concept that has gotten far too little attention from policy planners.

chambers of commerce, and any other local institution. They have to have something to do, and their responsibility has to be real.

So I am proposing that there is nothing mysterious about why people become atomized in modern urban settings. Individuals are drawn to community affiliations and attach themselves to them in direct proportion to the functional value of those organizations. As people attach themselves to individual community institutions the aggregate intangible called "community" itself takes on a life and values that are greater than the sum of the parts. Take away the functions, and you take away the community. The cause of the problem is not a virus associated with modernity, it is a centralization of functions that shouldn't be centralized, and this is very much a matter of political choice, not ineluctable forces.

IS ANYTHING BROKEN THAT NEEDS FIXING?

Even with the question put in those terms, one could ask, So what? Let us imagine an antagonist who has read faithfully to this point, and says:

"It is still not clear to me that we need any major reforms. I, for one, have a career that I enjoy. It both challenges me and interests me—it gives me a chance to 'exercise my realized capacities' just as the Aristotelian Principle prescribes. [Or: I do not have such a career, but nothing in social policy is preventing me from trying to find one.] I am deeply engaged in trying to be a good husband and father. [Or: I don't have a good marriage, or I have no marriage, but again, that's not the fault of social policy.] All the enabling conditions have been met for me—material resources, safety, self-respect, intrinsic rewards, friendships and intimate relationships with a few selected people.

"For me, there is nothing broken that needs fixing. I am, at this moment, under this system, living in very nearly the best of all possible worlds. Whatever the 'stopping point' for government must be, the government has so far not infringed upon it. On the contrary, I am quite busy enough already, and I prefer *not* to have to worry about all the things that contemporary social policy so conveniently takes care of for me. I want the poor and disadvantaged to be looked after and I am glad to pay taxes so that someone else will see that such things get done. It is precisely to escape from the demands of the old-fashioned community that I have moved to a housing division zoned in two-acre lots.

"The choice of a 'stopping point' is not such a difficult thing. It is to be solved pragmatically on the basis of costs and effectiveness. We are a rich enough country that we can make everybody comfortable and then let them pursue happiness as they see fit. If providing benefits to the less fortunate reaches a point that the work disincentives impair the nation's economy, then we should retrench. And costs must be kept within bounds. But these are practical economic calculations. As of now, I'm doing fine, the poor and disadvantaged don't seem to be complaining that they've got too many benefits, so what's the problem?"

In thinking about the position of this imaginary antagonist, I shift between two different responses, with different valences and implications. The first is to assume that he is right: He is living in the best of all possible worlds, for him. But such a world is not best for everyone, because of what I will call the problem of the upside-down pyramid. My second response is to argue that he is wrong. He doesn't know what he is missing. I will take up each response in turn.

THE PURSUIT OF HAPPINESS AND THE PROBLEM OF THE UPSIDE-DOWN PYRAMID

Privilege, like poverty, is often first imagined in terms of money. The distribution of the population in terms of privilege is symbolically imagined as a pyramid with a broad base of ordinary folk at the bottom and then successively narrow strata of more privileged people at the higher levels rising to a narrow peak at the top peopled by Rockefellers and Mellons.

But it takes only a little thought to realize how little money has to do with leading a privileged life, just as income has only a little to do with living an impoverished life. Money buys access to things and possibilities but not to the capacity to enjoy them. In that sense, the privileged are not those with the most money but those with other gifts—natural abilities, curiosity and interests, realized through education—and enough money (which is not necessarily a lot) to exercise them.

Conceived in this way, the most privileged people are those with the largest number of options for finding satisfying ways of filling up the hours of their lives. The more privileged you are, the more options you have for pursuing happiness. In terms of the Aristotelian Principle ("Other things equal, human beings enjoy the exercise of their realized capacities . . . and this enjoyment increases the more the capacity is realized, or the greater its complexity"), you have both more capacities to choose from and higher levels of complexity within your reach.

You also have latitude for "wastage." It is possible that you would have found great satisfaction in becoming an engineer, but no matter. You fell in love with biology in college and ended up being a biologist, in which you also find great satisfaction. And if it hadn't been engineering or biology, it could have been one of the many other satisfying vocations that your level of cognitive skills would have permitted you to follow.

Now, suppose that you have no gifts. You are not particularly smart, nor especially well-coordinated, nor musical. You are not beautiful or witty or charismatic. How, in the best of all possible worlds, will it come to pass that you reach the end of your life happy? It is not a rhetorical question. I begin from the assumption that in a good society, *everyone* may pursue happiness, not just the smart or the rich or the gifted. But the pyramid of options for achieving happiness narrows rapidly as gifts narrow, and the people at the bottom of the socioeconomic ladder are often not only the poorest people and the least educated, but also those with the fewest *options* for achieving happiness. Whence the upside-down pyramid.*

This logic admits of an ideological objection. We may decide that there is no such thing as the individual without special gifts; all that is required is a social system that liberates them. A revolution succeeded in Russia on just such expectations—in the best of all possible Soviet worlds "the average human type will rise to the heights of an Aristotle, a Goethe, or a Marx," as Leon Trotsky told us.

Against that, I propose this formulation: Yes, there are hidden resources in just about everyone, resources that can make just about everyone a self-determining, self-respecting, competent human being. But the medians in the many assets which humans possess are going

---

*I had better say explicitly what should be obvious: The socioeconomic relationship is a statistical tendency. Money and social status have very little inherent causal role. There are plenty of people high on the economic ladder who watch TV all day, plenty of people with less money who pursue varied and complex interests. Usually, however, people with greater gifts do better economically.

to remain about where they are now. And now and forevermore, half of the human race will at any moment be below the median on any given measure. Only a comparatively few will ever have any one asset that is so far above average that they can compete for the peaks in any field, whether the peak is defined as Nobel Laureate or California's top Chevrolet salesman. A system founded on the assumption that the only successful lives are the visibly brilliant ones is bound to define the bulk of the population as unsuccessful. Or to remain within the vocabulary of the pursuit of happiness, very large proportions of the population are not going to be achieving happiness by "the exercise of their realized capacities" in the sense that they excel in some specific vocational (or avocational) skill.

So how are we to construct society so that anyone, no matter what his gifts, can reach the age of seventy, look back on his life, and be able to say it has been a happy life, filled with deep and justified satisfactions? The answer is that, no matter what his gifts, he will in a properly run society be able to say things such as,

"I was a good parent to my children,"
"I was a good neighbor,"
"I always pulled my own weight,"

and that he lived among people who respected those achievements.

These are excellent things to be able to say of a life. They are probably the best there are. The point of the upside-down pyramid is that, for many people, these are the *only* options. There is no possibility of having been famous to offset having been a poor parent, no consolation of an absorbing career to compensate for having had too few friends. We are forced to this question: If we assume a man of no special skills, under what circumstances will society enable him to achieve these goals? And the answer centers on one particular little platoon of immense importance, the immediate physical neighborhood in which he lives.

This is not a bad thing, but it is to some extent a *necessary* thing. Consider the situation of a man who works hard at a low-skill, low-responsibility job—he is a baggage handler, let's say. He is not a potential surgeon just needing a chance to reveal his potential, he is not a prospective supervisor. He is an ordinary working stiff, as millions are. Consider first the surgeon's situation, then compare it with the baggage handler's.

The surgeon's world of affiliations (as the lawyer's or businessman's) may consist of many little islands: old school friends, golfing friends, fishing friends, doctor friends; professional affiliations at the clinic and the hospital; memberships in clubs and fashionable charities; season tickets for whatever is locally chic. His world doesn't have to include all of these islands, but it may if he so wishes. He has options. One of the reasons the surgeon buys the house with the two-acre lot is to have a refuge, to get away from the demands of the geographic community.

The surgeon's wider world also offers him protections against onslaughts on his self-esteem. He can be a failure at home, he can be inactive in his geographic community, and still see himself as "measuring up" in terms of his contribution to society. And as far as the esteem of others is concerned, *of course* he is esteemed by society at large—that's a given.

For the baggage handler, the immediate geographic community is much more his entire world. The baggage handler's friends are likely to come from the neighborhood, not across town, from a bar down the street, not the country club five miles away. A night out is likely to be at a local movie theater, not the Civic Arts Center. Equally importantly, the baggage handler's sense of who he is, both his self-respect and self-esteem, are rooted much more deeply in the immediate neighborhood than are the self-esteem and self-respect of the surgeon. No underlings scurry to assist him. No patients tell him how wonderful he is. If he gets respect, it is primarily from his family and neighbors. If he is appreciated, it is primarily by his family and neighbors.

And where are his satisfactions to come from? What are going to be for him the activities serving important functions for which he has responsibility? He is not going to save a life or develop a new procedure for arterial bypass or "exercise his realized capacities" in any other way that depends on unusual personal assets. What remains to him, however, is the one resource that he *can* contribute and that *will* be highly valued, if the circumstances are right. He can be a good neighbor.

He can help feed the hungry—especially if his neighborhood is enough of a functioning community not to be overwhelmed with them. He can comfort the bereaved. He can be a source of support to people who are having a hard time, just as they can help him. And in these most important of all possible "things to take trouble over," he can do as well as anyone.

This point needs emphasis. Throughout the discussion of the upside-down pyramid, I have been in one sense relentlessly elitist. Some people have more options than others, the reason they have more options is that they have more "realized capacities," and this difference in options is not going to disappear no matter what social system is in place. It cannot disappear because the latent capacities themselves differ. People vary in such things as cognitive skills, interpersonal skills, small motor skills, ambition, industriousness, and the rest. With this view of the situation goes an acceptance of such conclusions as: If we give the baggage handler the same income as the surgeon, he will not then acquire the same satisfactions that the surgeon enjoys. Having adopted this elitist argument, there is another that I must make at least as forcefully: The socioeconomically advantaged people in my hierarchical view have *more* options, but not *better* ones for achieving happiness.

I am trying to focus attention on one aspect of the situation facing the baggage handler: If it is true that the little platoon constituting the immediate geographic neighborhood is extremely important to the lives of many people—probably most—and *if there are few other alternatives,* especially to those at the bottom of the socioeconomic pyramid—then it becomes extremely important to consider how a neighborhood becomes a functioning little platoon that provides such sources of satisfaction.

First, because affiliations are both the basis for living according to one's values and the building blocks of a vital little platoon, it *becomes extremely important to let the low-income person affiliate with people who think as he does.* No effort is required to get him to do so, if he is given the choice. When he rents an apartment, he will choose a neighborhood where people share his values over a neighborhood where they don't, *if* he is given the choice. No effort is required to get landlords to give preference to tenants like the baggage handler over someone with the same amount of money who is less respectable. If the choice is left undistorted, neighborhoods of low-income working people, sharing common values, will form. All that social policy has to do is make sure that it doesn't interfere.

Second, because the important satisfactions are so bound up with the functions of community, social policy must be designed to leave those functions in the community. Or to bring the question back to my antagonist who prefers to pay other people to take care of such things for him: I concede his right to set up a system in which *he* pays other people to do these things but that does not mean it is appropriate to run the whole country that way.

Having worked through that argument, however, it must also be acknowledged that my imaginary antagonist has an excellent response. He says:

"You are really playing Lady Bountiful in reverse. I am satisfied with my life the way it is, including an arrangement whereby the government has the responsibility for taking care of all sorts of human needs I don't want to have to worry about. You seem to be saying that such a system impedes others from pursuing happiness. If that's the case, why don't you go out and find some of these people at the bottom of your upside-down pyramid who agree with you? You will fail to come close to a majority. Most people on the lower levels of the pyramid don't want fewer benefits; they want more. They don't want government to leave their communities on their own; they want more things done for them. Ultimately, isn't the argument of the upside-down pyramid just another instance of trying to tell other people what's good for them?"

My answer is: Yes and no. If the country is to be run by a sequence of national legislative decisions in which a majority may pass any law it pleases, then yes. Put it to an up-and-down vote, and a majority of people given the chance to get something from the government will take that chance more often than not, and over time the result will be similar to the process we have witnessed in modern Western democracies—indeed, in every democracy everywhere, throughout history.

But on another level I am arguing for a world in which no one is at the mercy of strangers' opinions about how he should live, neither mine nor anyone else's. I am arguing for a system in which we stop making ad hoc judgments about what other people "really" need, and obliging those others to live by them. I am arguing that we must try to step outside the exigencies of day-to-day politics and lay down a way of running society that will protect us from ourselves, and from each other, in years to come. This is why any nation needs a constitution, and why I believe that we should return to a more literal implementation of ours.

Let me leave the problem of the upside-down pyramid at that, and proceed to my other reason for thinking that all is not well with the current state of affairs, even for the privileged person who perceives no need for the little platoon called community.

COMMUNITY AS THE THIRD DIMENSION IN TWO-DIMENSIONAL LIVES

The story so far is that my imaginary antagonist on his two-acre lot has asked to opt out of becoming involved in his community. If the government stops doing certain things, let us say that he will respond by contributing more than he does now, in money and perhaps in personal time and effort. But even conceding this, he argues that for him the world will have changed for the worse. He *wants* the government to take the trouble out of the community functions I have described, so he can concentrate on the other little platoons through which he pursues happiness—work, and family.

Now I argue that he is ignoring the reverberations that a vital community has for the things that he does value in his life. Even for those who want to pay people to do the work of the community for them, there are good reasons to want to be paying that money to people nearby, not to people far away. Let me take as an example the little platoon known as the family, and try to trace just a few of the paths that interconnect the satisfactions of family with the satisfactions obtained by leaving communities with something to do.

A Functioning Community and a Functioning Family

Marriage, like other affiliations, acquires content over time. On the wedding day the two people are already attracted to each other and they have aspirations for what the marriage will become, but the things that constitute a good marriage are in embryonic form. The clichés are once again true: Marriage and family become satisfying cumulatively through years of shared experiences. Mutual reliance, respect, and trust are essential. And so on.

The question then becomes, What shared experiences? Mutual reliance for what purposes? Mutual respect for what accomplishments? Mutual trust based on what? For a comparatively few people, the answer might be something like, "Our shared love of opera," or "Mutual respect based on our accomplishments in our respective careers"; but commonly the raw materials center on paying the mortgage, raising the children, and the things that happen in the immediate physical vicinity of the home and work.

Specifically, one extremely important source of mutual respect, reliance, and trust involves *the way that the married couple interact with the people around them*. To gain the respect of a virtuous spouse, one must act virtuously, and to practice the habit of virtue requires an environment in which one has opportunities. A functioning community—which is to say, a community with functions to fulfill—provides an extremely important venue for practicing virtue. It is a stage upon which the partners in a marriage may reveal themselves to each other. It also provides a marriage with the room it needs to flourish: Husbands and wives who are everything to each other are in peril of one day being not nearly enough. Yet if their "communities" are entirely separate ones, they are likely to be pulled apart.

The same dynamics impinge on another of the central functions of marriage, the "passing on" of values from parent to child. It is one of the most satisfying of the roles of parenthood. It happens both through the parents' example and by having available for the child an environment in which the child can develop the habits of virtue that the parents have taught. In both cases, the existence of a community is important, for the process of passing things on once again involves the reality test. Suppose, for example, that you want to pass on to your children the virtue of compassion. Under what circumstances will this be a heritage that can be passed on? How does one bequeath a habit of helping others, of giving, of generosity, if this has not been part of one's own life? Once again, the activities immediately surrounding the home—the functions of the community—provide raw material. It is not necessary that the parent be engaged in every possible community activity. On the contrary, most of what is involved in being a "good neighbor" as I am using the term does not involve organized activity at all. It seems necessary, however, that there be an environment in which the child observes these things happening, knows people who are engaged in them, and comes to understand the concept of social obligation by observing other people living according to that concept. Watching parents support compassionate politicians just isn't the same.

These comments apply as well to parents who prefer to pay other people to perform the functions of community. If such parents are engaged in directly paying other people *in the community*—supporting local institutions—they at least must do such things as choose whom they will pay and how much. And even these actions provide a richer basis for instruction than signing a 1040 Form and then trying to explain compassion to the child in the abstract.

A Functioning Community and the Single-Parent Family

The interconnections linking functioning communities with functioning families go far beyond these. Many are self-evident (functioning communities tend to have low crime and good schools, which makes it much easier to have functioning families, for example). I will end the discussion of the interconnections with a less obvious example involving the single woman without a job, without education, without the support of a male, and with children to raise. She is receiving assistance. How is that assistance to be given so that it gives the woman and her children alike their best chance to live satisfying lives?

One answer is: in whatever way gives her the best chance to become self-determining and self-respecting by becoming economically self-sufficient. But that does not happen naturally no matter how much material support is provided during the process. To move from dependence to precarious independence to secure independence is an intimidating and exhausting experience, and *there has to be a reason to do it.* Functioning communities can provide that reason, both in the form of encouragement, holding out to the woman the prospect of something-worth-having (full-fledged membership in a community she wants to be a part of), and in the form of prodding, holding up to the woman the reasons why failing to become self-sufficient is a drain on the community.* And when the assistance itself is being provided by people in the locality, the pressures on her to become a self-determining, self-respecting person are going to be much greater than if the money comes from a bureaucracy. This is the reason for observing earlier that the fed child will be better off if fed by the church instead of by a social service bureaucracy. The goal is not just to feed the family and keep them in shelter, but to provide that family with the enabling conditions for pursuing happiness, and the more short-term encouragement *and* pressure on them to become self-sufficient in the long term, the better for the family.

But in some ways the more provocative case involves the single woman with children who for some reason cannot be expected to become self-sufficient, or for whom it is especially difficult. There are many reasons why this might be the case, and it raises intriguing questions. How can she still "measure up" to community norms and

---

*Functioning communities are also effective in discouraging males from making single mothers out of single women in the first place.

thereby achieve self-respect? How does she pass on to her children, by her example, a good way to live in the world? The options are few and forced. One of the most obvious and best is that *she has herself been a contributor to the community,* by being a good neighbor in all the ways that she indeed can be, economically self-supporting or not, if she lives in a vital community. One of the important reasons for leaving the functions of a community in the community is that doing so increases the chances for the recipients of help to be givers of help as well. The same institutions that are providing the dependent with help have some things they will be asking in return, and through that lies a possibility for authentic self-respect. The only way to "take the stigma out of welfare" is to provide a means of paying it back.

Perhaps I have used too many formal social service examples of community (feeding the hungry) and not enough informal ones (taking a casserole to the bereaved family). I should emphasize, therefore, that I am not envisioning an ideal society in which everyone is a social worker, but one in which the full dimensions of being a neighbor are played out in full view of everyone, on the local stage. The motivation underlying the vision is not to construct a more efficient way of delivering social services, but to permit communities to be communities.

THE GAIN

A summing-up: The ways in which people pursue happiness are rooted in, processed through, and enhanced by little platoons. Little platoons are vital insofar as they consist of people voluntarily doing important things together. To enable people to pursue happiness, good social policy consists of leaving the important things in life for people to do for themselves, and protecting them from coercion by others as they go about their lives.

The policy principle may be started as simply as this: No one has to teach people how to pursue happiness. Unless impeded, people form communities that allow them to get the most satisfaction from the material resources they have. Unless impeded, they enforce norms of safety that they find adequate. Unless impeded, they develop norms of self-respect that are satisfying and realistic for the members of that community. Unless impeded, people engage in activities that they find to be intrinsically rewarding, and they know (without being taught) how to invest uninteresting activities with intrinsic rewards.

The behaviors that lead to these happy results do not have to be prompted by or mandated for anyone, neither for people with wealth and education nor for people with little money and little education. Does everyone always act in every way to achieve these positive results? No. My assertion rather is that these behaviors reach a maximum on their own. Unless impeded, people continually make small, incremental changes in their lives that facilitate their pursuit of happiness, and the mechanism whereby they accomplish this is voluntary affiliations with other people. To encourage, nourish, and protect vital little platoons, the government's main task is to make sure that no one interferes with people coming together in these voluntary acts of mutual benefit.

But aren't my fears after all more theoretical than real? Aren't we muddling through, most of us, reasonably well? What, finally, is to be gained?

My sense of the present state of affairs is captured by one of Adam Smith's thought experiments in *The Theory of Moral Sentiments,* and it provides a fitting conclusion to this discussion. In this passage, Smith begins by asking his readers to "suppose that the great empire of China, with all its myriads of inhabitants, was suddenly swallowed up by an earthquake." How would a humane man in Europe be affected upon hearing the dreadful news? Smith sketches the predictable reactions. This humane gentleman would express his great sorrow. He would reflect upon the precariousness of life. He might then speculate upon the economic effects this catastrophe would have on the rest of the world. And then he would go about his business "with the same ease and tranquility as if no such accident had happened." This, Smith continues, is the understandable consequence of distance and disconnection, and he continues by discussing the very different response of the same man to people whose happiness he *does* affect. This is what Smith, the emblem of uncaring laissez-faire self-interest, has to say:

> When the happiness or misery of others depends in any respect upon our conduct, we dare not, as self-love might suggest to us, prefer the interest of one to that of many. The man within immediately calls to us, that we value ourselves too much and other people too little, and that, by doing so, we render ourselves the proper object of the contempt and indignation of our brethren.

Human nature has not changed since the eighteenth century. I am arguing that when we are disconnected from the elemental functions of community and "the happiness or misery of others" around us no longer depends in any meaningful way upon our conduct, we consign even our neighbors to a kind of China from which we become as detached as Smith's humane and otherwise compassionate gentleman. The loss this represents is not redeemed by satisfactions from career nor wholly compensated even by the satisfactions of family. No matter how much satisfaction we may derive from work and family, they are only two dimensions of life in a three-dimensional world.

The Original-Intent
Controversy

It seems almost quaint to read Alexander Hamilton's assurances (in the Federalist) *that of the "departments of power" the judiciary "will always be the least dangerous to the political rights of the Constitution." So prescience wasn't one of his gifts.*

Political judging—using black robes to make laws—is a very bad idea, and yet the Left has embraced it. Well, you think, doesn't he expect the Left to have just such bad ideas? Sure, but not to the point of suicide. Because if the law is simply to be what courts say it is today, and today the judges are liberals, that's fine. But what about tomorrow, when all the judges are reactionary?

Russell Kirk here makes the case for restraint among judges.

NO MATTER HOW PLAINLY AND LUCIDLY WRITTEN, any statute—let alone any constitution—requires interpretation by judges. It is presumed that judges must govern themselves, in interpreting, by the intentions of the framers of constitution or statute: for judges are not supposed to exercise legislative or executive functions.

Such concerns arose during the Reagan administration: the attorney-general of the United States expounding the doctrine of "original intent," one elderly justice of the Supreme Court declaring in public that the Constitution is whatever the Supreme Court wishes to make it. Hot disputes of this sort have occurred ever since the clash between

Federalists and Republicans in the first decade of the Republic. In this "original intent" debate there arises the question, "Is the Constitution an instrument for preservation, or an instrument for change?"

So in this chapter I discuss first the necessity for a doctrine of original intent; second, the difficulties of ascertaining such intent; third, I presume to examine the intellectual means which were employed in the past for interpreting the Constitution in the light of original intentions. And finally, I shall touch upon the alternatives to conformity to original intent.

The least controversial portion of the proposed new Constitution, in 1788, was Article III, concerning chiefly the federal judiciary. Who could obdurately oppose the establishment of federal courts, even though such had not existed under the Articles of Confederation? Obviously any effective general government must have judges to apply its laws. Few at the state ratifying conventions, or in the first Congress under the Constitution, could have fancied how powerful those federal judges might become two centuries later.

Certain Anti-Federalists, nevertheless, objected that federal courts might overshadow or overrule state courts, and that federal judges might impede the federal legislative branch, the Congress. Alexander Hamilton replied to these doubting Thomases in *The Federalist*. In Number LXXXI he declared, perhaps somewhat disingenuously, that never, under Article III, could citizens have recourse to federal courts for suing a state for debts—a point I will take up later. As for judicial usurping of power, Hamilton endeavored to refute that notion in more than one number of *The Federalist*.

"Whoever attentively considers the different departments of power must perceive, that, in a government in which they are separated from each other, the judiciary, from the nature of its functions, will always be the least dangerous to the political rights of the Constitution; because it will be least in a capacity to annoy or injure them . . ."So Hamilton wrote in Number LXXXVII. "The judiciary . . . has no influence over either the sword or the purse; no direction either of the strength or of the wealth of the society; and can take no active resolution whatever. It may truly be said to have neither *force* nor *will*, but merely judgment; and must ultimately depend upon the aid of the executive arm even for the efficacy of its judgments."

As for interpretation of the Constitution—well, the Federalists argued, how could judges ignore the plain details of a written constitution? It would be Congress and the state legislatures that would make the laws; the judges of the federal system would be restricted to applying the statutes passed by the Congress.

Presently I will return to this argument. Just now I remark that in 1787 and 1788 no political faction denied that a constitution must possess ascertainable original intentions: for a constitution is the fundamental law of a land. (In no country are the *decisions* and *rulings* of courts of law themselves the fundamental law of the land; rather, they are interpretations and applications of the law.) Clearly the Articles of Confederation had been intended for certain specified purposes, and had been interpreted literally. A principal purpose of the Constitutional Convention in 1787 was to define and clarify the purposes, the intentions, of the Union of the thirteen original states. Madison, Hamilton, and Jay published *The Federalist Papers* as a systematic explanation and definition of the original intent of the Framers at Philadelphia.

Yet nowadays, as I wander over the face of the land talking about the Constitution, sometimes a professor or a lawyer inquires of me, "Why need the United States be bound by this 'original intent' of the Framers? Why aren't we free to choose today—to make the Constitution mean whatever we think it should mean?"

To people unfamiliar with the concept of political and historical continuity, it may not be easy to explain the necessity for a *permanent* fundamental law—susceptible of change, indeed, but enduring in essence. A country's constitution is a pattern for the maintenance of order in a society. In the case of the Constitution of the United States, it is a written compact, a formal agreement among the people of the United States to "form a more perfect Union, establish Justice, insure domestic Tranquillity, provide for the common defence, promote the general Welfare, and secure the Blessings of Liberty to ourselves and our Posterity." It is a binding social compact—not the fanciful contract or compact of Locke or Rousseau, derived from a human "state of nature" which never did exist; no, a practical, realistic instrument of government resulting from genuine consensus. (It is perfectly true, of course, as Max Farrand and others have remarked, that the Constitution is a bundle of compromises; that is how the Framers achieved consensus.)

In other words, the Constitution is a solemn agreement on a national scale as to how the American people shall live together in peace.

The purpose of law is to keep the peace, we cannot too often remind ourselves. If this solemn pact that we call the Constitution should come to be regarded as a mere formula of words, to be set aside for present seeming convenience whenever a temporary majority or strong-willed minority may choose—why, the peace soon would be breached. For in such circumstances, the terms of the pact called the Constitution would fall null and void; the fundamental law would crumble for lack of an enduring consensus; and every faction or interest would feel free, or perhaps obliged, to pursue its own objects in disregard of the general public interest. That condition of society is called anarchy.

People assume that there exists a fundamental body of law in the United States which does not change very much from year to year, and by which they are protected. If they cease so to assume, every man's hand is against every other man's, and habitual obedience to the rule of law ceases. Then we can be kept from one another's possessions and one another's throats only by force. Yet as Talleyrand instructs us, "You can do everything with bayonets—except sit upon them." If a generally-accepted basic law, a constitution, dissolves in confusion, even an arbitrary master with troops at his disposal cannot long maintain order.

The American people believe that some original intent may be found within the seven Articles of the original Constitution and the amendments of the Bill of Rights. They are right in so believing; for without such a web of intentions, the public is at the mercy of the whims of the hour's dominant faction of politicians, intellectuals, or ideologues.

Men and women in a tolerable society ought to be able to feel confident that the body of rules which we call the law will be much the same tomorrow as it was yesterday. It becomes difficult to obey the law if the law is changed greatly from time to time, and changed almost unpredictably. People like to live by rules; to have the assurance that if they behave conformably to certain rules called the law, mischief will not be done to them. Permanence and continuity in the law are virtually essential to a society's material success. Take commercial contracts: if the laws concerning such contracts vary swiftly and unpredictably under various changes of political regime, commerce will dwindle and much of a population may be impoverished. (The Framers, in 1787, were especially concerned for the enforcement of contracts.) If this need for constancy and enduring precedent is of very high importance in all laws, it is of supreme importance in basic constitutions. Men and women give implicit assent to living by a nation's constitution because they take it for granted that they live under a basic body of law that makes possible certain agreed-upon intentions of general benefit.

That is the case for recognizing and respecting, so far as possible, the original intent of the Framers of the Constitution.

Yet it is no easy business to ascertain precisely the intentions of the Framers in this or that particular. Large differences of opinion existed among factions and individual delegates at the Constitutional Convention; these were bridged over by large and small compromises; but the language of the compromises sometimes remains ambiguous and perhaps sometimes intentionally so, lest awkward inquiries be raised at state ratifying conventions.

Does the power to coin money, conferred upon the Congress in Article I, Section 7, include the power to print paper money? Does the power to "establish Post Offices and post Roads" imply the power to construct turnpikes and canals at the general expense—or, later, to subsidize railroads and then airlines? What are the limits, if any, to the authorization "To make all Laws which shall be necessary and proper for carrying into Execution the foregoing Powers"?

In Article II, the President is empowered to "require the Opinion, in writing, of the principal Officer in each of the executive Departments, upon any Subject relating to the Duties of their respective Offices . . ." Has he no greater authority over members of the cabinet than this? Has the President power to undertake military actions short of a declaration of war? No such power is specified in Article II.

As for Article III, concerning the judicial power, what is meant, for instance, by its granting to federal courts appellate jurisdiction in actions "between a State and Citizens of another State"? (I will comment presently on that provision.) What about judicial review of acts of the Congress or of actions by the Executive? Such powers of the judiciary are not specified.

In other instances as well, the original intent of the Constitution is not crystal clear. What, for example, is comprehended in the term "general welfare"? It does not follow that the original intent is quite impossible to ascertain; but search must be undertaken, and differences of opinion are conceivable.

Some light may be obtained through study of Madison's and Yates' notes on the Convention's proceedings, and other fragmentary accounts by delegates. The *Federalist Papers* are a principal source of information about intent—although in part those newspaper articles were special pleading. The correspondence of the men who were Convention delegates provides some clues. Story's and Kent's respective commentaries on the Constitution are of great value here; more of them later. It may be said that in general the intentions of the Framers may be ascertained by study; but that some points always have been in dispute.

Also considerable latitude as to original intent must be indulged when courts endeavor to apply provisions of the Constitution to cases that involve circumstances very different from the circumstances of 1787. For the United States do not stand still, and occasionally *stare decisis* must give ground to accommodate technological change. Consider the power of Congress "to regulate Commerce . . . among the several States," which eventually produced the multitudinous activities of the Interstate Commerce Commission. Did the Framers intend to establish the present jurisdiction of that body? I offer you a simple illustration of how powers are expanded.

On a warm day late in August, 1787, many members of the Constitutional Convention went down to the banks of the Delaware River to observe the demonstration of John Fitch's new contraption, an oared boat propelled by steam. (The Convention had recessed that day so that a committee might discuss proposals to empower Congress to pass navigation acts.) Edmund Randolph, governor of Virginia, and Dr. William Samuel Johnson, the learned delegate from Connecticut, were among the spectators; both gave to Fitch certificates attesting his experiment's success. It is doubtful whether Randolph, or Johnson, or any other delegate present on the banks of the Delaware, then foresaw that steamboats would become the subject of an action at law which would greatly affect interpretations of the Constitution they were drawing up that August.

Yet by 1824, Chief Justice Marshall and his colleagues of the Supreme Court would be deliberating over *Gibbons* v. *Ogden,* the "Steamboat Case," concerning a monopoly granted to Livingstone and Fulton by New York's legislature for commercial navigation of the Hudson River by steamboats. In his opinion, John Marshall expounded the doctrine that the Constitution should be liberally construed, not confined to strict limits, as against a previous decision by Chancellor James Kent in the same litigation that the general government's powers, originating with the sovereign states, ought to be hedged. Marshall's doctrine has prevailed. Incidentally, in this case Marshall ruled that Congress' power extended to vessels propelled by steam as well as to those propelled by wind—even though no practicable commercial steamboats had existed when the Constitution was drawn up.

In such concerns, as the complexity of American life increased, not only the judicial branch, but the legislative and the executive branches of government, would find it necessary or convenient to resort to the doctrines of implied powers and liberal construction. Some extensions of federal jurisdiction or activity seemed extravagant and pernicious to many people in the first half of the nineteenth century; other such enlargements have seemed yet more baneful to many citizens in the closing half of the twentieth century. As a specimen of protest against liberal construction of the Constitution, take a passage from the long speech of Representative John Randolph of Roanoke in the House of Representatives, on January 31, 1824—only a few days before *Gibbons* v. *Ogden* was taken up by the Supreme Court.

The Framers of the Constitution had intended to grant Congress only a minimum power over the economy, Randolph declared; indeed, if when submitted for ratification the Constitution had included a specific provision for laying a duty of ten per cent *ad valorem* on imports, the Constitution never would have been adopted. Here are Randolph's sardonic words.

"But, sir, it is said . . . we have a right to regulate commerce between the several states, and it is argued that 'to regulate' commerce is to prescribe the way in which it shall be carried on—which gives, by a *liberal* construction, the power to *construct* the way, that is, the roads and canals on which it is to be carried: Sir, since the days of that unfortunate man, of the German coast, whose name was originally Fyerstein, Anglicized to Firestone, but got, by translation, from that to Flint, from Flint to Pierre-a-Fusil, and from Pierre-a-Fusil to Peter Gun—never was greater violence done to the English language, than by the construction, that, under the power to prescribe the way in which commerce shall be carried on, we have the right to construct the way on which it is to be carried. Are gentlemen aware of the colossal power they are giving to the General Government? . . . Sir, there is no end to the purposes that may be effected under such constructions of power."

Too true, then and now. Yet it may be said that at least the centralizers of 1824, John Marshall among them, endeavored to produce a constitutional warrant for their decisions and policies, purportedly derived from some clause of the Constitution; while in 1987 at least one justice of the Supreme Court professed that he sees no need to justify any decison of the Supreme Court by reference to the text of the Constitution: any plausible decision, founded upon expediency or moral impulses, will serve perfectly well. As an earlier justice of the Supreme Court remarked informally, "The Constitution is what the judges say it is."

There remain today in the law schools, the courts, and the Congress no "strict constructionists," strictly defined. The defense of "original intent" is carried on in our time by the juristic heirs of Chief Justice Marshall and Justice Story, the early advocates on the Supreme Court of "liberal construction" of the Constitution. In certain academic departments of literature, in this bent world of ours, the school of thought styled "deconstructive criticism" prevails. On the Supreme Court, certain justices now represent what we may call the deconstructive school of jurisprudence. To their minds, what does "original intent" matter? Construe or deconstrue, as fits your ideology and prejudices—so we are advised by certain judges and certain professors of law.

One reason why the doctrine of original intent has fallen into disuse is that considerable historical knowledge and reading of dusty law commentaries are necessary if one tries to find what a particular provision or phrase of the Constitution signified to the Framers or (more difficult yet) to the delegates at the state ratifying conventions. I have mentioned already the provision in Article III, Section 2, that "The judicial Power shall extend to Controversies;—between a State and Citizens of another State . . ." On the face of this clause, surely it appears that the Constitution assigns to the Supreme Court an appellate jurisdiction over suits by citizens of one state against another state, "both as to Law and Fact, with such Exceptions, and under such Regulations as the Congress shall make." A literal reading of this provision of Article III would seem to guarantee that a state government might be sued, against its wish, by citizens of some other state.

And yet in truth it appears that this clause probably was not so understood by many of the fifty-five delegates to the Constitutional Convention; and certainly not so understood by the people who elected delegates to the state ratifying conventions, or by most of the delegates to those state conventions. The several states owed huge debts; their governors and legislatures had been insistent that they must not be sued for these debts, against their will, in federal courts. That federal courts might assume jurisdiction over such suits was one of the principal arguments against ratification of the Constitution, in several states, New York among them.

Thus Hamilton, eager to persuade citizens of New York to approve the Constitution, wrote in *The Federalist,* Number LXXXI, "It has been suggested that an assignment of the public securities of one State to the citizens of another, would enable them to prosecute that State in the federal courts for the amount of those securities; a suggestion which the following considerations prove to be without foundation." Hamilton went on to declare "that there is no color to pretend that the State governments would by the adoption of that plan, be divested of the privilege of paying their own debts in their own way, free from every constraint but that which flows from the obligations of good faith. The contracts between a nation and individuals are only binding on the conscience of the sovereign, and have no pretensions to a compulsive force.... To what purpose would it be to authorize suits against States for the debts they owe? How could recovery be enforced? It is evident, it could not be done without waging war against the contracting State; and to ascribe to the federal courts, by mere implication, and in destruction of a pre-existing right of the State governments, a power which would involve such a consequence, would be altogether forced and unwarrantable."

That passage from a high Federalist is clear denial of what the offending clause in Article III seems to imply. It appears to have been the understanding at the state ratifying conventions that states could not, under the new Constitution, be sued by citizens of other states.

This notwithstanding, in the case of *Chisholm* v. *Georgia* (1793), the Supreme Court ruled that the state of Georgia might be sued by a citizen of another state. The decision was written by Justice James Wilson, a centralizer and an advocate of democratic political theories, who in his opinion asserted vigorously that the American people formed a nation, transcending state boundaries.

Although this Supreme Court decision might pretend to be a literal interpretation of the pertinent provision in Article III of the Constitution, the ruling in *Chisholm* v. *Georgia* was received with fury in Georgia and with apprehension in other states. So when Congress convened, the Eleventh Amendment was passed by overwhelming majorities in both Senate and House, almost immediately, and speedily ratified in the several states. "The Judicial power of the United States shall not be construed to extend to any suit in law or equity, commenced or prosecuted against one of the United States by Citizens of another State, or by Citizens or Subjects of any Foreign State," the amendment read; and so it has stood unchallenged, to the present day.

I have digressed here to show how "literal interpretation" and "original intent" may not always coincide. Much knowledge is required for plumbing the well where original intent lies. Incidentally, constitutional amendment is one method, obviously, for overturning a Supreme Court decision believed to contravene the original intent of a constitutional provision; but ordinarily the amendment-process is an awkward tool, and only in this undoing of *Chisholm* v. *Georgia* has retribution been so swift.

I have said that the doctrine of original intent is necessary, but that often it becomes snared in difficulties. We turn now to the question of how provisions of the Constitution have been adapted to changed American circumstances, without abandoning the doctrine of original intent.

Change is the means of our preservation, Edmund Burke said— meaning that social institutions, like the human body, must experience change and renewal, or else perish. Responding to great social alterations, the law too must change—but gradually, with high regard for continuity, and not "unfixing old interests at once." Why cannot the executive or the legislative branch of a representative government work out necessary change by statute or executive order? Why, either can; but such abrupt changes on a grand scale may be too sudden and sweeping, or on the other hand may be effected too tardily. It seems preferable usually to permit judges to modify laws by degrees than to take the risk of damaging the whole frame and spirit of law by frequent legislative or executive intervention.

Therefore in every civilized society the judges have enjoyed some degree of latitude in administering and interpreting the laws of the land. Just how far judges rightfully may go in changing the organic law through reinterpretation—why, that has become a much-debated question nowadays, in Britain as in the United States. In America, judges have been given a larger share in power than in any other country, ever. A good many people now accuse them of judicial usurpation.

Judges' thirst for power seemed highly improbable in 1787–88: Alexander Hamilton, James Madison, James Monroe, and other gentlemen politicians remarked the feebleness of the judicial branch, assuring the public that judges never could be a menace to the separation of powers or to public liberties. Yet only fifteen years after the Constitution's ratification, the executive and legislative branches of the American government were at war with the judicial branch, which had begun to assert its independent authority most forcefully. President Jefferson privately urged the House of Representatives, dominated then by Democratic Republicans, to impeach the Federalist Justice Samuel Chase (formerly a radical); John Randolph, leader of the House, passionately did so, winning a large majority for impeachment. But Chase was acquitted in 1805, on his trial by the Senate. Never since then has a justice of the Supreme Court been impeached, although during President Lyndon Johnson's administration Justice Abe Fortas resigned from the Court, rather than face probable impeachment.

The Framers, in 1787, had created a very powerful Supreme Court. It appears probable that most of the delegates at the Great Convention expected the Court to be able to rule in some fashion on the constitutionality of federal or state statutes. Beginning about 1801, the Supreme Court would assert successfully its power to decide whether or not an act of Congress should conform to the Constitution of the United States. President Jefferson, infuriated at this, hoped at the time of the trial of Aaron Burr for treason that he might succeed in having Chief Justice Marshall impeached and convicted of failing to maintain "good Behaviour"—for Article III of the Constitution permits impeachment of a judge on grounds far less serious than the "Treason, Bribery, or other high Crimes and Misdemeanors" required for the impeachment of President, Vice President, and all civil Officers of the United States. But Marshall, a shrewd and humorous man, foiled the President in this.

Until the second administration of Jefferson, it had been thought by many leading Americans that the power of impeachment might serve to confine federal judges to the limits of "original intent." Alexander Hamilton, in Number LXXXI of the *Federalist Papers,* had assured New Yorkers that the judiciary could not conceivably usurp any powers, a principle "greatly fortified by the consideration of the important constitutional check which the power of instituting impeachments in one part of the legislative body, and of determining upon them in the other, would give to that body [the legislature] upon the members of the judicial department. This is alone a complete security."

But this fancied "complete security" was undone by the boldness and strength of mind of Chief Justice John Marshall, who was convinced that the Constitution conveyed to the Supreme Court the implied power of judicial review of legislation and of executive orders. Mr. Justice Marshall had his own concept of original intent; he had known many of the Framers, and was the biographer of George Washington, who had been the Constitutional Convention's presiding officer. A Supreme Court dominated by Federalists interpreted the Constitution throughout the control of the Executive Force by the Virginia Dynasty of Democratic Republicans.

Liberal construction of the Constitution during those years, however, and for long thereafter, did not signify repudiation of the doctrine of original intent. After the death of Chief Justice Marshall, after the death of his learned colleague Justice Joseph Story, still the Supreme Court adhered, by and large, to the concept that there could be discerned an original intent, in most matters, of the framers and the ratifiers of the Constitution.

How were those intentions to be known? At first, through the *Federalist Papers* and St. George Tucker's American edition of *Blackstone's Commentaries on the Laws of England;* somewhat later, through two learned works, Joseph Story's *Commentaries on the Constitution of the United States,* and James Kent's *Commentaries on American Law.* In both federal and state courts, throughout most of the nineteenth century, the analyses of Story and Kent of constitutional points were cited with high respect; and both writers on jurisprudence were studied in American law schools. The dispassionate writings of these two scholars in the law strongly affected interpretation of the Constitution for decade upon decade, imparting an attachment to the intentions of the Framers. Story's *Commentaries* were carefully edited and enlarged by Professor Thomas Cooley in

1873, and the revised version of Story went through various large printings, remaining a major influence in courts and law schools down to the early years of the twentieth century.

I lack space to touch upon the rise of the schools of jurisprudence known as legal positivism and legal realism, here in the United States. Gradually those innovating doctrines of law carried the day in American courts and law schools, despite stubborn resistance. Yet until half a century ago, the Supreme Court of the United States continued conservative in its decisions, for the most part; exercised judicial restraint; and (whatever the eccentricity of some decisions) did not advance the theory that the Court is entitled to do as it likes with the text of the Constitution—although Justice Holmes and some others broadly hinted at that notion.

The doctrine of original intent did not perish utterly when Story and Kent went out of fashion; and today there is being carried on a strong endeavor to restore an understanding of the Constitution in the light of what the Framers and their generation were trying to achieve. Perhaps the best argument in favor of such a restoration is the bleak prospect of what is liable to occur if recent tendencies of the federal judiciary are much prolonged.

If a reasonable attachment to the written text of the Constitution— which does not mean a blinkered literalism at all times—is not retained or restored as the standard for interpretation of the basic law of the United States, we will be left with a most unpromising alternative.

That alternative mode would be the domination of American public policy, and much of American private life, by the impulses, prejudices, and ideological dogmata of the nine justices of the Supreme Court. Those justices having received no systematic preparation for serving as a kind of oligarchy or council of ephors, they would make many blunders, some disastrous. They have made a good many grave blunders already, over the past forty years and more. Their power to do mischief would become almost infinite; their ability to rule prudently would be improbable. In any event, such a scheme would abolish the American democracy and enfeeble both Congress and the presidency—if the justices were permitted to perpetuate their assumption of haughty authority, power that courts of law never were intended to exercise.

But presumably the Supreme Court would not be permitted to continue in this usurping of power. The Congress and the Executive Force, if pushed to the wall, have means for repelling this juridicial insolence.

The executive branch, given a strong-willed president, could undo the Supreme Court simply by refusing to enforce its writs: extreme medicine, that, but it has been swallowed down as a bitter dose in other countries and times, for good or ill.

The Congress could much curb and chasten the Supreme Court, did it decide to do so, in two ways: first, by greatly reducing the categories of cases over which the Supreme Court exercises appellate jurisdiction, as is authorized in Article III of the Constitution. (Senator Sam Ervin, of North Carolina, a considerable constitutional authority, urged Congress to do just this with respect to compulsory "busing" of school pupils.) Such contraction of appellate jurisdiction, in effect leaving whole classes of actions at law within the jurisdiction of state courts only, or at least outside the sphere of federal courts, has happened before in the history of American law.

Second, the Congress could resort to its power of impeaching justices, whose tenure of office depends on "good behavior." Deliberately ignoring constitutional texts and confessedly substituting one's own juridical notions is not good behavior in a justice of the Supreme Court; it might be called subversive of the spirit of laws.

It would be a melancholy day if either of these remedies had to be applied: for it would mean some interruption of the usual rule of law, or at least of accustomed processes. But if the Court should be thoroughly dominated by a majority of justices who might not think themselves confined in the least by respect for the terms of the Constitution itself—why, for every action there is an equal and opposite reaction.

The temper of public opinion nowadays will not abide much more eccentricity or perversity of Supreme Court decisions. The odder or more arbitrary those rulings become, the more swiftly does the public's respect for the federal judiciary decline. The Court's decisions in recent years have invaded some of the more intimate concerns and interests of the American democracy; and resentments have accumulated. As Edmund Burke said of the governmental notion that the people ought to accept a rational explanation of why their interests are being damaged by public policy, "No man will be argued into slavery."

In recent years the tone of the Supreme Court has been improved by the appointment of three new vigorous commonsensical jurists who, to judge from their performance thus far, do not think that justice was born yesterday, or that the Constitution of 1787 is altogether obsolete. One is somewhat surprised to find that such judges still have survived the deluge of mingled positivism and social sentimentality which has left awash many courtrooms, federal, state, and municipal.

The original intent of the Framers of the Constitution was to give the American people a Republic of elevated views and hopes. They desired to establish an independent judiciary; they did not mean to create a new form of government, unknown to Plato or Aristotle, that might be termed an *archonocracy*—a domination of judges. As Randolph of Roanoke observed, with reference to certain tendencies of the federal courts in his own time, "I can never forget that the Book of Judges is followed by the Book of Kings."

The Revival of Classical Republicanism

In my opinion, two reforms loom large in our political future: a flat-rate income tax, and term limits on our various elected representatives. I believe I'll see both in my lifetime. Come to think of it, I already have seen one term limit passed: the Twenty-second Amendment in February, 1951, which holds the president to two terms. I was three. Before I'm one hundred and three, I'd like to see similar limits placed on Congress.

Many libertarian conservatives argue that we already have term limits, namely elections. How can one not have sympathy with that argument? Wouldn't term limits be a diminishment of our freedom to vote for whomever we wish? Well, yes, they would. But the current sclerotic condition of the American political system demands a little open-heart surgery.

Mr. Will has chosen the right word, restoration, *and presents a sound argument.*

ON DECEMBER 23, 1783, George Washington went before Congress in Annapolis to tender his resignation as commanding general of what remained of the army that had made a nation and thereby moved mankind onto a new and ascending path. Earlier that year he had rendered perhaps the most crucial of his many vital services to the nation. He had restrained the rebelliousness and reinforced the loyalty of the understandably restive soldiers. In what arguably still stands as the most critical moment in more than two centuries of American history, Washington had held back the rebellious despair of an army whose justifiable grievances could have caused it to overthrow civilian authority, such as it then was. That would have presaged the disintegration of the nation into a clutter of weak and probably warring little entities. The army's bloody footprints in the snows of the wartime winters had testified to the poor provision made for it by the Continental Congress. That Congress was too institutionally weak to compel assistance from the states, which were jealously guarding their sovereignty. The soldiers had often lived off the land "like beetles off a leaf," and when many of them left the army they were as destitute as they were triumphant.

So in December, 1783, Congress, in its civilian plainness and political impotence, would have been an object of Washington's disdain, had he blamed it, as many of his soldiers did, for the destitution they had endured while many Americans prospered. But that was not how Washington probably saw the legislature as he was ushered into the Hall of Congress. In the words of Washington's finest biographer, James Flexner, "His physical eye saw a tiny, powerless body of some twenty men, hardly worth, Napoleon would have thought, the whiff of grapeshot that would so easily have sent them flying; but in his mind's eye, Washington saw gathered before him the power that was to grow down the centuries, the dignity of a great nation."

General Washington, like the American officers at the surrender of Charleston three years earlier, thought of Congress not as what it was but as what it could and should be. He thought of it not as a frail vessel of flawed men and their rivalries but as the incarnation of a free nation.

Dignity is in the eye of the beholder, and few who behold Congress today consider it dignified. To some extent Americans are judging Congress severely to avoid judging themselves at all. It may be that the nation today is faithfully portrayed in Congress the way Dorian Gray was portrayed in his portrait. Be that as it may, the brute fact is that most Americans regard Congress with contempt. But a republic can not long despise its legislature and respect itself.

If the flinty realists who framed this Republic saw the condition of Congress today, they probably would be saddened but not shocked. They knew that what they accomplished—a judicious founding—

could do no more than increase the probability of political happiness. Nothing is guaranteed in politics. That is why political philosophers are great worriers. They often gaze upon the social order and conclude:

> Take but degree away, untune that string,
> And, hark! what discord follows . . .

The philosophic politicians among America's Founders were like that. They were anxious lest they make small mistakes at the nation's beginning that would have large consequences later. In this anxiety they were men of their age. The eighteenth century is known to us as the Age of Reason, but its most reasonable statesmen knew the limited role of reason in human affairs. A sense of permanent impermanence was in the eighteenth-century air.

The most famous work of history written in the English language was published during the American founding and dealt with a recurring fascination of Western political thinkers, the decline and fall of the Roman empire. Gibbon's six-volume work, published between 1776 and 1788, was avidly read by people apprehensive about something that had made Plato, and has made many philosophers since him, apprehensive. It was the possibility that societies—all sorts of societies—can easily slip into the grip of decay. This worry linked Machiavelli with the ancients. Machiavelli, so unlike the ancients in so many ways, shared with them an intense interest in the problem of preventing decay, and the possibility of regenerating a society when decay has not been kept at bay. These are the themes—degeneration and regeneration—that connect today's two controversies about the condition of Congress and the meaning of representation with the largest and most enduring arguments of the Western political tradition.

If the term limitation movement can not convincingly connect itself with a political philosophy—with perennial themes and values of the Western tradition and American political experience rather than with merely epiphenomenal discontents of a season—then it will not succeed, and should not. Fortunately, it can connect. In fact, term limitation is an idea nourished by two intellectual streams. One is the Founders' understanding of the institutional prerequisites for deliberative democracy. Another intellectual stream is the idea of classical republicanism. That idea had a larger role in the American founding, and hence has a larger relevance to contemporary American governance, than most Americans realize.

In a justly famous aphorism, John Maynard Keynes said that "practical men, who believe themselves to be quite exempt from any intellectual influences, are usually the slaves of some defunct economist." Keynes was an economist, so forgive his belief in the primacy of economists. His larger point, put with his customary verve, is valid: "I am sure that the power of vested interests is vastly exaggerated compared with the gradual encroachment of ideas." Those whom Keynes rather unkindly called "academic scribblers" sometimes are, in fact, if not on purpose, people of considerable practical consequence. There are today, for example, some American historians whose arguments might, and should, shape the thinking of people who have never heard of them. It would be particularly desirable for those historians' arguments to percolate among the people now participating in arguments about the depressing trajectory of America's representative institutions. Fortunately, the slow seepage of scholarly disputation into the broader culture may already be quietly exerting a gravitational pull on people who do not consciously feel it. Cultural osmosis is at work. The vocabulary of public discourse is being leavened by the revival, in academic settings, of some sturdy old concepts and categories, such as those of classical republicanism.

A timely survey of current thinking about the role of classical republicanism in the founding era is *The Political Philosophy of Thomas Jefferson*. The author, Garrett Ward Sheldon, is a professor of political science at the Clinch Valley College of the University of Virginia. While describing some intellectual currents in the late eighteenth and early nineteenth centuries, he illuminates how those arguments echo in the late twentieth century. He is doing intellectual archeology, tracing the several threads of thought that Jefferson wove into the fabric of his philosophy. However, one result of his research is a deepened understanding of today's dissatisfaction with the functioning of contemporary American democracy. To read his essay is to understand that the term limits movement has a richer intellectual pedigree than it knows.

The American Revolution arose not only, or even primarily, from grievances about such material matters as taxation and regulation of trade. To be sure, sparks struck by the Stamp Act, the Townsend Acts and other provocations from Westminster set the colonies ablaze. But why were the colonies such combustible tinder? What is the explanation for such a swift coalescing of the new American consciousness, and the consequent rapid unraveling of the British position in the American colonies? Between 1760 and 1776 something that had seemed unthinkable and indeed had barely been thought of—a desperate revolutionary wager for independence—came to seem (in the title of the most important nongovernmental publication in American history, published in 1776) as a matter of "common sense." What happened to cause this abrupt change?

What happened is that some ideas got spread around. Ideas account for the astonishing acceleration of events in the decade and a half that midwifed the modern world. Ideas explain what seems to be the disproportion between the colonists' grievances and their world-shaking and history-making response. Perhaps never before or since has philosophy been such an intensely practical subject. The era of the founding of the United States is especially powerful evidence for the school of historians that says not only that ideas have consequences, but that only ideas have large and lasting consequences.

Sheldon's book is part of an argument currently enlivening the writing of early American history. From the mother lode of Jefferson's philosophy, Sheldon mines a gleaming nugget of an insight. It is that we have too often slighted one of the two strands of philosophy that deserve equal dignity as intellectual progenitors of this Republic. The strand that has not been neglected is the liberalism derived from the writings of John Locke, especially from his *Two Treatises on Government*. The insufficiently appreciated strand is that of classical republicanism. The ways in which these two philosophies complement each other, and the tension between them, is relevant to America today.

For several decades now, historians have debated the sources and qualities of the Ameican Revolution. The debate has turned on the supposed primacy of John Locke's ideas of individualism, natural rights and limited government. Individualism: Locke portrayed mankind as a loose—very loose—aggregation of autonomous and almost asocial individuals. Natural rights: These individuals possess, prior to political association with others, certain rights by virtue of their nature. Limited government: These rights-endowed individuals ("endowed by their Creator," says the Declaration of Independence) associate politically only to make more commodious each individual's enjoyment of these rights.

Recently, however, there has been increased appreciation of the saliency of other notions, those of classical republicanism. These include the ideas of social man, the central importance of public participation in civic life and the struggle of the virtuous people out in the country to contain the corruption associated with those who cluster around the central power, like a court around a king.

Until recent decades—until, we may say, the late 1960s—there was a broad and, it seemed, durable consensus among historians. It held that an understanding of Lockean liberalism was not merely necessary but was virtually sufficient for understanding this Republic's origins, its founding and its early course. An influential and characteristic formulation of the consensus was that "Locke dominates American political thought as no thinker anywhere dominates the political thought of a nation." That was written in 1955, when, from the center of Europe to the South China Sea, Marxism was an established civil religion enforced by state terror. Nevertheless, Louis Hartz, who wrote that, had a point. Marxism was only an imposed and alien orthodoxy; we now know how utterly it failed to sink roots into the social soil. In contrast, Locke's liberalism permeates America's political vocabulary and institutions.

Locke portrayed man as a mild and essentially congenial creature, semisocial but basically isolated while in a "state of nature." In that state he is a materialist. He possesses a "natural right" to life, liberty and property. In Locke's understanding of government, men make a rational, if unenthusiastic, choice to leave the state of nature. They enter into a social contract with kindred spirits who seek from government a severely limited service. They seek only relief from the generally mild inconveniences and insecurities of the state of nature. These inconveniences and insecurities are primarily the results of disputes between people exercising their natural rights. The government they create is essentially an arbitrator—a referee. Thus the government that arises from Lockean liberalism is inherently limited in its purposes and scope by the impulse that gives rise to it. That impulse is the desire for the protection of the private rights and acquired interests that predate government.

For many years the practice of locating the intellectual origins of the American polity entirely in Lockean liberalism had, for historians and other intellectuals, the attraction of tidiness. It also had, in this century, the advantage of political utility. As Sheldon says, "Locke's emphasis on private property and conflicting material interests led quite easily into the progressive (and later Marxist) school of historical interpretation that focused upon economic, social and institutional factors in explaining political ideas and actions in America."

Then the consensus began to fray.

In the 1960s classical republicanism became a rival of Lockean liberalism as an explanatory concept in the writing of early American history. The crucial difference with Lockean liberalism is the emphasis classical republicanism gives to man's natural sociability. That sociability entails both a need and a disposition to participate in civic life and to develop and display public virtue. In 1969, J. G. A. Pocock, backed by rich and persuasive scholarship, said, in effect: Mr. Locke, move over and make room for credit to be given to another philosophic contribution to the making of the first modern nation. Pocock extracted from the writings of Aristotle, Cicero, Machiavelli and others a coherent political philosophy that first appeared in Ancient Greece and Rome, later resurfaced in Renaissance Italy, then resonated in eighteenth-century England and became a fighting faith in revolutionary and postrevolutionary America. But in America it was alloyed with Lockean liberalism and was often lost sight of.

Classical republicanism is rooted in Aristotle's notion that man is a political animal. Man, to Aristotle, is not political in the tentative, limited and diffident manner of the Lockean man who enters into political society only negatively, as a necessary concession to inconveniences. Rather, said classical republicans, man is political in the sense that his nature can not be realized, and his natural inclinations can not be fulfilled, without active involvement in a political order— a particular kind of political order. It is a kind that makes possible political participation, which Aristotle considered a defining attribute of citizenship. Such a political order is right for man's nature. Which is to say, it is a natural right.

Classical republicanism stressed the economic independence of the individual as a prerequisite for satisfying the individual's social nature through political participation in a virtuous republic. Virtue, Sheldon notes, is a decidedly non-Lockean concept, because it involves the individual in sacrificing some self-interest for the common good.

The reappearance of classical republicanism in eighteenth-century England reflected a quickened concern about civic virtue and the decay of political life. Classical republicanism was the rallying doctrine of the country gentry. That gentry saw itself as the force of countervailing virtue against the wealthy, corrupt and dependent "court" faction that inevitably flourishes when great power is concentrated in a central government in a vast metropolis. In England in the sixteenth and seventeenth centuries considerable political tension existed between the sovereign and the class of landowners who had to bear most of the financial burden of the sovereign's government. The tension was not just about money. It also concerned the apportionment of power and respect, and different visions of how English society and government should evolve. This struggle for supremacy was often spoken of as a contest between "court and country." The "country" party—if it is not too anachronistic to use the word "party" about this faction—thought of the court not just as the sovereign but as the gaggle of interests that fastened like leeches on the seat of government in a corrupt and corrupting political city.

It would be crashingly incongruous to call the "country" faction democrats. They did not seek substantial extension of political participation to those below them. Neither were they republicans. They wanted to tame and trim the crown's prerogatives, but they did not seek to abolish it. On the other hand, they were making more than a narrow argument on behalf of the material and political interests of their class. They also were formulating a moral stance. It was, in a sense, an echo of earlier political philosophers and would soon reverberate in America. It was an echo of the tradition of those ancients in Greece and Rome, and subsequent thinkers such as Machiavelli, who worried about political arrangements that work against the very virtues that the political arrangements presuppose. And the English "country" faction was an anticipation of the revival, across the ocean, of an intense, and intensely practical, debate about the problems of defining and nurturing republican virtue.

In the last decade of the eighteenth century in America, as the two-party system began to coalesce from the cooling dust of the revolutionary explosion, the "court versus country" distinction was a useful analogy that Jeffersonians put to partisan use. They invoked it in their rivalry with Hamiltonians. Jeffersonians were grounded in, and spokesmen for, the rural yeomanry who, Jeffersonian theory held, were disciplined by agrarian life to the virtues requisite for freedom: individualism, hardihood, self-reliance. It suited Jeffersonian political purposes to portray Hamiltonians as sunk in metropolitan corruption. Hamiltonians, said Jeffersonians, were seeking private gain from proximity to an overreaching and overbearing central government.

This was a caricature, but like all caricatures it was a distortion developed from a kernel of truth. Jeffersonians did, indeed, believe in a sociology of virtue. Their sociology entailed agrarianism, localism and decentralism. And Hamiltonians did in fact favor considerable (for that day) concentrations of power in the federal government. Hamiltonians wanted that government to possess power sufficient to promote credit, commerce and industry. That would necessarily mean urbanization, which would sever many people, and hence popular government, from what Jeffersonians considered indispensable—the ennobling influences of life on the land.

To be fair (as Jeffersonians and Hamiltonians rarely were to one another), Hamilton himself had a clear and noble moral vision. It involved a social revolution as important, Hamilton thought, as the political revolution that had just been effected. And Hamilton thought that without the second—the social—revolution, the political revolution would prove to have been a barren achievement. He cast his cool gaze on history and on this contemporary situation and came to a conclusion many others have come to before and since. He concluded that social progress is always propelled by the exertions of an industrious minority. For this minority, in the modern age, money must be the means as well as the measure of achievement. A society plastic to the power of money may be susceptible to crassness, vulgarity and corruption, but it also is apt to be an open society, with a large cohort of the industrious. Thus, Hamilton thought, it would be decidedly superior to a Jeffersonian society.

Hamilton's best modern biographer, Forrest McDonald, rightly insists that Hamilton saw the free working of sound money as a solvent to wash away the rigidities of a Jeffersonian society, a form of society that Hamilton thought would suffocate social energies. Hamilton considered Jeffersonianism partly a sentimental celebration of rural existence and partly (sometimes simultaneously) the self-interested ideology of a retrograde class. Against this, and on behalf of a more fluid and vital America, Hamilton proposed to unleash the creative force of money. "For money," McDonald writes, "is oblivious to class, status, color, and inherited social position; money is the ultimate, neutral, impersonal arbiter. Infused into an oligarchical, agrarian social order, money would be the leaven, the fermenting yeast, that would stimulate growth, change, prosperity, and national strength."

Jefferson said: Keep the factories, financiers and cities in Europe.

Democracy depends on yeomen dispersed over vast spaces (hence the Louisiana Purchase). Hamilton saw cities in America's future. Although in 1790 America's largest city, Philadelphia, had a population of 54,391 (about the size of Rapid City, South Dakota, today), Hamilton was the first political thinker for urban America. He saw in Jefferson's vision not the romance of bucolic life but an indolent, oligarchic caste society suffocating America's promise.

Hamilton's rival vision was contained in one of the most important public documents in American history. His "Report on Manufactures" made the case for tariffs, a central bank, public works and other government assistance to commercial development, but was not just a statement of economic policy. The "Report" was an exercise in statecraft as soulcraft. He aimed at nothing less than a change in the American character. Like Jefferson, Hamilton took seriously the social ecology of virtue. He wanted a different society because he had a different idea of virtue for individuals and the nation.

America never really had a choice between Hamiltonian and Jeffersonian futures. The forces—scientific, industrial, financial, organizational—that made the modern world were going to erupt. Nothing Jeffersonians could have done would have made the Atlantic a barrier to them. Furthermore, it is, on balance, good that they erupted. Modernity has meant a vast improvement in conditions for the mass of mankind. And when Hitler and Stalin got factories, it was good that we had some, too.

Still, there is a tragic dimension to Hamiltonianism, and to American history. Hamilton had a healthy distrust of human nature but was not wary enough. He underestimated the difficulty—the impossibility, it seems—of keeping government limited and reasonable once it becomes a big player in the game of creating and allocating wealth. Hamilton had an austere, even noble, vision of a people energized by the spirit of perpetual improvement. He did not foresee the degradation of political and economic life that would result when government became an arena for entrepreneurship, engulfed in a feeding frenzy of people bending public power to private purposes.

Prescient Jeffersonians saw that the kind of government Hamilton favored would lend itself to exploitation by individuals and interests animated by lust for private gain. However, in extenuation of Hamilton's responsibility for our current discontents, let us stress that we have today a central government that has grown mighty beyond Hamilton's dreams of federal supremacy. Still, he planted the intellec-

tual and institutional seeds from which today's regulatory and thera-
peutic welfare state grew into the huge engine it is. Therefore the sys-
temic problems of this government, particularly the deep
dissatisfaction with the style and substance of the politics such a state
generates, are, in a sense, part of Hamilton's mixed legacy. Hence it is
reasonable to consult the Jeffersonian tradition for guidance concerning possible corrective measures.

Jefferson's life of public involvement was so long, and his intellectual life had so many facets, that one comes upon portions of the Jeffersonian tradition wherever one turns when examining the American
political tradition. This is certainly true when considering the tradition—one might better say the ethic—of term limitation. George
Washington's voluntary retirement after two terms in the presidency
established the ethic by example. But it might not have done so if Jefferson had not chosen to make the ethic explicit.

Halfway through President Jefferson's second term the nation
found itself sailing in increasingly choppy waters. It was embroiled in
disputes with France and Britain over the rights of neutral nations'
shipping during the war between those two nations. In June, 1807, the
issue of impressment of members of U.S. ships' crews by British Navy
ships reached a crisis point. The U.S. frigate *Chesapeake* was fired
upon by the British frigate *Leopard*. The *Chesapeake* struck its colors,
four Americans were taken away on the *Leopard,* and the new nation's sense of dignity was lacerated. Jefferson's proclamation ordering British warships out of American territorial waters was followed
by a British proclamation ordering still more aggressive searches for
British subjects serving on the crews of American ships. Congress
then passed the Embargo Act, which divided the nation in the most
dangerous way, along its regional fault line, North against South.
New England merchants were especially injured and angry.

Meanwhile, the American public was increasingly alarmed by evidence of Aaron Burr's conspiracy to separate Western states from the
Union. So it was not surprising that, beginning in November, 1806,
and with increasing urgency, local meetings of Jefferson's party, the
Republican Party, began petitioning him to seek a third term. Soon
nine of the seventeen state legislatures and one territorial government
joined the call for him not to retire.

Jefferson did not respond until December, 1807, and then he replied
only to the addresses from state legislatures. He was emphatic. He

said he felt as obligated to put down the burdens of the presidency as he had felt duty-bound to take them up. Because the Constitution had not limited presidential terms, custom must do so. Otherwise the office might become, *de facto,* one held for life. "I should unwillingly be the person who, disregarding the sound precedent set by an illustrious predecessor, should furnish the first example of prolongation beyond the second term of office." Jefferson's position was praised by the editor of the *Richmond Enquirer.* He said that if Jefferson had allowed himself to be persuaded by the nation's emergency to serve another term, a "less virtuous and more ambitious" successor might "seize upon any lowering speck in the distant horizon, perhaps to conjure up an imaginary danger, that he might shield his ambition under a similar excuse. Mr. Jefferson's retirement wrests this plausible pretext from the hands of his successors. They will see from his example, that no crisis, however fruitful in danger or in war *can* justify the prolongation of their term of office."

Jefferson surely knew that the question of improper "prolongation" of tenure in office involves values that were first, and arguably best, discussed by the ancients. Historian Bernard Bailyn maintains that although other American thinkers of the founding era used classical allusions "ornamentally," Jefferson was a "careful reader" of the ancients. However, he was not an acolyte in awe of them. Aristotle and other Greeks, said Jefferson, never mastered the task that confronted the American Founders. It was the task of preparing a middle ground "between a democracy (the only pure republic, but impractical beyond the limits of a town) and an abandonment of themselves to an aristocracy, or a tyranny independent of the people."

The American solution was a government of what Jefferson called "the second grade of purity." We should not be distracted by the resonance his language has today. The added ingredient of representation was—is—not an impurity. Representation is a necessity "where the citizens can not meet to transact their business." And the idea of representation contains its own standard of purity. That standard can be expressed negatively, as the avoidance of what Jefferson called the "detestable game" and "base scramble" for public funds and other private advantages from public power. That game rages today on a scale far beyond Jefferson's worst nightmares.

This twentieth-century scramble may be in part a consequence of seventeenth- and eighteenth-century theories of human nature. Are human beings only mildly social creatures, moved primarily by the desire for self-preservation and avoidance of the "inconveniences" that the state of nature has for property holders? Do they, therefore, enter into only chilly political associations with other materialistic individuals who are similarly motivated by private interests? If people are described this way—and therefore taught to be this way—by the public philosophy, we should not be surprised or aghast when the politics that results from such narrow utilitarian calculations turns out to be the sort of scramble that Jefferson detested.

Such scrambling, which legislative careerism intensifies and term limitation would abate, is incompatible with good citizenship. Civic virtue means a steady predisposition to prefer the public good to private advantages when they conflict. Term limitation would also help to reinvigorate our understanding of citizenship by reemphasizing the value of civic participation. Aristotle taught that citizenship in a republic implies participation. That is all very well for a compact city-state, but it gives little guidance for our age. Our task is to define the sort of participation that is prudent and practical in a complex and continental republic. To Jefferson, the key was localism.

In 1809 he rode out of Washington a week after Madison was inaugurated, never to return. Seven years later he was still strong in his faith in decentralization: "As Cato, then, concluded every speech with the words 'Carthago delenda est,'* so do I every opinion, with the injunction, 'divide the counties into wards.'" One can sympathize with Jefferson's yearning for centrifugal forces, but one can not deny the centripetal tendency of American history since—actually, even during—Jefferson's day. (President Jefferson's Louisiana Purchase, and the Embargo Act and its enforcing legislation, were early manifestations of the flow of power to the central government, however much Jefferson believed or pretended otherwise.) But this does not mean that we must meekly abandon participation as a value importantly implied by citizenship. One function of term limitation is to inscribe in fundamental law and infuse throughout political practice this sentiment: The essential act of republicanism—lawmaking in a representative institution—is not work that requires such a long apprenticeship that most citizens are effectively excluded from the pool of talent from which lawmakers can be drawn. Lawmaking is not the arcane province of a clerisy of experts and specialists whose ranks are

*Carthage must be destroyed.

open only to people prepared to commit substantial portions of their adult lives.

Term limitation covering 535 seats in the national legislature will affect only the minute fraction of the American public that will serve in those seats. But if term limitation is inscribed as a constitutional value it will perform, as law frequently does, an expressive and affirming function. It will express an idea central to the civic culture of republicanism (of the American, if not necessarily the Burkean, variety). The idea is that representation is not a function beyond the capacities of any reasonably educated and attentive citizen. Term limitation will affirm the democratic faith in the broad diffusion in the public of the talents necessary for the conduct of the public's business. Term limitation does not rest on the assumption that (as Lenin said but did not believe) any cook can run the state. However, term limitation does say, moderately and usefully, that democracy does not depend on any indispensable people.

The genius of American society, nicely distilled in Jefferson's idea of "natural aristocracy," is in the belief that the meritorious should rule but that merit can be found, or nurtured, in every social rank. And the merit of the public—of the nation itself—can be nurtured by the normal working of the institutions of self-government, especially the central institution of representation, Congress.

Many Americans reflexively flinch from the idea of government nurturing virtue. According to the instinctive notions of most Americans, politics generally should faithfully reflect, not seek to modify, the citizens' sentiments or characters. Americans have a bluff, commonsense belief that a government that has a hard enough time delivering the mail and patching potholes can not be expected to bring off anything as subtle and complex as moral improvement. Besides, even if government could do it, government should not do it, because soulcraft is incompatible with freedom. The boldness of the American experiment in liberal democracy is precisely this: Liberty is to be protected primarily by institutional arrangements rather than by reliance on the nurturing of virtue, either among the masses or in some saving elite.

However, although that is the primary reliance, it is not the only one. Virtue, too, is requisite. And the workings of the institutions of popular government are themselves supposed to nurture some of the virtues that their proper working presupposes.

The importance of the philosophy of classical republicanism in the

American founding means that America's intellectual and moral origins are not exclusively in modernity, not just in the liberalism that founds liberty on individualism, rights and materialism. America also arises from the ancient republicanism that stressed the fulfillment of man's political nature through political participation. But not through just any participation. It should be participation in the governance of a polity that nurtures what it presupposes, a modicum of public virtue. This virtue is a tendency to prefer the public good to personal interests; it is a readiness to define the public good as more than an aggregation of private interests.

Prior to the American—more precisely, the Madisonian—revolution in democratic theory, most political philosophers thought that a successful democracy needed a certain quantity of a particular quality. The quality was called virtue. And a sufficient supply of this quality could flourish only in a polity conducive to it. That meant a small polity. Only in a small, face-to-face society would there be sufficient homogeneity to avoid factions, which were presumed to be the bane of democracy.

However, a republic that is continental in scope and commercial in nature must welcome a multiplicity of factions. They make the machinery of government move, and their countervailing forces prevent it from moving to tyranny. This scheme of governance contrasts with the classic notion of a compact republic relying on virtue—both the virtue of the many who select the few that govern, and the virtue of the few.

The Madisonian scheme had, for the thoughtful statesmen who devised it, the intellectual charm of elegance and ingenuity. It also satisfied their rigorous realism. A system that relies on the physics of interestedness—that treats politics as a field of low but steady, predictable and manageable forces—is a system free from the inherently uncertain reliance on virtue. It is a system that will not count overmuch on virtue, either of the people or of the representatives the people select.

Not overmuch, but somewhat. America's Founders sought safety in both sociological and institutional factors. The sociological factors included diversity of factions and extensive territory. Two of the institutional factors were the constitutional principles of separation of powers and federalism. However, the Founders also counted on another constitutional factor to make democracy not only safe but a force for the steady, constant improvement of the nation's character. This third factor was supposed to be the conspicuous—and hence elevating—practice of deliberative democracy in Congress. Hence the Constitution itself was supposed to be, and should be seen to be, a moralizing force. Its dignity and its suitability as an object of veneration are partly a product of this grave function.

No sensible person lightly suggests amending it. Still, the Founders, by including the amending provisions, contemplated changes. And, anyway, the Constitution's meaning and force have been considerably changed by the nation's political and social evolution—sometimes seamless, sometimes with abrupt ruptures—during two centuries. In his history of Reconstruction, Eric Foner writes that it was fitting that as Congress debated a vast expansion of federal power "in February 1867, the last surviving veteran of the American Revolution died. For like the Revolution, Reconstruction was an era when the foundations of public life were thrown open for discussion." It would be excessive to suggest that America in the 1990s stands at such a potentially critical pivot in its history, when the nature of the regime itself is at issue, and the structure of the regime seems malleable. However, it is not too much to say that for the first time since the New Deal, political debates about practical measures are raising questions concerning the essential nature of American republicanism.

These questions were at issue in the birth of our party system, in the controversy between Jefferson and Hamilton. There is an elegant memorial in Washington to Jefferson, but none to Hamilton. However, if you seek Hamilton's monument, look around. You are living in it. We honor Jefferson, but live in Hamilton's country, a mighty industrial nation with a strong central government. Questions about how republicanism should be understood were again—were still—at issue in 1861, when the nation was torn by the "irrepressible conflict" about its nature. Four years of that conflict gave the national government a giant shove toward supremacy but also toward a strength that has proven to be problematic. "On the eve of the Civil War . . . one could live out one's life without ever encountering an official representative of national authority." Since the Civil War, and especially since the New Deal, the federal government has been woven into the fabric of daily life.

The 1932 presidential election inaugurated the modern era of American politics. What began then was only dimly perceived and only vaguely planned, but it was nothing less than a fundamental change in the relationship of the citizen to the central government. Ever since, Americans have been getting what they manifestly have wanted, a federal government taking responsibility for the nation's aggregate economic output, and for myriad lesser questions of distributive justice and social amelioration.

However, six decades have passed since the New Deal began to be improvised and Americans are not happy with the political process that has evolved in conjunction with the kind of government they have requested. Term limitation is an attempt, by a limited, surgical revision of the rules of representation, to restore a balance, a temperateness and—let us not flinch from the word—a virtue that has been lost from public life.

PART V

The Cultural Order

A leading critic lays bare the deeper meanings:

What must be questioned is what these compound terms mean, and what they say about democracy. It is clear that on the whole they use the immense prestige, the philosophical rhetoric, and the political trappings of democracy to advance particular social visions that are not necessarily democratic. A few explanations tell the story: economic democracy now means the achievement of socialism; social democracy means egalitarianism; capitalist democracy, free market economics; people's democracy, Stalinism; participatory democracy, the rule of a mob led by intellectuals; sexual democracy, libertinism; cultural democracy, the farther shores of behavioral relativism; even our own liberal democracy increasingly uses the appearances of tradition and conservatism to camouflage and make palatable a relentlessly secular and socially dynamic society.

SAMUEL LIPMAN, "Redefining Culture and Democracy,"
in *Arguing for Music, Arguing for Culture* (1990)

Assorted Dogmas

What's wrong with the West? What's wrong with English? What's wrong with being a (gulp!) white man? Plenty, according to the sensitivity police who now watch over American education from kindergarten through graduate school.

There have always been critics of "the system," but never before have they had license to act as commissars over their dreamed-of cultural revolution. Naturally they want to mold young minds. Predictably, as Thomas Sowell demonstrates, they fail.

Tenure notwithstanding, the failure is profound. Far from creating more understanding, the multiculturalists succeed only in deepening divisions. What about E pluribus unum?

AMONG THE MANY DOGMAS prevailing in American education, most can be divided into two broad categories—dogmas about society and dogmas about education. The most widespread of the social dogmas revolve around "multicultural diversity" and the educational dogmas include "relevance," educating "the whole person," and a general de-emphasis of authority. Not all these dogmas are exclusively American. Some have gotten a foothold in the educational systems of some other countries, usually with the same disastrous consequences as in the United States.

"MULTICULTURAL DIVERSITY"

Few catch-phrases have been so uncritically accepted, or so variously defined, as "multicultural diversity." Sometimes it refers to the simple fact that peoples from many racial, ethnic, and cultural backgrounds make up the American population. At other times, it refers to an agenda of separatism in language and culture, a revisionist view of history as a collection of grievances to be kept alive, and a program of both historical and contemporary condemnation of American society and Western civilization.

Despite frequent, chameleon-like changes in the meanings of multiculturalism, its basic components are three: (1) a set of ideological beliefs about society and the world, (2) a political agenda to make these beliefs the basis for the curriculum of the whole educational system, and (3) a set of beliefs about the most effective way to conduct an educational system.

Many critics of multiculturalism, such as former Secretary of Education William J. Bennett, have done battle over the ideological beliefs of the multiculturalists. What is most salient *educationally,* however, is the attempt of multiculturalists to make these beliefs a new orthodoxy, to be imposed institutionally by the political authorities. What is also salient are the multiculturalists' educational methods, geared toward leading students to a set of pre-selected beliefs, rather than toward developing their own ability to analyze for themselves, or to provide them with adequate factual knowledge to make their own independent assessments.

The ideological component of multiculturalism can be summarized as a cultural relativism which finds the prominence of Western civilization in the world or in the schools intolerable. Behind this attitude is often a seething hostility to the West, barely concealed even in public statements designed to attract wider political support for the multicultural agenda. That such attitudes or opinions exist, and are expressed by some people, is to be expected in a free society. It is not these beliefs, as such, which are the real problem. The real *educational* problem is the attempt to impose such views as a new orthodoxy throughout the educational system, not only by classroom brainwashing but also by institutional power—expressed in such things as compulsory indoctrination programs for teachers, making adherence to multiculturalism a condition of employment, and buying only those textbooks which reflect multiculturalism in some way, even if these are textbooks in mathematics or science.

Some or all of these patterns can be found in public schools across the United States, in leading American colleges, and in educational institutions as far away as Britain and Australia. In all these settings, what the general public sees are not the ideological foundations or the institutional mechanisms of multiculturalism, but only their educational arguments. These arguments fall into a few standard categories:

1. Multiculturalism is necessary to enable our students to participate in the emerging global economy.

2. Multiculturalism is necessary because an increasingly diverse population within the United States requires and demands education in a variety of cultures.

3. Intergroup relations are better when people are introduced to each other's cultures in school.

4. Education itself is better when presented from various perspectives, derived from culturally different social groups.

Whatever the plausibility of any of these beliefs, supporting evidence has seldom been asked or given. On the contrary, evidence contradicting each of these claims has been ignored.

When a 1991 commission report, prepared for the New York state Commissioner of Education, referred to "the need for preparing young people to participate in the world community," it was echoing a familiar theme in the multicultural literature. Yet neither argument nor evidence was offered to show how the particular things being done as part of the multicultural agenda would accomplish that purpose, which was itself left vague. It would be hard to think of a more monocultural, insular and self-complacent nation than Japan—and yet the Japanese are among the leading participants in the international economy, in international scientific and technological developments, as well as in international travel and tourism. This is not a defense of insularity or of the Japanese. It is simply a piece of empirical evidence to highlight the *non sequitur* of the claim that international participation requires the multicultural ideology or agenda.

Another equally reckless claim is that the ethnic diversity of the American population requires multicultural education. The United States has been ethnically diverse for more than a century. Yet successive massive waves of immigrants have arrived on these shores and become Americans without any such programs as have been proposed by the multiculturalists. Nor is there the slightest evidence, whether from the United States or from other countries where similar programs have been tried, that the transition has gone better as a result of multiculturalism.

Perhaps the most tendentious aspect of the claim that ethnic diversity requires multicultural education programs is the assertion that this demand comes from the various ethnic groups themselves—as distinguished from vocal activists. Non-English-speaking parents, for example, generally seek to get their children to be taught in English, rather than in the foreign-language programs promoted by activists under the label of "bilingualism." Asian Americans, as well as Hispanics, have been found in polls to prefer to have their children educated in English, and bilingual activists have had to resort to pressure and deception to maintain enrollments in bilingual programs.

The claim that groups will get along better when they are given multicultural education is a straightforward claim which might be straightforwardly tested against the facts—but it almost never is. Wherever group separatism appears or group animosity erupts in the wake of multicultural education, these are automatically attributed to the influence of the larger society. The educational benefits of multiculturalism are likewise often proclaimed but seldom documented. There is no *a priori* reason to believe such claims, especially in the face of multiple evidences of declining educational quality during the period when multiculturalism and other non-academic preoccupations have taken up more and more of the curriculum.

Multiculturalists themselves are quite clear that they do not see their philosophy as just one of many philosophies that different people may entertain, or as something to be optional in some parts of the school curriculum. "Multicultural perspectives should *infuse the entire curriculum, prekindergarten through grade 12*" (emphasis in the original), according to the official report to the New York State Commissioner of Education. Because this report considered "*commitment* to multicultural social studies education" to be crucial, it called for "*extensive staff development*" which would "address attitudes"—

i.e., indoctrination—and which would extend even to the schools' clerical staffs and bus drivers. In short, the call for cultural "diversity" is a call for ideological conformity.

This pattern is not peculiar to New York state or even to the United States. A study of a multiculturally orientated school in Manchester, England, found the very same buzzwords—"sensitive," "child centered,"—as well as a determination not to "bend to parents' prejudices," a similar disregard of teachers who criticized what was being done in the name of "multiculturalism," and a hiring and promotion of new teachers more in tune with the multicultural dogma. In Australia as well, there is the same dogmatic sense of exclusive rectitude in a multicultural educator's dismissal of "assimilationist and melting pot thinking from some reactionaries."

There are many variations on the theme of multiculturalism, but their basic ideological premises, political modes of implementation, and educational practices show a recurrent pattern, whether at the school level or the college level, and whether in the United States or abroad. In all these settings, a major ingredient in the political success of promoters of multiculturalism has been a concealment of both their ideological agendas and their educational results. One of the most politically successful of these "multicultural diversity" programs in the United States, so-called bilingual education, has owed much of its political success to concealment of its educational reality.

"Bilingual Education"

The theory behind bilingual education is that youngsters who do not understand English can best be taught school subjects in their native language, taking English classes as a separate subject, rather than be subjected to an all-English education from the first day. The children of immigrants from Spanish-speaking countries have been the principal focus of bilingualism, but once the idea caught on in the political arena and in the courtrooms, it expanded to include school children of Asian, Middle Eastern, and other backgrounds, and ultimately drew into its orbit even native-born American children whose only language was English. While most of the bilingual programs have featured the Spanish language, some have been in Chinese, Armenian, Navajo, and more than a hundred other languages.

A landmark on the road to bilingualism was the 1974 U.S. Supreme Court decision in *Lau v. Nichols* that it was an unconstitutional denial of equal protection to provide only an English-language education to non-English-speaking school children. While the Supreme Court did not specify what alternative education must be provided, organized ethnic activists now had leverage to push for bilingualism, using the threat of lawsuits and political charges of discrimination and racism against school systems which resisted the activists' agenda.

Both legally and educationally there were many possible ways of dealing with the language difficulties of foreign school children, and both school officials and parents might have been given discretion to choose among various options. For example, the foreign students might have been given a course on English as a second language, while taking their other school subjects in English as well, either immediately or after a transition period. At the other end of the range of possibilities, the children might be taught in a foreign language for years, perhaps with only token gestures toward making them English speakers. The relentless political pressures of ethnic activists have been directed toward the latter system—that is, establishing whole programs taught in a foreign language.

The political clout of these ethnic activists was reflected in Congress' restrictions on what percentage of federal spending in this area could be on programs teaching English as a second language, rather than on programs taught in foreign languages and given the label "bilingual." During the Carter administration, only 4 percent of the money could be spent on programs featuring English as a second language. Even under the Reagan administration (which was more critical of bilingualism) this rose only to 25 percent. In short, parents and school officials alike have been restricted in their ability to choose how to deal with foreign students' language problems, if their choice did not coincide with that of ethnic activists.

These ethnic activists—the Mexican American Legal Defense and Educational Fund, the National Council of La Raza, and others—have developed a whole agenda, going well beyond the language problems of school children. They argue that the "societal power structure" of white, Anglo-Saxon, English-speaking Americans handicaps non-English-speaking children, not only by presenting education in a language with which these children will have difficulty, but also by making these children ashamed of their own language and culture, and by making the abandonment of their ancestral culture the price of acceptance in the educational system and in American society. Consistent with this general vision, the educational deficiencies and high drop-out rates of Hispanic students, for example, are blamed on such assaults on their culture and self-esteem.

Given this vision, the agenda of the ethnic activists is not one of transitional programs to acquire English-language skills, but rather a promotion of the foreign language as a medium of instruction throughout the curriculum, promotion of the study and praise of other aspects of the foreign culture in the schools, and (whether openly avowed or not) promotion of a sense of historic grievances against American society, both on their own behalf and on behalf of other presumed victims of American and Western civilization, at home and around the world. In short, the activist agenda goes well beyond language education, or even education in general, to encompass political and ideological issues to be addressed in the public schools at taxpayer expense—and at the expense of time available for academic subjects. This activist agenda has provoked counter-responses by various individuals and groups, including school teachers, parents, and such civic organizations as "U.S. English" and "LEAD" (Learning English Advocates Drive). The resulting clashes have ranged from shouting matches in school meetings to legal battles in the federal courts. Bilingual education has been characterized by the *Washington Post* as "the single most controversial area in public education."

Studies of the educational effectiveness of bilingualism and of alternative approaches have been as much shrouded in controversy as every other aspect of this issue. Yet the preponderant weight of the political system and the educational system has been solidly behind bilingualism, just as if it were a proven success, and its advocates have kept bilingual programs well supplied with school children, through methods which often circumvent the parents of both foreign and native-born children.

In San Francisco, for example, thousands of English-speaking children with educational deficiencies were assigned to bilingual classes, blacks being twice as likely to be so assigned as whites. Hundreds of other youngsters, who in fact had a foreign language as their mother tongue, were assigned to bilingual classes in a *different* foreign language. Thus a Chinese immigrant child could be assigned to a bilingual program because of speaking a foreign language—but then be put into a Spanish language class. Similarly, a Spanish-speaking child might be put into a Chinese language class—all this being based on where space happened to be available, rather than on the actual educational needs of the particular child. "Bilingual-education classes," according to the leader of a Chinese American organization, have also been "used as a 'dumping ground' for educationally disadvantaged students or students with behavior problems."

In short, maintaining or expanding enrollment in bilingual programs has clearly taken priority over educating children. Moreover, the deception common in other programs promoted by zealots has also been common in bilingual programs. District administrators interviewed by the *San Francisco Examiner* "downplayed the number of black students assigned to bilingual classes, first estimating the number at three"—an estimate subsequently raised to about a hundred, though the real figure turned out to be more than 750. A civil rights attorney representing minority children characterized the whole approach as a "mindless" practice of "assigning kids to wherever there is space." It is not wholly mindless, however. Children whose parents are poorer, less educated, and less sophisticated are more likely to be assigned, or to remain, in bilingual programs. "More vocal white parents manage to maneuver their kids out of bilingual classes," as the civil rights attorney noted.

The San Francisco situation is by no means unique. A national study of bilingual programs found large numbers of English-speaking minority students in programs taught in foreign languages and ostensibly designed for youngsters unable to speak English. Only 16 percent of all students in such programs were students who spoke only Spanish—the kind of student envisioned when bilingual programs were instituted. A study in Texas found that most school districts automatically categorized as "limited English proficiency" students— eligible for bilingual programs—even those Hispanic children who spoke *only* English and whose parents only occasionally spoke Spanish at home. The study concluded that English was "the dominant language" of most of the students participating in the bilingual programs surveyed. Again, the whole thrust of the policy was toward maximizing enrollments.

Hispanic youngsters are not spared in the ruthless sacrifices of school children to the interests of the bilingual lobby. American-born, English-speaking students with Spanish surnames have often been targeted for inclusion in bilingual programs. Forced to speak Spanish during so-called bilingual classes, such youngsters have been observed speaking English among themselves during recess. A bilingual education teacher in Massachusetts reported speaking to Puerto Rican children in Spanish and having them reply in English. Research in several California school districts showed that children classified as "limited English proficient" ranged from being predominantly better in Spanish than English in districts closer to the Mexican border to being predominantly better in English than in Spanish in districts farther north, with about two-thirds being equally proficient (or deficient) in the two languages in the intermediate city of Santa Barbara. A large-scale national study of bilingual programs found that two-thirds of the Hispanic children enrolled in such programs were already fluent in English, and more than four-fifths of the directors of such programs admitted that they retained students in their programs after the students had mastered English.

While the rationale for so-called bilingual programs has been presented to the public in terms of the educational needs of children whose native language is not English, what actually happens in such programs bears little relationship to that rationale. It bears much more relationship to the careers and ideologies of bilingual activists. A study of Hispanic middle-school students in Boston, for example, found that 45 percent had been kept in bilingual programs for six years or more. The criteria for being taken out of such programs are often based on achieving a given proficiency in English, so that students are retained in bilingual programs even when their English is better than their Spanish. A bilingual education teacher in Springfield, Massachusetts, reported her frustration in trying for years to get such students transferred into regular classrooms:

> Each year we had the same disagreement. I argued that the students, according to test scores and classroom performance, had made enough progress in English to be able to work in a regular classroom, with some further attention to their reading and writing skills. The department head argued that they must remain in the bilingual program as long as they were not yet reading at grade level. It did not matter when I countered that many American students who speak only English do not read at grade level, or that after six or seven years of heavy instruction in Spanish without achieving good results it was probably time to try a different approach.

Students retained in bilingual programs for years, without mastering either English or Spanish, have sometimes been characterized as "semi-lingual," rather than bilingual. The bilingual label is often grossly misleading also in terms of the token amount of time spent on English—perhaps a couple of hours a week—in programs which are predominantly foreign language programs, where students may spend years before taking a single subject taught in English.

The great majority of Hispanic parents—more than three-fourths of Mexican American parents and more than four-fifths of Cuban American parents—are opposed to the teaching of Spanish in the schools at the expense of English. Many Asian refugee parents in Lowell, Massachusetts, likewise declared their opposition to bilingual education for their children. In Springfield, Massachusetts, the Spanish-speaking bilingual teachers themselves put their own children in private schools, so that they would not be subjected to bilingual education. Parents in Los Angeles who did not want their children enrolled in bilingual programs have been pressured, deceived, or tricked into agreement or seeming agreement. By and large, ethnic activists oppose giving parents an option.

That the wishes of both majority and minority parents have been over-ridden or circumvented suggests something of the power and the ruthlessness of the bilingual lobby. Much of this power comes from the U.S. Department of Education, where ethnic activists have been prominent among those writing federal guidelines, which go much further than the courts or the Congress in forcing bilingual programs into schools and forcing out alternative ways of dealing with the language problems of non-English-speaking children. However, bilingual activists have also been active in state and local agencies, and have been ruthless in smearing or harassing those who do not go along with their agenda.

More than ideological zealotry is involved in the relentless drive to maintain and expand enrollment in bilingual programs, at all costs. Federal and local subsidies add up to hundreds of dollars per child for students enrolled in bilingual programs, and teachers proficient in Spanish receive bonuses amounting to thousands of dollars each annually. Bilingualism has been aptly described as "a jobs program for Spanish-speaking teachers."

Teachers from foreign countries who speak one of the languages used in bilingual programs can be hired in California without passing the test of basic skills required of other teachers, even if they lack a college degree and are not fluent in English. At the University of Massachusetts, candidates for their bilingual teacher program were, for a number of years, not even tested in English—all testing being done in Spanish. Moreover, a non-Hispanic woman who was fluent in Spanish, and who had taught for years in Mexico, was rejected on grounds that she was not sufficiently familiar with Puerto Rico. Among the questions she was asked was the name of three small rivers in the interior of the island—a tactic reminiscent of the questions once asked by Southern voter registrars to keep blacks from being eligible to vote.

The costs of bilingualism add up. In Dade County, Florida, it cost 50 percent more to educate an immigrant child than the cost of educating a non-immigrant child. Oakland, California, found that it was spending $7 million annually to provide native-language instruction. Nationally, expenditures on bilingual education have tripled in a decade. The largest costs, however, are paid by the students who go through programs which claim to teach them two languages but often fail to teach them mastery of one. Among adults, Hispanics fluent in English earn incomes comparable to other Americans of the same age and education level. To deny them that fluency is to create a life-long economic handicap.

The virtually unanimous support of bilingualism among Hispanic activists, "leaders" and "spokesmen"—in contrast to Hispanic parents—is understandable only in terms of the self-interest of those activists, "leaders" and "spokesmen," who benefit from the preservation of a separate ethnic enclave, preferably alienated from the larger society. This is not peculiar to Hispanics. Similar patterns can be found around the world. Activists, "leaders" and "spokesmen" for Australian aborigines promote the teaching of aboriginal languages to aborigines who already speak English, just as Maori activists in New Zealand push the teaching of the Maori language to Maoris who have grown up speaking English. In these and other countries, separate language maintenance has been part of a larger program of separatism and alienation in general. In all these disparate settings, the education of school children has been sacrificed to the financial and ideological interests of activists.

Promoters of so-called bilingual education, like the promoters of other forms of separatism, often claim that they are promoting intergroup harmony and mutual respect. "Language diversity within a society reduces ethnocentrism," one such promoter claims, but it would be hard to find concrete examples of this anywhere on this planet, while there are all too many counter-examples of nations torn apart by ethnic polarization in Malaysia, murderous riots in India, and outright civil war in Sri Lanka, to name just a few. Sri Lanka is an especially poignant example, for it was at one time justly held up to the world as a model of intergroup harmony—*before* language politics became a major issue.

One of the most widely used, and most tendentious, arguments in favor of the foreign-language and foreign-culture programs operating under the bilingual label is that a changing racial and cultural mix in the United States requires such programs, in order for American society to accommodate the newcomers. "People of color will make up one-third of the net additions to the U.S. labor force between 1985 and 2000," according to one bilingual advocate, who has urged "second-language competencies by all students," because otherwise a merely transitional bilingual program for minorities will lead to "the erosion, rather than the maintenance of, the minority languages."

First of all, when people say that racial, ethnic, or linguistic minorities will make up some projected percentage of "net additions to the U.S. Labor force," there is much less there than meets the eye. The American population and labor force are growing slowly, so that any given fraction of that small *increment* is not a major factor in the overall composition of the country's population or labor force. Even if it were, it is a *non sequitur* to say that special language programs must be established for newcomers, in a country where millions of newcomers have flooded in for generations on end, without any such programs being established.

Inflating the size of the population affected by language policy by speaking of "people of color" ignores the fact that most of those people of color are black, native-born, English-speaking people. Finally, even for those people who come to the United States speaking a different language, they not only can learn English but are in fact learning English, just as other immigrants did before them. Virtually all second-generation Hispanics speak English and more than half of all third-generation Hispanics speak *only* English. All the sound and fury of the bilingual advocates is directed toward countering this natural evolution, which will otherwise deprive them of the separate and alienated ethnic enclaves so useful to "leaders"—and so detrimental to minorities as a whole and to the society as a whole.

The political success of bilingual activists—despite the opposition of parents and teachers, and despite both scholarly studies and journalistic exposés revealing the fraudulence of their claims—has wider implications for the vulnerability of the political process to strident special interests who are organized and ruthless. Education at all levels is especially vulnerable to promoters of their own ideological or financial interests in the name of some group for whom they claim to speak. In Los Angeles, which has one of the largest bilingual programs in the country, more than three-quarters of the school teachers oppose such programs—but to no avail. Bilingual activists have been so successful in branding critics as "racists" opposed to Hispanic people that an organization critical of bilingualism keeps their membership secret. Intimidation and character assassination tactics have proved effective all the way up to the college and university levels, and for other groups besides Hispanics. Sometimes it is sufficient to accuse people merely of "insensitivity" to accomplish the same political result.

One of the most tendentious words in the vocabulary of multiculturalism is "sensitivity." When it is proclaimed that one must become more "sensitive" to various ethnic, linguistic, sexual, or lifestyle groups, neither a reason nor a definition usually accompanies this opaque imperative. Moreover, what is called "sensitivity" often involves being *less* sensitive, in order to be more ideologically in fashion. For example, it is considered "insensitive" to use the word "Orientals" instead of "Asians" (even though the Orient or east is ultimately just a direction—and no one considers it insensitive to refer to the West or to Westerners). But, where there is a substantive difference between "Orientals" and "Asians," the former is the more specific term referring to persons of Chinese, Japanese, and related racial ancestry, while the latter geographical term encompasses as well the racially different peoples of India, Malaysia, Indonesia, and the Philippines.

In other countries as well, to be "sensitive" in the ideological sense is to be *insensitive* to finer distinctions. In Britain, for example, to be ideologically sensitive is to call all non-white Britons "black," whether they are in fact Chinese, Pakistani, or West Indian. In Canada, the phrase that lumps all non-whites together is "visible minorities." In the United States, the corresponding phrase is "people of color."

In plain English, to make finer distinctions is to be more sensitive, but in educational Newspeak "sensitivity" means going along with current ideological fashions. When racially and culturally heterogeneous groups are lumped together—whether as "Asians" in the United States, "blacks" in Britain or "visible minorities" in Canada—the ideological point is to depict them all as victims of whites, and their economic, educational, or other problems as being due to that victimization. What a finer breakdown would reveal is that some of these groups differ as much from one another as they do from whites, whether in race, income, education, or cultural patterns. In some cases, particular ethnic groups within the broad category depicted as victims actually exceed the income or occupational status of whites. The taboo against finer distinctions among such groups serve to conceal such ideologically inconvenient facts.

"Sensitivity" goes in only one direction. It is seldom considered insensitive to refer to individuals or groups as "Anglos" or "WASPs" (white, Anglo-Saxon Protestants), even when they are in fact Celtic, Semitic, or Slavic in ancestry or Catholic, Judaic, or agnostic in religion. Nor are the most sweeping stereotypes about "Anglos" or "WASPs" likely to be questioned, either as to taste or accuracy.

The charge of "insensitivity" applies far more widely than to names, though usually with the same one-sidedness. To be sensitive, as ideologically defined, requires that one not merely accept but "affirm" other people's way of life or even "celebrate" diversity in general. Like other demands for "sensitivity," this demand offers no reason—unless fear of being disapproved, denounced, or harassed is a reason. If the thought is that anyone who really understood, or tried to understand, others' cultures would necessarily approve, then this is simply an unsubstantiated dogma posing as a moral imperative. Moreover, automatic approval has no meaning, except as a symptom of successful intimidation.

If you have no right to disapprove, then your approval means nothing. It may indeed be distressing to someone to have you express your opinion that his lifestyle is disgusting and his art, music or writing is crude, shallow, or repugnant, but unless you are free to reach such conclusions, any praise you bestow is hollow and suspect. To say that A has a right to B's approval is to say that B has no right to his own opinion. What is even more absurd, the "sensitivity" argument is not even consistent, because everything changes drastically according to who is *A* and who is *B*. Those in the chosen groups may repudiate any aspect of the prevailing culture, without being considered insensitive, but no one from the prevailing culture may repudiate any aspect of other cultures.

The Flow of Racism

One of the claims for multicultural programs in schools and colleges is that they reduce intergroup conflict by making all groups aware of, and sensitive to, racial, ethnic, and cultural differences—and more accepting of these differences. Whatever the plausibility of these claims, they are seldom, if ever, backed up with any evidence that schools or colleges with such programs have less intergroup conflict than institutions without them. The real dogmatism of such claims comes out most clearly, however, where mounting evidence of *increasing* animosities among students from different backgrounds, in the wake of multicultural programs, is met by further claims that this only shows the racism of the larger society overflowing into the schools and colleges.

An editor of *The American School Board Journal* was all too typical in asserting—without a speck of evidence—that "the effects of society's racism are spilling over into the schools," and adding (also without evidence), "public schools are society's best hope of battling racism." He urged adding multicultural programs to the school curriculum and quoted an education professor who said: "Few other instructional techniques promise to make such improvements." That statement is no doubt true enough in itself. The real question is whether multiculturalism delivers on that promise—or whether it in fact makes racism worse. That empirical question is not even asked, much less answered, either by this editor or by numerous other advocates of "multicultural diversity."

This dogmatism by multicultural zealots is found from the elementary schools to the colleges and universities. It stretches across the country and internationally as well.

The chairman of a committee of inquiry into a race-related murder on a school playground in Manchester, England, reported: "At several stages of our inquiry, we were told that racism in school derives from racism in the wider community." Yet, after reviewing the zealous "multicultural" and "anti-racist" policies of the schools—policies which the committee chairman generally favored—he was forced to conclude that, in this instance at least, the actual implementation of these policies was "one of the greatest recipes for the spread of racism from the school out into the community." The *very possibility* that racism is flowing in the opposite direction to that assumed is never considered in most of the vast international literature on multiculturalism.

The Manchester multicultural program was instituted despite a warning that such programs in the London area had proved to be "a fiasco," and "divisive," and had created "suspicion" and "squabbles." Ordinary people in the neighborhood near the Manchester school, where a Pakistani boy was killed by a white boy, also had no difficulty considering the possibility that multiculturalism could be counterproductive.

"I feel that this enforced focus on multi-culturalism produces prejudices," one said.

"I feel that the best way to bring about avoidance of racial hostility would be to ignore people's ethnic origins and characteristics," another said.

Double standards in treating students were cited among the counterproductive fruits of multiculturalism: "The teachers are scared, they are frightened to take the white side in case they are accused of racism." Such complaints of double standards, favoring non-white students, also came from white students in the school—and were confirmed by the predominantly *non-white* committee of inquiry, dominated by Labor Party members. This panel's findings could not be dismissed in the usual way by labeling them white male conservatives.

Some of the criticisms of multiculturalism as a counterproductive factor in race relations may be only statements of plausibility—but so are the opposite statements of the multicultural zealots. Yet these zealots operate as intolerantly as if they had the certainty of a proven fact. Belief in multiculturalism became a litmus test for applicants for teaching positions in the Manchester school, for example, and initiatives from the principal and other multicultural zealots "were presented in a way that assumed everybody was racist." None of this was peculiar to Manchester or to England. Such things as enforcement of ideological conformity, *a priori* accusations of racism, and double standards for judging students' behavior are common features of multicultural programs in the schools and colleges of the United States. So too is trying to force people to take part in foreign cultural experiences—in religion, food, and a useless smattering of foreign words, for example—whether they want to or not, and regardless of the academic or other costs.

"Why do we have to eat their food?" a student in Manchester asked. Their parents' questions included: Why are English children being taught to count in Punjabi, when they are having trouble counting in English? Why are they being forced to take part in Moslem religious rites? Similar questions can be raised wherever multicultural zealots gain dominance—and such questions are likely to be ignored elsewhere, as they were in Manchester.

In the United States, multiculturalism not only covers the kinds of practices and attitudes found in England. In the U.S., the very pictures in textbooks must reflect the multicultural ideology. As one education writer noted:

> . . . the textbooks teachers rely on are required to reflect the growing insistence on inclusion of "underrepresented populations"—mainly racial and ethnic minorities, women, and the handicapped.

In the two biggest textbook markets in the country, Texas and California, committees of the state legislature have "set up exacting goals for depicting these groups in a book's stories and illustrations." One free-lance artist stopped illustrating children's readers after receiving a set of "multicultural" instructions running to ten pages, single-spaced. As she described the pictures resulting from these instructions:

> The hero was a Hispanic boy. There were black twins, one boy, one girl; an overweight Oriental boy, and an American Indian girl. That leaves the Caucasian. Since we mustn't forget the physically handicapped, she was born with congenital malformation and had only three fingers on one hand. . . .

The Hispanic boy's parents could not have jobs that would seem stereotypical, so they had to be white collar workers and eat non-Hispanic food—"spaghetti and meatballs and a salad." The editor even specified to the artist what kind of lettuce should be in the salad. "Make sure it's not iceberg: it should be something nice like endive."

There also had to be a picture of a "senior citizen"—jogging. Such nit-picking is neither unusual nor the idiosyncrasy of a particular editor or publisher. A specialist in textbook production pointed out that virtually every textbook "has to submit to ethnic/gender counts as to authors, characters in stories, references in history books, etc. Even humanized animal characters—if there's two boy bears, there have to be two girl bears."

Part of the double standards of multiculturalism often involves a paternalistic sheltering of disadvantaged minority children from things remote from their immediate experience. As one former teacher on a Wyoming Indian reservation put it, in asking for "textbook relevance" for his Indian students:

> The concept of an ocean would be foreign to them. The children of Wind River know Ocean Lake, so named because of its considerable size, and the occasional wind-driven waves. They couldn't fathom the idea of a real ocean.

No such claim was made for the white children in Wyoming, or in any of the other land-locked states of the United States. More fundamentally, it did not address the question whether education is meant to open a window on a larger world or to paint the student into his own little corner.

With so many people bending over backward to be "sensitive," with so much attention to mixing people from different groups, not only in real life (through "busing" and the like), but even in textbook pictures, what has been the net result? A San Francisco high school presented a lunchtime scene all too typical of many American schools and colleges where "multicultural diversity" is only statistical:

> In the brick-lined courtyard, a group of black students gathers on benches. Outside a second-floor classroom, several Chinese girls eat chow mein and fried rice from takeout cartons. Inside the dreary cafeteria, a clique of Vietnamese students sprawls across two tables—where they have spent every lunch since September. Against the back wall, two lone Russian boys pass lunch in conversation.
>
> San Francisco schools have spent two decades and more than $100 million on integration programs. Yet outside the classroom—at the lunch counters, on the playground and in the hallways—many ethnic groups still mix as well as oil and water.

It should be noted again that California is one of the states where the very textbook pictures must conform to the multicultural ideology. Moreover, it is not at all clear that there was this much ethnic separatism in multi-ethnic schools in times past. This is not simply a California problem, however. Researchers around the country report internal self-segregation among students in schools racially "integrated" statistically. A two-year study by a professor at the University of Pittsburgh found that, on a typical day at a school being studied, only 15 out of 250 students ate lunch sitting next to someone of a different race, even though the school had equal numbers of black and white students.

The more fundamental question—whether racism is increased or decreased in the schools by multiculturalism, and therefore whether the flow of racism is primarily from the schools to the larger society, or vice-versa—can be better addressed in discussions of multiculturalism in American colleges and universities. It is sufficient here to point out that that question is seldom even considered in the massive outpourings of words on "multicultural diversity."

MISCELLANEOUS PSYCHO-BABBLE

"Relevance"

Everyone wants education to be relevant. It is hard even to conceive why anyone would wish it to be irrelevant. Those who proclaim the need for "relevance" in education are fighting a straw man—and evading the crucial need to define what *they* mean by "relevance," and why that particular definition should prevail.

Beginning in the 1960s, insistence on "relevance" became widespread and the particular kind of "relevance" being sought was typically a relevance judged *in advance* by students who had not yet learned the particular things being judged, much less applied them in practice in the real world. Relevance thus became a label for the general belief that the usefulness or meaningfulness of information or training could be determined *a priori*.

"No one should ever be trying to learn something for which one sees no relevance," according to Carl Rogers. The student should be asked:

"What do you want to learn? What things puzzle you? What are you curious about? What issues concern you? What problems do you wish you could solve?"

It is easy to see how this particular concept of relevance is consonant with trends toward more student choice, whether individually in choosing among elective courses in schools and colleges, or collectively in designing or helping to design the curriculum. Because the student has neither foreknowledge of the material to be learned nor experience in its application in the real world beyond the walls of the school, his emotional response to the material must be his guide. As Carl Rogers envisioned the process:

> I am talking about LEARNING—the insatiable curiosity that drives the adolescent boy to absorb everything he can see or hear or read about gasoline engines in order to improve the efficiency and speed of his "cruiser." I am talking about the student who says, "I am discovering, drawing in from the outside, and making that which is drawn in a real part of *me*." I am talking about any learning in which the experience of the learner progresses along this line: "No, no, that's not what I want"; "Wait! This is closer to what I'm interested in, what I need"; "Ah, here it is! Now I'm grasping and comprehending what I *need* and what I want to know!"

At the heart of the "relevance" notion is the belief that current emotional responses are a reliable guide to the future usefulness or meaningfulness of education. Although this assumption is essential to the logic of the argument for "relevance," Carl Rogers was one of the few who made that assumption explicit when he said that the man who would "do what 'felt right' in this immediate moment" would "find this in general to be a trustworthy guide to his behavior." If emotions are indeed so prescient and virtually omniscient, then of course there is little reason to rely on experience—which must mean the experience of others, in the case of inexperienced students.

It is hard to imagine how a small child, first learning the alphabet, can appreciate the full implications of learning these particular 26 abstract symbols in an arbitrarily fixed order. Yet this lifelong access to the intellectual treasures of centuries depend on his mastery of these symbols. His ability to organize and retrieve innumerable kinds of information, from sources ranging from encyclopedias to computers, depends on his memorizing that purely arbitrary order. There is not the slightest reason in the world why a small child should be expected to grasp the significance of all this. Instead, he learns these symbols and this order because his parents and teachers want him to learn it—not because he sees its "relevance."

Experience would be virtually worthless if it were possible to know *a priori* what will and will not be needed in the future. If an economist who has done 20 years of research and analysis has no better idea how much statistical analysis a beginner should master than that beginner himself has, then one can only marvel that 20 years of experience have been such a complete waste. In a new recruit beginning basic training in the army knows just as much as a battle-scarred veteran as to what one should do to prepare for battle, then there is no justification for putting experienced officers in charge of troops and no excuse for differences in rank. In no other field of endeavor besides education would such reasoning even be taken seriously, much less be made the basis of institutional policy.

The "relevance" argument becomes especially dangerous when it is used to justify teaching different things to students from different racial or ethnic groups, on the basis of those students' immediate emotional responses, or their uninformed sense of plausibility as to what might, for example, be "relevant to the black experience"—at a time of life when they do not have enough experience of any color to make such a determination. How can someone who sets out to study things "relevant to the black experience" know whether such statistical concepts as multicollinearity or such economic concepts as dynamic equilibrium will turn out to be among those things which provide a whole new perspective on racial issues? To say that such questions can be answered *a priori* is to assume at the outset the very competence which education is supposed to produce as an end result.

Although many who use the "relevance" argument may not see clearly how it depends crucially on the reliability of current emotions as a guide to the future value of education, the inner logic of the argument nevertheless shows through in the frequency with which people of this persuasion use the word "exciting" as a recommendation for some educational policy. Other investments—that is, current costs incurred for future benefits—are seldom assessed in terms of how "exciting" they are. Farmers do not say that planting a given crop is exciting. Their justification for choosing a particular crop, or for planting it in a certain soil at a particular time of year, is much more apt to be in terms of the likelihood of producing a good harvest. Similarly, a financial investor seldom characterizes his choice of portfolio as "exciting." Instead, his justification for choosing the particular investments in his portfolio is likely to run in terms of his assessment of future rewards.

Education is one of the largest investments in the society, running into hundreds of billions of dollars annually. Yet this investment is often, and increasingly, assessed in terms of its current emotional appeal to students or teachers. In short, it is not treated as an investment but as current consumption. The Bible said: "By their fruits ye shall know them." Educators too often seem to be saying: "By their excitement ye shall know them." For those less blatant, the word "relevance" is a roundabout way of saying the same thing.

The idea that inexperienced young people can judge in advance what will later turn out to be relevant over the next half-century or more of their life is part of a more general and romantic social vision. This vision underlies such things as denigration of authority derived from experience or specialized training. This vision has been not only part of many radical experiments in American education, beginning during the 1960s, but was also the foundation of even more radical educational experiments in schools and colleges in China during the "great cultural revolution." The results were very similar in these very different settings.

In China, as in the United States, ideologically defined "relevance" superseded traditionally defined skills, as academic criteria in general were subordinated to such social goals as group "representation," while elitism in general was decried. College entrance examinations were abolished, grades were no longer unilaterally assigned by teachers but were discussed or negotiated, and off-campus activities substituted for academic work. Educators' authority was so undermined that teachers were "afraid to take firm charge of their students." The educational results in China were also similar to those in the United States. Nearly half the middle-school students failed the tests of basic knowledge in science and technology, and more than two-thirds failed the mathematics examination. By 1979, a group of American educators found that China's college entrance examinations were no longer as sophisticated as they had been 20 years earlier.

The biggest difference between China's educational experiments and those in the United States has been that the Chinese learned from their mistakes, and abandoned such policies, while American education continues on the same course. Chinese political leaders recognized that China was falling further behind world standards in science and technology as a result of its educational debacles, and proceeded to re-introduce the teaching of traditional subjects and college entrance examinations. Ideologically defined "relevance" was no longer a sacred cow in China, though it remains so in the United States.

The "Whole Person"

The idea that one should teach "the whole child" goes back at least as far as John Dewey. Some today call it "child-centered education" at the elementary school level and teaching "the whole person" in high school or college. The idea of tailor-made education, varying with the social background and psychology of each student, is related to the notion of "relevance." It is also reminiscent of an idea once popular among some ambitious economists, that they could "fine tune" the economy—until embarrassing experience taught them that they were lucky to get the right channel.

Ambitious educational goals seldom seem to evoke the question as to whether we have the capability of achieving them. Nor are these ambitions noticeably moderated by the educational system's abysmal failure at teaching the most basic skills. That educators who have repeatedly failed to do what they are hired to do, and trained to do, should take on sweeping roles as amateur psychologists, sociologists, and social philosophers seems almost inexplicable—except that they are doing it with other people's money and experimenting on other people's children.

There is only one way to deal with "the whole person"—and that is superficially. Anyone who is serious about understanding just one small aspect of the whole person—the endocrine glands, for example—knows that it is the labor of a lifetime for highly trained people, working with unrelenting dedication. Merely to develop the whole person's photographic talents can take many years, as anyone can see by looking at the nondescript early photographs taken by the great photographer Ansel Adams. The reason for teaching mathematics, instead of teaching "the whole person," is that one may have had some serious training in mathematics, and so at least have the possibility of being competent at it.

Educational theory too often focuses on the *desirability* of doing something, to the complete exclusion of the question of our *capability* of doing it. No doubt it would be far more desirable to travel through the air like Superman, instead of inching along in a traffic jam. But that is no reason to leap off skyscrapers. Our educational system is full of the results of leaping off skyscrapers.

Other countries whose educational systems achieve more than ours often do so in part by attempting less. While school children in Japan are learning science, mathematics, and a foreign language, American school children are sitting around in circles, unburdening their psyches and "expressing themselves" on scientific, economic and military issues for which they lack even the rudiments of competence. Worse than what they are *not* learning is what they *are* learning—presumptuous superficiality, taught by practitioners of it.

The "whole person" philosophy is not simply a theory of education. It has become an open floodgate through which all sorts of non-educational activities have poured into the schools, relieving many teachers of the drudgery of teaching, and substituting more "exciting" world-saving crusades in place of the development of academic skills.

Whether the crusade concerns the environment, AIDS, foreign policy, or a thousand other things, it is far more often pursued as a crusade than as an issue with arguments on both sides. Moreover, it is not sufficient that the students be propagandized in the classroom; they are taught to *act* on the one-sided superficiality they have been given. At one time, the President of the United States received more letters from school children fulfilling classroom assignments on nuclear war than letters from any other group on any other subject.

In the San Francisco public schools in 1991, teachers organized a letter-writing campaign in which thousands of students sent letters to elected state officials, protesting cuts in the school budget. One letter from an elementary school student said: "I hate you. I would like to kill you." Another letter asked about the official's wife and children and said, "I'm going to set your house on fire and get my homies to beat you up!" In response to public outcry and to angry officials, California's State Superintendent of Public Instruction, Bill Honig, sent out a memorandum to county and district superintendents, warning that "it would be legally safer to avoid such activities." As for the ethics and propriety of using the children in this way, a spokesman for Honig's office was quoted in the *San Francisco Examiner* as justifying such school assignments:

> "It's appropriate to have kids responding to a current issue directly in-volving their lives," she said. "So having kids use class time to address public officials on current events is appropriate."

Those who emphasize the teaching of "issues" rather than acade-mic skills fail to understand that "issues" are infinitely more complex and difficult to master than fundamental principles of analysis. The very reason why there is an issue in the first place is usually because no single principle can possibly resolve the differences to the mutual satisfaction of those concerned. Innumerable principles are often in-teracting in a changing environment, creating vast amounts of com-plex facts to be mastered and assessed—*if* one is serious about resolving issues responsibly, as distinguished from generating excite-ment. To teach issues instead of intellectual principles to school chil-dren is like teaching calculus to people who have not yet learned arithmetic, or surgery to people lacking the rudiments of anatomy or hygiene. Worse, it is teaching them to go ahead and perform surgery, without worrying about boring details.

"Role Models"

One of the most widely accepted—or at least unchallenged—dogmas in American education today is that students need "role models" from the same social background as themselves. From the kinder-garten to the colleges and universities, the dogma holds sway that stu-dents are taught more effectively by people of the same race, ethnicity, culture, and sex as themselves. Empirical evidence is almost never asked for, much less given.

Many of those who espouse this doctrine have the most obvious self-interest in doing so. Teachers and directors of bilingual edu-cational programs, Afro-centric programs in schools and various ethnic studies programs in college, all preserve jobs and careers for themselves—free of competition from members of the majority population—by using the "role model" dogma. So do feminists, homosexuals, and others. Administrators who have caved in to demands for various enclaves and preserves for particular groups likewise have a vested interest in this dogma, as a defense against critics. Around this solid core of supporters of the "role model" idea, there is a wider penumbra of those who wish to be *au courant* with the latest buzzwords, or to be on the side of the angels, as currently defined.

Historically, there have been good, bad, and indifferent schools where students and teachers were of wholly different backgrounds and all sorts of combinations in between. There is no empirical evidence that any of those similarities or differences are correlated with educational results, and considerable indications that they are not.

One of the most academically successful of the all-black schools was Dunbar High School in Washington, D.C., during the period from its founding in 1870 until its rapid deterioration in the late 1950s, in the wake of new rules for selecting students. In addition to producing good academic results in general during this period, Dunbar also produced an impressive list of "the first black" to enter a number of fields and institutions, ranging from West Point and Annapolis to the federal judiciary and the Presidential Cabinet. Its curriculum, however, was hardly Afro-centric and was in fact so traditional as to include Latin, long after most American schools had abandoned that ancient language. While Dunbar's teachers were black, another equally high-quality high school, St. Augustine's in New Orleans, was founded and manned by whites of the Josephite order.

Among the European immigrant groups, the first Irish Catholic children were taught by Protestant Anglo-Saxon teachers, at a time when such differences were very important socially and economically. Later, when the Jewish immigrant children began flooding into the public schools, they were far more likely to be taught by Irish Catholic teachers than by Jewish teachers. Still later, among the Chinese and Japanese children of immigrants, it was virtually unknown for them to be taught by teachers of their own race, religion, or culture. Yet, from all this vast experience, no one has yet produced evidence that "role models" from the student's own background are either necessary or sufficient, or in fact make any discernible academic difference at all.

The "role model" dogma is pork barrel politics, masquerading as educational philosophy. That this wholly unsubstantiated claim has been taken seriously in the media and by public officials is one more sign of the vulnerability of our minds and our institutions to vehement assertions—and to strident attacks on all who question them.

"Self-Esteem"

The notion that self-esteem is a precondition for effective learning is one of the more prominent dogmas to have spread rapidly through the American educational system in recent years. However, its roots go back some decades, to the whole "child-centered" approach of so-called Progressive education. Like so much that comes out of that philosophy, it confuses cause and effect. No doubt valedictorians feel better about themselves than do students who have failed numerous courses, just as people who have won the Nobel Prize probably have more self-esteem than people who have been convicted of a felony.

Outside the world of education, few would be confident, or even comfortable, claiming that it is a lack of self-esteem which leads to felonies or its presence which leads to Nobel Prizes. Yet American schools are permeated with the idea that self-esteem precedes performance, rather than vice-versa. The very idea that self-esteem is something *earned*, rather than being a pre-packaged handout from the school system, seems not to occur to many educators. Too often, American educators are like the Wizard of Oz, handing out substitutes for brains, bravery, or heart.

The practical consequences of the self-esteem dogma are many. Failing grades are to be avoided, to keep from damaging fragile egos, according to this doctrine. Thus the Los Angeles school system simply abolished failing grades in the early years of elementary school and many leading colleges and universities simply do not record failing grades on a student's transcript. Other ways of forestalling a loss of self-esteem is to water down the courses to the point where failing grades are highly unlikely. A more positive approach to self-esteem is simply to give higher grades. The widespread grade inflation of recent decades owes much to this philosophy.

While the "role model" dogma is more obviously self-serving than the "self-esteem" dogma, the latter is not wholly free of self-interest. It is much easier to water down academic courses, replace them with non-academic activities, or give automatic high grades for either, than to take on the serious and difficult task of developing intellectual competence among masses of school children. Whatever the intentions of John Dewey or other pioneers of the Progressive education philosophy, its practical conseqences have been a steady retreat from the daunting task of making mass education a serious attempt to raise American school children to a standard, rather than bringing the standard down to them.

The history of American education, from the time when high schools ceased to be a place reserved for an academic or social elite, has been a history of a steady displacement, or swamping, of academic subjects by non-academic subjects or academic subjects increasingly watered down. A blue-ribbon committee formed in the 1890s indentified 40 subjects being taught in American high schools but, within two decades, the number of subjects expanded to 274. As of the period from 1906 to 1910, approximately two-thirds of all subjects taught in American high schools were academic subjects, but by 1930 only one-third were academic subjects.

Even when the educational reform movements of the 1980s were successful politically in getting academic-subject requirements written into law and public policy, the response of many school systems across the country was simply to increase the number of academic subjects taught at a lower level—including courses taught remedially or even meretriciously, as former non-academic courses were renamed to look academic on paper. Sometimes the proliferation of pseudo-academic courses led to an absolute decline in the number of students taking challenging academic subjects.

The "self-esteem" doctrine is just one in a long line of educational dogmas used to justify or camouflage a historic retreat from academic education. Its success depends on the willingness of the public, elected officials, and the media to take such dogmas seriously, without the slightest evidence. American school children and American society are the ultimate victims of this gullibility.

Sex and Separateness

The publication of The Closing of the American Mind *was as important a cultural event as has happened in the last twenty-five years. Allan Bloom was the first to attack publicly what was to become known as political correctness. But the scope of his criticism encompassed most of the excesses of our age.*

He wrote about sex. He was not a religious man and yet his analysis suited orthodox tastes, although, God knows, not always. A scholar of the first order who clearly loved his students—and listened to them—Professor Bloom understood as well as anyone the price that men and women, perhaps especially women, pay for "liberation."

What follows is Dan Quayle's "Murphy Brown" speech, for intellectuals.

SEX

Contrary to the popular prejudice that America is the nation of unintellectual and anti-intellectual people, where ideas are at best means to ends, America is actually nothing but a great stage on which theories have been played as tragedy and comedy. This is a regime founded by philosophers and their students. All the recalcitrant matter of the historical *is* gave way here before the practical and philosophical *ought to be,* as the raw natural givens of this wild continent meekly submitted to the yoke of theoretical science. Other peoples were autochthonous, deriving guidance from the gods of their various places. When they too decided to follow the principles we pioneered, they hobbled along awkwardly, unable to extricate themselves gracefully from their pasts. Our story is the majestic and triumphant march of the principles of freedom and equality, giving meaning to all that we have done or are doing. There are almost no accidents; everything that happens among us is a consequence of one or both of our principles—a triumph over some opposition to them, a discovery of a fresh meaning in them, a dispute about which of the two has primacy, etc.

Now we have arrived at one of the ultimate acts in our drama, the informing and reforming of our most intimate private lives by our principles. Sex and its consequences—love, marriage and family—have finally become the theme of the national project, and here the problem of nature, always present but always repressed in the reconstruction of man demanded by freedom and equality, becomes insistent. In order to intuit the meaning of equality, we have no need for the wild imaginative genius of Aristophanes, who in *The Assembly of Women* contrives the old hags entitled by law to sexual satisfaction from handsome young males, or of Plato, who in the *Republic* prescribed naked exercises for men and women together. We only have to look around us, if we have eyes to see.

The change in sexual relations, which now provide an unending challenge to human ingenuity, came over us in two successive waves in the last two decades. The first was the sexual revolution; the second, feminism. The sexual revolution marched under the banner of freedom; feminism under that of equality. Although they went arm in arm for a while, their differences eventually put them at odds with each other, as Tocqueville said freedom and equality would always be. This is manifest in the squabble over pornography, which pits liberated sexual desire against feminist resentment about stereotyping. We are presented with the amusing spectacle of pornography clad in armor borrowed from the heroic struggles for freedom of speech, and using Miltonic rhetoric, doing battle with feminism, newly draped in the robes of community morality, using arguments associated with conservatives who defend traditional sex roles, and also defying an authoritative tradition in which it was taboo to suggest any relation between what a person reads and sees and his sexual practices. In the background stand the liberals, wringing their hands in confusion because they wish to favor both sides and cannot.

Sexual liberation presented itself as a bold affirmation of the senses and of undeniable natural impulse against our puritanical heritage, society's conventions and repressions, bolstered by Biblical myths about original sin. From the early sixties on there was a gradual testing of the limits on sexual expression, and they melted away or had already disappeared without anybody's having noticed it. The disapproval of parents and teachers of youngsters' sleeping or living together was easily overcome. The moral inhibitions, the fear of disease, the risk of pregnancy, the family and social consequences of premarital intercourse and the difficulty of finding places in which to have it—everything that stood in its way suddenly was no longer there. Students, particularly the girls, were no longer ashamed to give public evidence of sexual attraction or of its fulfillment. The kind of cohabitations that were dangerous in the twenties, and risqué or bohemian in the thirties and forties, became as normal as membership in the Girl Scouts. I say "particularly" girls because young men were always supposed to be eager for immediate gratification, whereas young women, inspired by modesty, were supposed to resist it. It was a modification or phasing out of female modesty that made the new arrangements possible. Since, however, modesty was supposed to be mere convention or habit, no effort was required to overcome it. This emancipation had in its intention and its effect the accentuation of the difference between the sexes. Making love was to be the primary activity, so men and women were to be more emphatically male and female. Of course, homosexuals were also liberated, but for the great mass of people, being free and natural meant achieving heterosexual satisfactions, opposite sexes made for each other.

The immediate promise of sexual liberation was, simply, happiness understood as the release of energies that had been stored up over millennia during the dark night of repression, in a great continuous Bacchanalia. However, the lion roaring behind the door of the closet turned out, when that door was opened, to be a little, domesticated cat. In fact, seen from a long historical perspective, sexual liberation might be interpreted as the recognition that sexual passion is no longer dangerous in us, and that is is safer to give it free course than to risk rebellion by restraining it. I once asked a class how it could be that not too long ago parents would have said, "Never darken our door again," to wayward daughters, whereas now they rarely protest when boyfriends sleep over in their homes. A very nice, very normal, young woman responded, "Because it's no big deal." That says it all. This passionlessness is the most striking effect, or revelation, of the sexual revolution, and it makes the younger generation more or less incomprehensible to older folks.

In all this, the sexual revolution was precisely what it said it was—a liberation. But some of the harshness of nature asserted itself beneath the shattered conventions: the young were more apt to profit from the revolution than the old, the beautiful more than the ugly. The old vein of discretion had had the effect of making these raw and ill-distributed natural advantages less important in life and marriage. But now there was little attempt to apply egalitarian justice in these matters, as did Aristophanes' older Athenian women who, because of their very repulsiveness, had a right to enjoy handsome young men before beautiful young women did. The undemocratic aspects of free sex were compensated for in our harmless and mildly ridiculous way: "Beauty is in the eye of the beholder" was preached more vigorously than formerly; the cosmetics industry had a big boom; and education and therapy in the style of Masters and Johnson, promising great orgasms to every subscriber, became common. My favorite was a course in sex for the elderly given at a local YMCA and advertised over the radio with the slogan "Use It or Lose It." These were the days when pornography slipped its leash.

Feminism, on the other hand, was, to the extent it presented itself as liberation, much more a liberation from nature than from convention or society. Therefore it was grimmer, unerotic, more of an abstract project, and required not so much the abolition of law but the institution of law and political activism. Instinct did not suffice. The negative sentiment of imprisonment was there, but what was wanted, as Freud suggested, was unclear. The programmatic language shifted from "living naturally" (with reference to very definite bodily functions) to vaguer terms such as "self-definition," "self-fulfillment," "establishing priorities," "fashioning a lifestyle," etc. The women's movement is not founded on nature. Although feminism sees the position of women as a result of nurture and not nature, its crucial contention is that biology should not be destiny, and biology is surely natural. It is not self-evident, although it may be true, that women's roles were always determined by human relations of domination, like those underlying slavery. This thesis requires interpretation and argument, and is not affirmed by the bodily desires of all concerned, as was the sexual revolution. Moreover, it is very often asserted that science's *conquest* of nature—in the form of the pill and labor-saving devices—has made woman's emancipation from the home possible. It is certain that feminism has brought with it a unrelenting process of consciousness-raising and -changing that begins in what is probably a permanent human inclination and is surely a modern one—the longing for the unlimited, the unconstrained. It ends, as do many modern movements that seek abstract justice, in forgetting nature and using force to refashion human beings to secure that justice.

Feminism is in accord with and encourages many elements of the sexual revolution, but uses them to different ends. Libertinism allows for what even Rousseau called the greatest pleasure. But in making sex easy, it can trivialize, de-eroticize and demystify sexual relations. A woman who can easily satisfy her desires and does not invest her emotions in exclusive relationships is liberated from the psychological tyranny of men, to do more important things. Feminism acted as a depressant on the Bacchanalian mood of the sexual revolution, as nakedness in Plato's *Republic* led not to great indulgences but to an unromantic regulation and manipulation of sexual desire for public purposes. Just as smoking and drinking overcame puritanical condemnation only to find themselves, after a brief moment of freedom, under equally moralistic attacks in the name not of God but of the more respectable and powerful names of health and safety, so sex had a short day in the sun before it had to be reined in to accommodate the feminist sensibility. As a people, we are good not at gratifying ourselves but at delaying gratification for the sake of projects which promise future good. In this case the project is overcoming what is variously called male dominance, machismo, phallocracy, patriarchy, etc., to which men and their female collaborators seem very attached, inasmuch as so many machines of war must be mounted against them.

Male sexual passion has become sinful again because it culminates in sexism. Women are made into objects, they are raped by their husbands as well as by strangers, they are sexually harassed by professors and employers at school and at work, and their children, whom they leave in day-care centers in order to pursue their careers, are sexually abused by teachers. All these crimes must be legislated against and punished. What sensitive male can avoid realizing how dangerous his sexual passion is? Is there perhaps really original sin? Men had failed to read the fine print in the Emancipation Proclamation. The new interference with sexual desire is more comprehensive, more intense, more difficult to escape than the older conventions, the grip of which was so recently relaxed. The July 14 of the sexual revolution was really only a day between the overthrow of the Ancien Régime and the onset of the Terror. The new reign of virtue, accompanied by relentless propaganda on radio and television and in the press, has its own catechism, inducing an examination of the conscience and the inmost sentiments for traces of possessiveness, jealousy, protectiveness—all those things men used to feel for women. There are, of course, a multitude of properly indignant censors equipped with loudspeakers and inquisitional tribunals.

Central to the feminist project is the suppression of modesty, in which the sexual revolution played a critical preparatory role, just as capitalism, in the Marxist scheme, prepared the way for socialism by tearing the sacred veils from the charade of feudal chivalry. The sexual revolution, however, wanted men and women to get together bodily, while feminism wanted them to be able easily to get along separately. Modesty in the old dispensation was *the* female virtue, because it governed the powerful desire that related men to women, providing a gratification in harmony with the procreation and rearing of children, the risk and responsibility of which fell naturally—that is, biologically—on women. Although modesty impeded sexual intercourse, its result was to make such gratification central to a serious life and to enhance the delicate interplay between the sexes, which makes acquiescence of the will as important as possession of the body. Diminution or suppression of modesty certainly makes attaining the end of desire easier—which was the intention of the sexual revolution—but it also dismantles the structure of involvement and attachment, reducing sex to the thing-in-itself. This is where feminism enters.

Female modesty extends sexual differentiation from the sexual act to the whole of life. It makes men and women always men and women. The consciousness of directedness toward one another, and its attractions and inhibitions, inform every common deed. As long as modesty operates, men and women together are never just lawyers or pilots together. They have something else, always potentially very important, in common—ultimate ends, or as they say, "life goals." Is winning this case or landing this plane what is most important, or is it love and family? As lawyers or pilots, men and women are the same, subservient to the one goal. As lovers or parents they are very different, but inwardly related by sharing the naturally given end of continuing the species. Yet their working together immediately poses the questions of "roles" and, hence, "priorities," in a way that men work-ing together or women working together does not. Modesty is a con-stant reminder of their peculiar relatedness and its outer forms and inner sentiments, which impede the self's free creation or capitalism's technical division of labor. It is a voice constantly repeating that a man and a woman have a work to do together that is far different from that found in the marketplace, and of a far greater importance.

This is why modesty is the first sacrifice demanded by Socrates in Plato's *Republic* for the establishment of a city where women have the same education, live the same lives and do the same jobs as men. If the difference between men and women is not to determine their ends, if it is not to be more significant than the difference between bald men and men with hair, then they must strip and exercise naked together just as Greek men did. With some qualifications, feminists praise this passage in Plato and look upon it as prescient, for it culminates in an absolute liberation of women from the subjection of marriage and childbearing and -rearing, which become no more important than any other necessary and momentary biological event. Socrates pro-vides birth control, abortion and day-care centers, as well as mar-riages that last a day or a night and have as their only end the production of sound new citizens to replenish the city's stock, cared for by the city. He even adds infanticide to the list of conveniences available. A woman will probably have to spend no more time and ef-fort on children's business than a man would in curing a case of the measles. Only then can women be thought to be naturally fit to do the same things as men. Socrates' radicalism extends to the relation of parent and child. The citizens are not to know their own children, for, if they were to love them above others, then the means that brought them into being, the intercourse of this man and this woman, would be judged to be of special significance. Then we would be back to the private family and the kinds of relatedness peculiar to it.

Socrates' proposal especially refers to one of the most problematic cases for those who seek equal treatment for women—the military. These citizens are warriors, and he argues that just as women can be liberated from subjection to men and take their places alongside them, men must be liberated from their special concern for women. A man must have no more compunction about killing the advancing fe-male enemy than the male, and he must be no more protective of the heroine fighting on his right side than of the hero on his left. Equal opportunity and equal risk. The only concern is the common good, and the only relationship is to the community, bypassing the intermediate relationships that tend to take on a life of their own and were formerly thought to have natural roots in sexual attraction and love of one's own children. Socrates consciously rips asunder the delicate web of relations among human beings woven out of their sexual nature. Without it, the isolation of individuals is inevitable. He makes explicit how equal treatment of women necessitates the removal of meaning from the old kind of sexual relations—whether they were founded on nature or convention—and a consequent loss of the human connections that resulted from them which he replaces with the common good of the city.

In this light we can discern the outlines of what has been going on recently among us. Conservatives who have been heartened by the latest developments within the women's movement are mistaken if they think that they and the movement are on common ground. Certainly both sides are against pornography. But the feminists are against it because it is a reminiscence of the old love relationship, which involved differentiated sexual roles—roles now interpreted as bondage and domination. Pornography demystifies that relationship, leaving the merely sexual component of male-female relationships without their erotic, romantic, moral and ideal accompaniments. It caters to and encourages the longing men have for women and its unrestrained if impoverished satisfaction. This is what feminist antipornographers are against—not the debasement of sentiment or the threat to the family. That is why they exempt homosexual pornography from censorship. It is by definition not an accomplice to the domination of females by males and even helps to undermine it. Actually, feminists favor the demystifying role of pornography. It unmasks the true nature of the old relationships. Their purpose is not to remystify the worn-out systems but to push on toward the realm of freedom. They are not for a return to the old romances, *Brief Encounter*, for example, which gave charm to love in the old way. They know that is dead, and they are now wiping up the last desperate, untutored, semicriminal traces of a kind of desire that no longer has a place in the world.

It is one thing, however, to want to prevent women from being ravished and brutalized because modesty and purity should be respected and their weakness protected by responsible males, and quite another to protect them from male desire altogether so that they can live as they please. Feminism makes use of conservative moralism to further its own ends. This is akin to, and actually part of, the fatal old alliance between traditional conservatives and radicals, which has had such far-reaching effects for more than a century. They had nothing in common but their hatred of capitalism, the conservatives looking back to the revival of throne and altar in the various European nations, and to piety, the radicals looking forward to the universal, homogeneous society and to freedom—reactionaries and progressives united against the present. They feed off the inner contradictions of the bourgeoisie. Of course fundamentalists and feminists can collaborate to pass local ordinances banning smut, but the feminists do so to demonstrate their political clout in furthering their campaign against "bourgeois rights," which are, sad to say, enjoyed by people who want to see dirty movies or buy equipment to act out comically distorted fantasies. It is doubtful whether the fundamentalists gain much from this deal, because it guarantees the victory of a surging moral force that is "antifamily and antilife." See how they do together on the abortion issue! People who watch pornography, on the other hand, are always at least a little ashamed and unwilling to defend it as such. At best, they sound a weak and uncertain trumpet for the sanctity of the Constitution and the First Amendment, of which they hope to be perceived as defenders. They pose no threat in principle to anything.

Similarly, some conservatives are heartened by recent feminist discussion about the differences between men and women and about the special fulfillment of "parenting," forbidden subjects at earlier stages of the movement, when equal rights was the primary theme. However, this discussion has really only been made possible by the success of those earlier stages. There may indeed be a feminine nature or self, but it has been definitively shaken loose from its teleological moorings. The feminine nature is not in any reciprocal relation to the male nature, and they do not define one another. The male and female sexual organs themselves now have no more evident purposiveness than do white and black skin, are no more naturally pointed toward one another than white master and black slave, or so the legend goes. Women do have different physical structures, but they can make of them what they will—without paying a price. The feminine nature is a mystery to be worked out on its own, which can now be done because the male claim to it has been overcome. The fact that there is today a more affirmative disposition toward childbearing does not imply that there is any natural impulse or compulsion to establish anything like a traditional fatherhood to complement motherhood. The children are to be had on the female's terms, with or without fathers, who are not to get in the way of the mother's free development. Children have always been, and still are, more the mother's anyway. Ninety percent or more of children of divorced parents stay with their mothers, whose preeminent stake in children has been enhanced by feminist demands and by a consequent easy rationalization of male irresponsibility. So we have reproduction without family—if family includes the presence of a male who has any kind of a definite function. The return to motherhood as a feminist ideal is only possible because feminism has triumphed over the family as it was once known, and women's freedom will not be limited by it. None of this means returning to family values or even bodes particularly well for the family as an institution, although it does mean that women have become freer to come to terms with the complexity of their situation.

The uneasy bedfellowship of the sexual revolution and feminism produced an odd tension in which all the moral restraints governing nature disappeared, but so did nature. The exhilaration of liberation has evaporated, however, for it is unclear what exactly was liberated or whether new and more onerous responsibilities have not been placed on us. And this is where we return to the students, for whom everything is new. They are not sure what they feel for one another and are without guidance about what to do with whatever they may feel.

The students of whom I am speaking are aware of all the sexual alternatives, and have been from early on in their lives, and they feel that all sexual acts which do not involve real harm to others are licit. They do not think they should feel guilt or shame about sex. They have had sex education in school, of "the biological facts, let them decide the values for themselves" variety, if not "the options and orientations" variety. They have lived in a world where the most explicit discussions and depictions of sex are all around them. They have had little fear of venereal disease.* Birth-control devices and ready abor-

---

*It remains to be seen what effect AIDS will have. The wave of publicity about herpes a couple of years ago had almost no discernible psychological fallout.

tion have been available to them since puberty. For the great majority, sexual intercourse was a normal part of their lives prior to college, and there was no fear of social stigma or even much parental opposition. Girls have had less supervision in their relations with boys than at any time in history. They are not precisely pagan, but there is an easy familiarity with others' bodies and less inhibition about using their own for a broad range of erotic purposes. There is no special value placed on virginity in oneself or in one's partners. It is expected that there were others before and, incredibly to older folks, this does not seem to bother them, even though it provides a ground for predictions about the future. They are not promiscuous or given to orgies or casual sex, as it used to be understood. In general, they have one connection at a time, but most have had several serially. They are used to coed dormitories. Many live together, almost always without expectation of marriage. It is just a convenient arrangement. They are not couples in the sense of having simulacra of marriage or a way of life different from that of other students not presently so attached. They are roommates, which is what they call themselves, with sex and utilities included in the rent. Every single obstacle to sexual relationships between young unmarried persons has disappeared, and these relationships are routine. To strangers from another planet, what would be the most striking thing is that sexual passion no longer includes the illusion of eternity.

Men and women are now used to living in exactly the same way and studying exactly the same things and having exactly the same career expectations. No man would think of ridiculing a female premed or prelaw student, or believe that these are fields not proper for women, or assert that a woman should put family before career. The law schools and medical schools are full of women, and their numbers are beginning to approach their proportion in the general population. There is very little ideology or militant feminism in most of the women, because they do not need it. The strident voices are present, and they get attention in the university newspapers and in student governments. But, again, the battle here has been won. Women students do not generally feel discriminated against or despised for their professional aspirations. The economy will absorb them, and they have rising expectations. They do not need the protection of NOW any more than do women in general, who see they are doing at least as well with Reagan as they did with Carter. Academically, students are comfortably unisexual; they revert to dual sexuality only for the sex act. Sex no longer has any political agenda in universities except among homosexuals, who are not yet quite satisfied with their situation. But the fact that there is an open homosexual presence, with rights at least formally recognized by university authorities and almost all students, tells us much about current university life.

Students today understandably believe that they are the beneficiaries of progress. They have a certain benign contempt for their parents, particularly for their poor mothers, who were sexually inexperienced and had no profession to be taken as seriously as their fathers'. Superior sexual experience was always one of the palpable advantages that parents and teachers had over youngsters who were eager to penetrate the mysteries of life. But this is no longer the case, nor do students believe it to be so. They quietly smile at professors who try to shock them or talk explicitly about the facts of life in the way once so effective in enticing more innocent generations of students to pay attention to the world of their elders. Freud and D. H. Lawrence are very old hat. Better not to try.

Even less do students expect to learn anything about their situation from old literature, which from the Garden of Eden on made coupling a very dark and complicated business. On reflection, today's students wonder what all the fuss was about. Many think their older brothers and sisters discovered sex, as we now know it to be, in the sixties. I was impressed by students who, in a course on Rousseau's *Confessions,* were astounded to learn that he had lived with a woman out of wedlock in the eighteenth century. Where could he have gotten the idea?

There is, of course, literature that affects a generation profoundly but has no interest at all for the next generation because its central theme proved ephemeral, whereas the greatest literature addresses the permanent problems of man. Ibsen's *Ghosts,* for example, lost all its force for young people when syphilis ceased to be a threat. Aristotle teaches that pity for the plight of others requires that the same thing could happen to us. Now, however, the same things that used to happen to people, at least in the relations between the sexes, do not happen to students anymore. And one must begin to wonder whether there is any permanent literature for them. As I have suggested earlier, this is the first fully historical or historicized generation, not only in theory but also in practice, and the result is not the cultivation of the vastest sympathies for long ago and far away, but rather an exclusive interest in themselves. Anna Karenina and Madame Bovary are adulteresses, but the cosmos no longer rebels at their deed. Anna's son today would probably have been awarded to her in the amicable divorce arrangements of the Karenins. All the romantic novels with their depictions of highly differentiated men and women, their steamy, sublimated sensuality and their insistence on the sacredness of the marriage bond just do not speak to any reality that concerns today's young people. Neither do Romeo and Juliet, who must struggle against parental opposition, Othello and his jealousy, or Miranda's carefully guarded innocence. Saint Augustine, as a seminarian told me, had sexual hang-ups. And let us not speak of the Bible, every *no* in which is now a *yes*. With the possible exception of Oedipus, they are all gone, and they departed in the company of modesty.

When young people today have crushing problems in what used to be called sexual relationships, they cannot trace them back to any moral ambiguity in man's sexual nature. That was, of course, what was erroneously done in the past.

SEPARATENESS

Civilization has seemingly led us around full circle, back to the state of nature taught to us by the founding fathers of modern thought. But now it is present not in rhetoric but in reality. Those who first taught the state of nature proposed it as a hypothesis. Liberated from all the conventional attachments to religion, country and family that men actually did have, how would they live and how would they freely reconstruct those attachments? It was an experiment designed to make people recognize what they really care about and engage their loyalties on the basis of this caring. But a young person today, to exaggerate only a little, actually begins *de novo,* without the givens or imperatives that he would have had only yesterday. His country demands little of him and provides well for him, his religion is a matter of absolutely free choice and—this is what is really fresh—so are his sexual involvements. He can now choose, but he finds he no longer has a sufficient motive for choice that is more than whim, that is binding. Reconstruction is proving impossible.

The state of nature should culminate in a contract, which constitutes a society out of individuals. A contract requires not only a common interest between the contracting parties but also an authority to enforce its fulfillment by them. In the absence of the former, there is no relationship; in the absence of the latter, there can be no trust, only diffidence. In the state of nature concerning friendships and love today, there is doubt about both, and the result is a longing for the vanished common ground, called roots, without the means to recover it, and timidity and self-protectiveness in associations guaranteed by neither nature nor convention. The pervasive feeling that love and friendship are groundless, perhaps the most notable aspect of the current feeling of groundlessness, has caused them to give way to the much vaguer and more personal idea of commitment, that choice in the voice whose cause resides only in the will or the self. The young want to make commitments, which constitute the meaning of life, because love and nature do not suffice. This is what they talked about, but they are haunted by the awareness that the talk does not mean very much and that commitments are lighter than air.

At the origins of modern natural rights teachings, freedom and equality were political principles intended to bring both justice and effectiveness to the relationships of ruling and being ruled, which in the conventional order were constituted by pretended rights of strength, wealth, tradition, age and birth. The relations of king and subject, master and slave, lord and vassal, patrician and pleb, rich and poor, were revealed to be purely manmade and hence not morally binding, apart from the consent of the parties to them, which became the only source of political legitimacy. Civil society was to be reconstructed on the natural ground of man's common humanity. Then it would appear that all relationships or relatedness within civil society would also depend on the free consent of individuals. Yet the relationships between man and woman, parent and child, are less doubtfully natural and less arguably conventional than the relations between rulers and ruled, especially as they are understood by modern natural rights teachings. They cannot be understood simply as contractual relationships, as resulting from acts of human freedom, since they would thereby lose their character and dissolve. Instead they seem to constrain that freedom, to argue against the free arrangements of consent dominant in the political order. But it is difficult to argue that nature both does and does not prescribe certain relations in civil soci-

ety. The radical transformation of the relations between men and
women and parents and children was the inevitable consequence of
the success of the new politics of consent.

It might be said, with some exaggeration, that the first state-of-
nature teachers paid little attention to the natural teleology of sex because they were primarily concerned with analyzing away the false
appearances of teleology in the existing political arrangements. (I
mean by teleology nothing but the evident, everyday observation and
sense of purposiveness, which may be only illusory, but which ordinarily guides human life, the kind everyone sees in the reproductive
process.) Hobbes and Locke marshaled their great talents to explode
myths of rulership that protected corrupt and selfish regimes, such as
Menenius' tale:

> There was a time when all the body's members
> Rebelled against the belly; thus accused it:
> That only like a gulf it did remain
> I' the midst o' the body, idle and unactive,
> Still cupboarding the viand, never bearing
> Like labor with the rest; where the other instruments
> Did see and hear, devise, instruct, walk, feel,
> And, mutually participate, did minister
> Unto the appetite and affection common
> Of the whole body. The belly answered . . .
> To the discontented members, the mutinous parts
> That envied his receipt; even so most fitly
> As you malign our senators for that
> They are not such as you . . .
> 'True is it, my incorporate friends,' quoth he,
> 'That I receive the general food at first
> Which you do live upon; and fit it is,
> Because I am the storehouse and the shop
> Of the whole body. But, if you do remember,
> I send it through the rivers of your blood,
> Even to the court, the heart, to the seat o' the brain;
> and, through the cranks and offices of man,
> The strongest nerves and small inferior veins
> From me receive that natural competency
> Whereby they live. And . . .
> . . . though all at once cannot
> See what I do deliver out to each,

Yet I can make my audit up, that all
From me do back receive the flour of all,
and leave me but the bran. . . .
The senators of Rome are this good belly,
And you the mutinous members; for, examine
Their counsels and their cares, digest things rightly
Touching the weal o' the common, you shall find
No public benefit which you receive
But it proceeds or comes from them to you,
and no way from yourselves.

(SHAKESPEARE, Coriolanus, 95–156)

In the place of such an "organic" tale they provided a rational account of legitimacy that made each individual the judge of his own best interests and gave him the right to choose rulers who were bound to protect him, abstracting from the habits of thought and feeling that permitted patricians under the colors of the common good to make use of plebs for their own greedy purposes. Hobbes and Locke gave the plebs equal rights to selfishness. The ruled are not directed by nature to the rulers any more than the rulers naturally care only for the good of the ruled. Rulers and ruled can consciously craft a compact by which the separate interests of each are protected. But they are never one, sharing the same highest end, like the organs in Menenius' body. There is no body politic, only individuals who have come together voluntarily and can separate voluntarily without maimimg themselves.

Hobbes and Locke supposed that, although the political order would be constituted out of individuals, the subpolitical units would remain largely unaffected. Indeed, they counted on the family, as an intermediate between individual and the state, partially to replace what was being lost in passionate attachment to the polity. The immediate and reliable love of one's own property, wife and children can more effectively counterpoise purely individual selfishness than does the distant and abstract love of country. Moreover, concern for the safety of one's family is a powerful reason for loyalty to the state, which protects them. The nation as a community of families is a formula that until recently worked very well in the United States. However, it is very questionable whether this solution is viable over the very long run, because there are two contrary views of nature present here. And, as the political philosophers have always taught, the one that is authoritative in the political regime will ultimately inform its parts. In the social contract view, nature has nothing to say about relationships and rank order; in the older view, which is part and parcel of ancient political philosophy, nature is prescriptive. Are the relations between men and women and parents and children determined by natural impulse or are they the product of choice and consent? In Aristotle's *Politics,* the subpolitical or prepolitical family relations point to the necessity of political rule and are perfected by it, whereas in the state-of-nature teachings, political rule is derived entirely from the need for protection of individuals, bypassing their social relations completely. Are we dealing with political actors or with men and women? In the former case, persons are free to construct whatever relations they please with one another; in the latter, prior to any choice, a preexisting frame largely determines the relations of men and women.

There are three classic images of the polity that clarify this issue. The first is the ship of state, which is one thing if it is to be forever at sea, and quite another if it is to reach port and the passengers go their separate ways. They think about one another and their relationships on the ship very differently in the two cases. The former case is the ancient city; the latter, the modern state. The other two images are the herd and the hive, which oppose each other. The herd may need a shepherd, but each of the animals is grazing for itself and can easily be separated from the herd. In the hive, by contrast, there are workers, drones and a queen; there is a division of labor and a product toward which they all work in common; separation from the hive is extinction. The herd is modern, the hive ancient. Of course, neither image is an accurate description of human society. Men are neither atoms nor parts of a body. But this is why there have to be such images, since for the brutes these things are not a matter for discussion or deliberation. Man is ambiguous. In the tightest communities, at least since the days of Odysseus, there is something in man that wants out and senses that his development is stunted by being just a part of a whole, rather than a whole itself. And in the freest and most independent situations men long for unconditional attachments. The tension between freedom and attachment, and attempts to achieve the impossible union of the two, are the permanent condition of man. But in modern political regimes, where rights precede duties, freedom definitely has primacy over community, family and even nature.

The spirit of this choice must inevitably penetrate into all the details of life. The ambiguity of man is well illustrated in the sexual passion and the sentiments that accompany it. Sex may be treated as a pleasure out of which men and women may make what they will, its promptings followed or rejected, its forms matters of taste, its importance or unimportance in life decided freely by individuals. As such, at least according to thinkers like Hobbes and Locke, it would have to give precedence to objective natural necessity, to the imperatives of self-love or self-preservation. Or sex can be immediately constitutive of a whole law of life, to which self-preservation is subordinated and in which love, marriage and the rearing of infants is the most important business. It cannot be both. The direction in which we have been going in obvious.

Now, it is not entirely correct to say that mankind at large is able to treat sex as a matter of free choice, one which initially does not obligate us to others. In a world where the natural basis of sexual differentiation has crumbled, this choice is readily available to men, but less so to women. Man in the state of nature, either in the first one or the one we have now, can walk away from a sexual encounter and never give it another thought. But a woman may have a child, and in fact, as becomes ever clearer, may want to have a child. Sex can be an indifferent thing for men, but it really cannot quite be so for women. This is what might be called the female drama. Modernity promised that all human beings would be treated equally. Women took that promise seriously and rebelled against the old order. But as they have succeeded, men have also been liberated from their old constraints. And women, now liberated and with equal careers, nevertheless find they still desire to have children, but have no basis for claiming that men should share their desire for children or assume a responsibility for them. So nature weighs more heavily on women. In the old order they were subordinated and dependent on men; in the new order they are isolated, needing men, but not able to count on them, and hampered in the free development of their individuality. The promise of modernity is not really fulfilled for women.

The decay of the natural ground for the family relationships was largely unanticipated and unprepared for in the early modern thinkers. But they did suggest a certain reform of the family, reflecting the movement away from the constraints of duty, toward reliance on those elements of the family that could be understood to flow out of free expressions of personal sentiment. In Locke, paternal authority is turned into parental authority, a rejection of a father's divine or nat ural right to rule and to rule permanently, in favor of a father's and a mother's right to care for their children as long as they need care, for the sake of the children's freedom—which the child will immediately recognize, when he reaches majority, to have been for his own benefit. There is nothing left of the reverence toward the father as the symbol of the divine on earth, the unquestioned bearer of authority. Rather, sons and daughters will calculate that they have benefited from their parents' care, which prepared them for the freedom they enjoy, and they will be grateful, although they have no reciprocal duty, except insofar as they wish to leave behind a plausible model for the conduct of their own children toward them. They may, if they please, obey their father in order to inherit his estate, if he has one, which he can dispose of as he pleases. From the point of view of the children, the family retains its validity on the basis of modern principles, and Locke prepares the way for the democratic family, so movingly described by Tocqueville in *Democracy in America.*

So far, so good. The children are reconciled to the family. But the problem, it seems to me, is in the motive of the parents to care for their children. The children can say to their parents: "You are strong, and we are weak. Use your strength to help us. You are rich, and we are poor. Spend your money on us. You are wise, and we are ignorant. Teach us." But why should mother and father want to do so much, involving so much sacrifice without any reward? Perhaps parental care is a duty, or family life has great joys. But neither of these is a conclusive reason when rights and individual autonomy hold sway. The children have unconditional need for and receive unquestionable benefits from the parents; the same cannot be asserted about parents.

Locke believed, and the events of our time seem to confirm this belief, that women have an instinctive attachment to children that cannot be explained as self-interest or calculation. The attachment of mother and child is perhaps the only undeniable natural social bond. It is not always effective, and it can, with effort, be suppressed, but it is always a force. And this is what we see today. But what about the father? Maybe he loves imagining his own eternity through the generations stemming from him. But this is only an act of imagination, one that can be attenuated by other concerns and calculations, as well as by losing faith in the continuation of his name for very long in the shifting conditions of democracy. Of necessity, therefore, it was understood to be the woman's job to get and hold the man by her charms and wiles because, by nature, nothing else would induce him to give up his freedom in favor of the heavy duties of family. But women no longer wish to do this, and they, with justice, consider it unfair according to the principles governing us. So the cement that bound the family together crumbled. It is not the children who break away; it is the parents who abandon them. Women are no longer willing to make unconditional and perpetual commitments on unequal terms, and, no matter what they hope, nothing can effectively make most men share equally the responsibilities of childbearing and child-rearing. The divorce rate is only the most striking symptom of this breakdown.

None of this results from the sixties, or from the appeal to masculine vanity begun by advertisers in the fifties, or from any other superficial, pop-culture events. More than two hundred years ago Rousseau saw with alarm the seeds of the breakdown of the family in liberal society, and he dedicated much of his genius to trying to correct it. He found that the critical connection between man and woman was being broken by individualism, and focused his efforts, theoretical and practical, on encouraging passionate romantic love in them. He wanted to rebuild and reinforce that connection, previously encumbered by now discredited religious and civil regulation, on modern grounds of desire and consent. He retraced the picture of nature that had become a palimpsest under the abrasion of modern criticism, and he enticed men and women into admiring its teleological ordering, specifically the complementarity between the two sexes, which mesh and set the machine of life in motion, each differing from and needing the other, from the depths of the body to the heights of the soul. He set utter abandon to the sentiments and imaginations of idealized love against calculation of individual interest. Rousseau inspired a whole genre of novelistic and poetic literature that lived feverishly for over a century, coexisting with the writings of the Benthams and the Mills who were earnestly at work homogenizing the sexes. His undertaking had the heaviest significance because human community was at risk. In essence he was persuading women freely to be different from men and to take on the burden of entering a positive contract with the family, as opposed to a negative, individual, self-protective contract with the state. Tocqueville picked up this theme, described the absolute differentiation of husband's and wife's functions and ways of life in the American family, and attributed the success of American democracy to its women, who freely choose their lot. This he contrasted to the disorder, nay, chaos, of Europe, which he attributed to a misunderstanding or misapplication of the principle of equality—only an abstraction when not informed by nature's imperatives.

This whole effort failed and now arouses either women's anger, as an attempt to take from them rights guaranteed to all human beings, or their indifference, as irrelevant in a time when women do exactly the same things as men and face the same difficulties in ensuring their independence. Rousseau, Tocqueville and all the others now have only historical significance and at most provide us with a serious alternative perspective for analyzing our situation. Romantic love is now as alien to us as knight-errantry, and young men are no more likely to court a woman than to wear a suit of armor, not only because it is not fitting, but because it would be offensive to women. As a student exclaimed to me, with approval of his fellows, "What do you expect me to do? Play a guitar under some girl's window?" Such a thing seemed as absurd to him as swallowing goldfish.

But the parents of this same young man, it turned out, were divorced. He strongly, if incoherently, expressed his distress and performed the now ritualistic incantation for roots. Here Rousseau is most helpful, for he honestly exposed the nerve of that incantation, whereas the discussion of roots is an evasion. There is a passage in *Emile,* his educational novel, which keeps coming back to me as I look at my students. It occurs in the context of the teacher's arrangements with the parents of the pupil whose total education he is undertaking, and in the absence of any organic relation between husbands and wives and parents and children after having passed through the solvent of modern theory and practice:

> I would even want the pupil and the governor to regard themselves as so inseparable that the lot of each in life is always a common object for them. As soon as they envisage from afar their separation, as soon as they foresee the moment which is going to make them strangers to one another, they are already strangers. Each sets up his own little separate system; and both engrossed by the time they will no longer be together, stay only reluctantly. (*Emile,* p. 53, ed. Bloom, Basic Books, 1979)

That is it. Everyone has "his own little separate system." The aptest description I can find for the state of students' souls is the psychology of separateness.

The possibility of separation is already the fact of separation, inasmuch as people today must plan to be whole and self-sufficient, and cannot risk interdependence. Imagination compels everyone to look forward to the day of separation in order to see how he will do. The energies people should use in the common enterprise are exhausted in preparation for independence. What would, in the case of union, be a building stone becomes a stumbling block on the path to secession. The goals of those who are together naturally and necessarily must become a common good; what one must live with can be accepted. But there is no common good for those who are to separate. The presence of choice already changes the character of relatedness. And the more separation there is, the more there will be. Death of a parent, child, husband, wife or friend is always a possibility and sometimes a fact, but separation is something very different because it is an intentional rebuff to the demand for reciprocity of attachment which is the heart of these relations. People can continue to live while related to the dead beloved; they cannot continue to be related to a living beloved who no longer loves or wishes to be loved. This continual shifting of the sands in our desert—separation from places, persons, beliefs—produces the psychic state of nature where reserve and timidity are the prevailing dispositions. We are social solitaries.

Postscript

Consequently one might with reason think there is too little snoring done—snoring with a purpose to guide it, snoring deliberately directed towards a salutary end which is otherwise unattainable—and that our society would doubtless be better off if its value of the practice were more fully recognized. In our public affairs, for instance, I have of late been much struck by the number of persons who professedly had something. The starry-eyed energumens of the New Deal were perhaps the most conspicuous examples; each and all, they were quite sure they had something. They had a clear premonition of the More Abundant Life into which we were all immediately to enter by the way of a Planned Economy. It now seems, however, that the New Deal is rapidly sinking in the same Slough of Despond which closed over poor Mr. Hoover's head, and that the More Abundant Life is, if anything, a little more remote than ever before.

I do not disparage their premonition or question it; I simply suggest that the More Abundant Life might now be appreciably nearer if they had put enough confidence in their premonition to do a great deal less thinking, planning, legislating, organizing, and a great deal—oh yes, a very great deal—more snoring.

—ALBERT JAY NOCK, "Snoring as a Fine Art," in *The Atlantic Monthly*
(November, 1938)

Contributors to *Good Order*

Allan Bloom's *The Closing of the American Mind* was the most talked-about book of the last decade. He was codirector of the John M. Olin Center for inquiry into the Theory and Practice of Democracy at the University of Chicago, and a renowned translator of Plato and Rousseau. He was the author of *Shakespeare's Politics, Giants and Dwarfs,* and *Love and Friendship.*

G. K. Chesterton was one of this century's most enduring writers, critics, and novelists. In scores of books he analyzed the challenges of modernity, nowhere more cogently than in *Orthodoxy.* He wrote *The Everlasting Man, St. Thomas Aquinas, St. Francis of Assissi,* and the ever-popular Father Brown detective stories. His collected works are currently being issued by Ignatius Press in San Francisco.

George Gilder is contemporary conservatism's most visionary writer. His *Sexual Suicide* (reissued as *Men and Marriage*) was one of the 1970s most controversial books. *Wealth and Poverty* seemed to define the view sometimes referred to as the Reagan Revolution, and *The Spirit of Enterprise* put Silicon Valley on America's spiritual and economic map. He has been a contributor to *The Wall Street Journal, Harper's,* and many other magazines.

Carol Iannone is a literature professor in the Gallatin Division of New York University. Her articles have appeared in *National Review, Commentary,* and many other magazines. In 1990 she was nominated for a seat on the National Endowment for the Humanities.

George Kelling is a professor of criminal justice at Northeastern University and a fellow of Harvard University in criminal justice.

Russell Kirk has often been called the founder of the modern conservative movement. His most famous book is *The Conservative Mind: From Burke to*

Eliot. Among his more than twenty-five books are *The Conservative Constitution, The Roots of American Order,* and *Eliot and His Age*. He was a recipient of the Presidential Citizens Medal for Distinguished Service to the United States. Professor Kirk died in April, 1994.

Peter Kreeft is professor of philosophy at Boston College. His numerous books include *Making Choices: Finding Black and White in a World of Grays, Heaven: The Heart's Deepest Longing,* and *Three Philosophies of Life*.

Myron Magnet is a member of the board of editors of *Fortune,* and a fellow of the Manhattan Institute. In addition to *The Dream and the Nightmare: The Sixties' Legacy to the Underclass,* he is the author of *Dickens and the Social Order*.

Charles Murray's most famous book is *Losing Ground,* which changed the terms of our ongoing debate about American social policy. He has been a fellow at the Manhattan Institute and the American Enterprise Institute. In addition to *In Pursuit: Of Happiness and Good Government,* Mr. Murray is the author with his wife, Catherine Cox, of *Apollo: Race to the Moon*.

Richard John Neuhaus is editor of *First Things: A Monthly Journal of Religion and Public Life*. He is religion editor of *National Review,* and a frequent contributor to *The Wall Street Journal*. Notable among his many books—in addition of course to *The Naked Public Square*—are: *To Empower People* (with Peter L. Berger), *The Catholic Moment,* and *Doing Well and Doing Good: The Challenge to the Christian Capitalist*.

Thomas Sowell is a senior fellow at the Hoover Institution, where he specializes in economic policy and the history of ideas. He writes a syndicated newspaper column, and is a contributor to *Forbes* magazine. Among his many books—in addition to *Inside American Education*—are: *A Conflict of Visions, Civil Rights: Rhetoric or Reality?, Ethnic America, Marxism, Markets and Minorities,* and *Preferential Policies*.

Richard M. Weaver's *Ideas Have Consequences* is a seminal work of modern conservatism. When it was first published in 1948, Paul Tillich called it "brilliantly written, daring and radical. . . ." and Reinhold Niebuhr hailed it as "a profound diagnosis of the sickness of our time." Among Professor Weaver's other works was *The Southern Tradition at Bay*.

George F. Will is a commentator for ABC News and a nationally syndicated columnist. In addition to *Restoration: Congress, Term Limits and the Recov-*

ery of Deliberative Democracy, he is the author of *Statecraft as Soulcraft,* and *Men at Work.*

James Q. Wilson is author of *the Moral Sense* and many other books. He teaches sociology at UCLA.

Acknowledgments

Every book has it genesis. The usual beginning is the writer's own idea, which makes *Good Order* unusual. Gail Winston thought a collection of conservative writing would be timely, and pitched *her* idea to the editors in Simon & Schuster's trade paperback division. They agreed, and editor-in-chief Marilyn Abraham suggested I might be interested in compiling the book. I am grateful to both of them.

Ms. Winston promptly took a new job at another company, and *Good Order* became the responsibility of Mitch Horowitz. He has been a steadfast, sympathetic, and enthusiastic editor. More than this, he has been a tough critic, challenging me at every step not to "preach to the choir." All this, and the man has patience too.

As I began thinking about a selection of essays that would suitably describe what is sometimes called the "classical liberal" point of view, I decided to seek other opinions. I sent a questionnaire to more than 400 conservative intellectuals. There are at least that many in these United States; there may actually be more. Most of the names came from a list provided to me by the Media Research Center in Alexandria, Virginia. I'm especially grateful to Annette Jarred for her helpfulness.

Nearly 100 questionnaires came back. If I'd been selling something, I'd be rich. I can't list the names of all those who so kindly responded, in part because not every returned questionnaire contained the correspondent's name. But more than a few did, and some were helpful beyond measure. Thanks to: M. D. Aeschliman, John Baden, Calvin Beisner, Mark Belling, Bob Blandford, Daniel Buksa, George F. Cahill, Jameson Campaigne, Allan C. Carlson, Don Carson, Bryce Christensen, Betsy Clarke, Charles Coulombe, Bob Chitester, John P. Cregan, Harry Crocker, Mark Davis, Sam Francis, Neal Freeman, Jeff Hart, George Grant, Wayne Grudem, John C. Hirschfield, Carl Horowitz, Lari McDonald, Tibor Machan, Keith Mano, Gene Methvin, Mark Miller, Brian Mitchell, Jacob Neusner, Wally Olson, Howard Philips, Jere Real, Alan Reynolds, Peter C. Rollins, John Penninger,

Ramesh Ponnuru, Russell Pulliam, James C. Roberts, Ed Rubenstein, Patrick Shaughness, Jane Shaw, Robert A. Sirico, Thomas Szasz, George W. Rutler, Cal Thomas, Lenore G. Thomas, David Theroux, William H. Wild, and Phyllis Zagano.

And there were a half dozen more who went further than most. They wrote to me, talked to me, and a couple of them even had lunch with me. I paid though. Doug Bandow, Rick Brookhiser, David Frum, Sim Johnston, George Marlin, and Terry Teachout. Thanks to each of them.

I am especially pleased to have received letters and suggestions from two very distinguished Americans, not that everyone I've mentioned so far isn't of that ilk. Missives from Senator Orrin Hatch and Professor Russell Kirk gladdened my heart and improved this book.

A note at the front of this book indicates that *Good Order* was supported in part by a grant from the Lynde and Harry Bradley Foundation in Milwaukee, Wisconsin. Indeed it was, and I'm pleased now to thank Michael Joyce and William Schambra of Bradley for their support. And I'd never have been able to understand the foundation world if it weren't for the advocacy of Robert Royal at the Ethics and Public Policy Foundation in Washington.

Penultimately, I thank Wick Allison, who generously gave me his opinions about every aspect of this book at every step along the way.

Finally, I thank my wife, Sydny Weinberg Miner. Writers always acknowledge the forbearance of their spouses, and I do. But there's more. Syd loves me. I don't know why, but she does, and it changes everything.

About the Editor

Brad Miner was born in Columbus, Ohio. He is currently Visiting Olin Professor at Adelphi University, where he teaches creative writing. Following a distinguished career in the book publishing industry, he became Literary Editor of *National Review,* America's leading journal of conservative opinion. Mr. Miner conceived of and, with Charles J. Sykes, wrote and edited *The National Review College Guide: America's Top Liberal Arts Schools,* which is now in its second edition.

He has published fiction and nonfiction, and is currently at work on an encyclopedia of conservatism. He is a board member of the Fulton J. Sheen Society, and a former president of the Religion Publishing Group. He lives in Pelham Manor, New York, with his wife, Sydny W. Miner, a publishing executive, and his sons, Robert, seven, and Jonathan, five.